The New Zealand Birdwatchers' Book

The New Zealand
Birdwatchers' Book

Brian Ellis

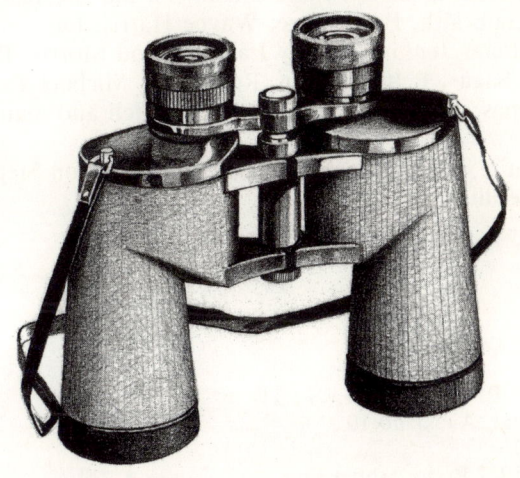

Illustrated by S. P. Ellis

REED METHUEN

Acknowledgements

My thanks are due to a great number of people who have
encouraged, guided or taught me over the years, from the
professor of zoology who reluctantly answered the questions of
a persistent schoolboy to numerous companions out in the field
all around New Zealand, especially members of the Wildlife
Service. There have been lots of days in wind, rain and sleet on
riverbeds, ocean beaches and offshore islands, but in my
memory they all seem like sunny days. If ever the birds didn't
come up to expectations, the good company made even the
toughest conditions worthwhile.

Many thanks to my wife Nancy for her support and help in a
hundred different ways; she has often proved how valuable it is
to have a qualified librarian in the house. I particularly wish to
acknowledge the help of the following in the preparation of this
book: David Collingwood, Stuart Chambers, the late Peter
Child, Mel Galbraith, Peter Gaze, Wayne Harris, Les
Henderson, Peter Jenkins, Paddy Latham, Rod Morris, Ray
Pierce, Paul Sagar, Betty Seddon, Roy Slack, Michael Taylor,
Russell Thomas, Kathleen Todd, Richard Veitch and many
others.

It has been a special pleasure working with my son Stephen in
preparing the illustrations.

First published 1987

REED METHUEN PUBLISHERS LTD
39 Rawene Road, Auckland 10

ISBN 0 474 00198 9

Cover photograph: *South Island Rifleman* (Rod Morris)
Typeset by Glenfield Graphics Ltd, Auckland,
New Zealand
Printed by Kyodo-Shing Loong Printing Ind. Pte Ltd, Singapore

Contents

Part III: Where to find birds

Appendices

Index 241

Introduction

There are about 8,800 species of birds in the world, and many of these also have subspecies or separate races. In every corner of the world they attract our attention with their song or beautiful plumage, and in many cases they are also an important source of food. In New Zealand long separation from other land masses has meant that many of our birds have evolved in a unique way. The kiwi, wrybill and kakapo are so completely different from birds in other countries that it is a challenge to learn more about them.

Many thousands of New Zealanders spend their leisure time in the outdoors — beaches or in the bush, on mountain sides or in boats — and there are always birds around them. It is not surprising that New Zealand has such a high proportion of birdwatchers compared with other countries. Once you start noticing birds you become keen to know more about them. With competent identification and the keeping of simple records you will learn which birds live in an area: the next step is to find out how they live.

This book tells you a little of how birds live. It will help you to find birds in all their specialised habitats and it describes the most rewarding places to look for birds in each part of the country. The study project on the starling can be a framework for a study of any bird you choose.

The index will help the tourist or holiday-maker who wants to see a particular species. The first step is to find out which districts the species occurs in. Then discover what habitats it prefers in these locations. For example, to see yellowheads during your next South Island holiday, include a visit to the districts described on pages 213, 221 or 222. In these places they will probably be making use of the habitat as described on page 112.

Throughout the book I have used the term birdwatcher rather than ornithologist, which means one who studies birds. The latter term is more accurate because the activity entails more than just watching. However, so many people have trouble pronouncing or spelling ornithologist that I believe birdwatcher is the best and most widely-accepted compromise.

Ornithology is one science which receives a great contribution from amateurs, and many people who start birdwatching as a hobby gradually expand their knowledge and are led on to scientific study. With birdwatching you can stop at whatever level of study you most enjoy, or what you have time for, according to circumstances.

It is hoped that you will move from simple bird identification and the keeping of records to a study of one species, or of one feature of bird behaviour or anatomy, for example, song, moult, territory, nest building, feather structure. There are hundreds to choose from.

Part I
Getting started

1

Chapter 1

Understanding birds

Bird anatomy and physiology

Before starting to identify and study birds, it is
necessary to extend our knowledge of their anatomy
and the way they live. An inspection of the bird
skeleton shows that it conforms to the basic
vertebrate pattern with some major adaptations
centred around the ability to fly.

Wing bones are easily identifiable as forelimbs.
Pairs of fingers have been fused so that there are
only two fingers and the thumb. The carpal bones of
the wrist are extended and with the "fingers" these
form the outer wing to which primary flight feathers
are attached.

Leg bones are modified to the extent that the
backward-bending bird leg appears to have an extra
segment. The thigh is within the body and the visible
upper leg (the tibia) is the equivalent of our shin, so
it is actually the ankle which gives the backward-
bending joint. This ankle is very differently con-
structed, one bone being extended to form the lower
leg, which is therefore best called the tarsus (more
correctly the tibiotarsus). There is never a fifth toe in
birds. Most have four, the first being the backward-
pointing one, the second, third and fourth (outer)
pointing to the front. The strong feet of pukekos or
domestic fowls indicate this clearly. Many bird
families have only three toes, with none, or only a
tiny remnant, to the rear. The ostrich is unique in
having only two toes, presumably an adaptation for
running on hard ground.

Toe size, shape and arrangement have many variations. Perching birds have four toes with strong claws, one at the back. Parrots and cuckoos have four toes arranged two to the front and two to the back. The toes of owls are usually held two forward, two back, but when perched they can bring a third forward. The tiny foot of the kingfisher has a broad sole and the fourth toe is partly united with the third. The webs on the toes of swimming birds vary considerably. Ducks, geese and swans have webs joining three toes (right to the claw) and the rear toe is very small. Shags have four strong toes, all joined by webs to make an efficient paddle. This is the totipalmate foot. The toes of grebes and coots have lobes along them, not joining them. The toes of rails and crakes are long and thin to support them on soft mud. Skylarks have long claws on their hind toes, which probably explains their reluctance to land on anything smaller than the top of a large fencepost. The grasping claws on the feet of falcons and harriers are strong and sharp: it is the hind toe claw which first hits the prey when the falcon strikes.

There are other modifications for flying found in the internal anatomy. Several joints, including a large proportion of the vertebrae, are fused to provide the rigidity needed for a flying frame. From the lungs, airsacs extend to the body cavity, both thorax and abdomen, and into many of the major bone structures such as vertebrae, pelvis, sternum and humerus. As well as giving buoyancy, these airsacs serve to regulate heat and form a reservoir of air, additional to the lungs, which can be utilised when singing. No doubt the long underwater dives of grebes and shags are made possible by the air in these cavities.

The tail of a bird plays an important part in flight control. Tail feathers (retrices) and wing primaries and secondaries (remiges) together form the flight feathers. They have strong quills in contrast to the weaker body feathers, which take no direct part in flying. Tails provide steering in flight, and braking. The many different tail shapes are adaptations to serve the style of flight of the species. The tail of a

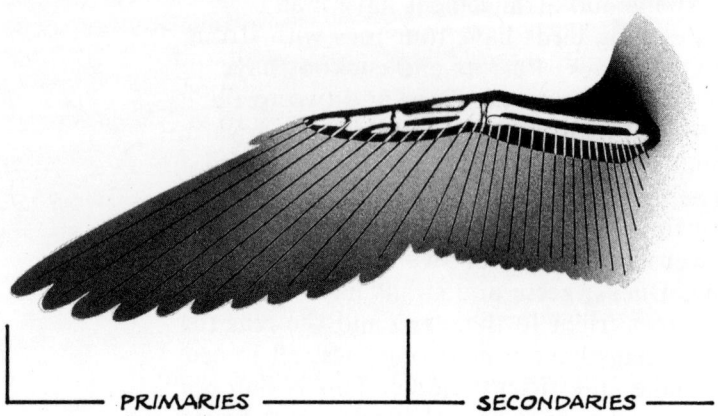

PRIMARIES ——————— SECONDARIES ———

gull is short and square, and if you watch a gull
hovering in a stiff breeze or gliding alongside a boat
you will see that the tail is in constant use to control
the bird in flight. When landing, a bird fans and
depresses its tail as an airbrake.

It may seem as though the flight of many common
birds is unspecialised and not much more than a
means of getting from one place to another, yet you
will notice that birds with an undulating bouncy
flight have short tails in contrast to the steady flight
of the longer-tailed blackbird. There are other more
interesting examples. The welcome swallow feeds on
flying insects scooped up in swift and swerving flight.
Its tail is deeply forked; long outer feathers provide
the control for swerving without drag, which would
reduce speed.

Tail shape is worth noting when trying to identify
a bird because it also provides a clue to the bird's
method of feeding. Be prepared for the tail to look
different when the bird is flying from when it is
perched. A deeply forked tail such as the white-
fronted tern's may look square when it is widely
fanned as the bird hovers. Fantails chase individual
insects, and this requires quick twists and turns at
low speed. The broad fan is obviously an important
balance for the bird, which appears to be able to
throw itself back on a widespread tail for a rapid
change of direction.

4

It is the feather which distinguishes birds from all other forms of life. Depending on their position on the body, contour feathers may be large or small and either functional, providing protection and insulation, or ornamental, as in the case of crests or decorative plumes.

Feathers are dressed and kept waterproof with regular applications of a fine oil which is produced by the uropygial gland, a little nipple-like structure situated on the bird's rump, above the tail. (It is easily seen on dressed poultry.) A preening bird rubs its bill under the feathers above the tail quite frequently to load this oil onto its bill. The oil is then smeared onto each feather as it is drawn through the bill. The nature of the oiling varies greatly between families. The saying "water off a duck's back" recognises that birds which spend their time in and under water are almost completely waterproof. However, shags are not, and they emerge from a diving session soaking wet and unable to fly properly. It is a common sight to see a shag, sometimes a row of them, perched near the water with wings held out as they dry their feathers in wind and sun.

Moult is the renewal of a bird's plumage — old feathers falling out and being replaced by new. Feathers are vital to survival, but as they wear, losing effectiveness both for flight and for protection and warmth, there must be a regular pattern of replacement. There is another cause of moult and renewal of plumage. Many species assume a temporary breeding plumage (the "nuptial plumage") in spring. Many families, such as sandpipers and duck, have winter or eclipse plumage. The moult for these is usually partial, more often in males than females, and usually involves contour feathers and not flight feathers.

Plumage colour may be an indication of age. Many species have an adult male plumage which is attained at the first full moult, the immatures being similar to the female, but others are more complicated. Black-backed gulls take three years to achieve the adult plumage of black and white with no traces of brown.

In any species, breeding will not take place until the individuals are in adult plumage.

Individual variation from the colour pattern of a species is a very rare thing except for some known conditions. Albinism is the best-known one, where all or some of the plumage is white instead of the usual colour. Melanism is where there is excessively dark pigmentation, and this may be recurring rather than accidental. The western weka has a melanistic form, most common in Fiordland. Leucism gives a paleness, often fawn or ginger in otherwise black birds, and the tui is subject to this.

Some species are dimorphic, with two colour forms. The fantail may be pied or black, and a mating of each form would produce chicks which may all be of either form, but usually some of each. The Stewart Island shag is also dimorphic, and its colonies always contain both pied and bronze birds. Sexual dimorphism describes a common situation where the sexes are different, and all dimorphism can be in things other than colour. Overall size difference is common between the sexes in pheasants and in birds of prey (where the female is normally larger). The extinct huia was unique in that male and female had markedly different bills.

More than any other part of the anatomy of the bird, the bill is adapted for its particular use, because it ensures survival through efficient food gathering. It is not difficult to recognise the main types of bill — probing by waders, tearing by hawks, grasping by petrels, spearing by herons, sifting by ducks, etc.

Commonly called the beak, and technically the rostrum, the projecting jaws of a bird consist of an upper (fixed) mandible and a lower (hinged) mandible attached to jaw bones similar to a mammal's. Parrots have the advantage of a limited hinge on the upper mandible, and in godwits and some other long-billed waders the upper mandible is flexible enough to bend upwards.

This flexibility, and the hook or sharp tip we see, are features of the horny sheath of the bill which is laid onto the bone structure. The sheath comes in many colours, and these are often a clue when identifying a species. The colour may change with the seasons; the yellow bill of the white heron changes to purplish black during nesting. It may change with age; some species do not have a brightly coloured bill until mature. The bill may be a different colour for male and female, as in the blackbird.

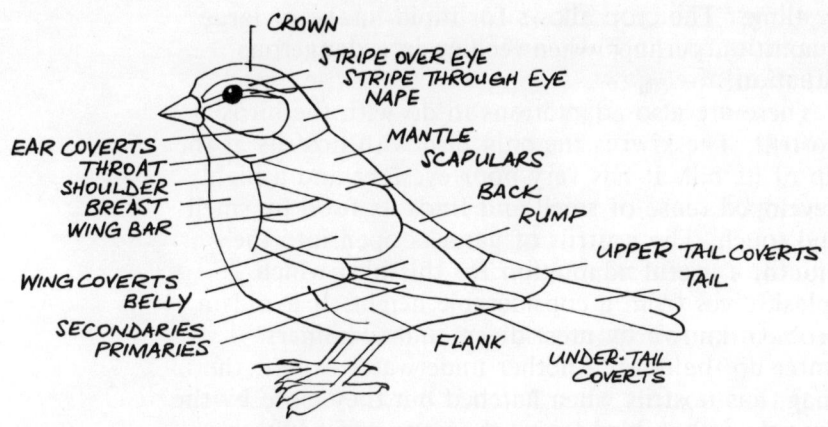

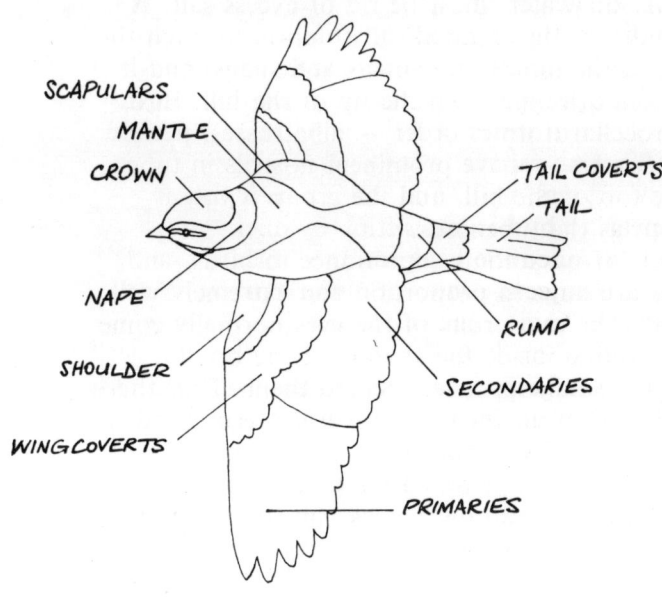

Since teeth have been replaced by the bill, which bites off but does not chew, there have been changes to the digestive system of birds. The gizzard is a muscly-walled sac which grinds and mixes food. Birds swallow small stones and pieces of shell to assist this grinding action. Some species have a crop which holds food immediately after swallowing, either for later, leisured digestion or for regurgitation to nestlings. The crop allows for rapid intake of large quantities, perhaps when feeding in a dangerous situation.

There are also adaptations to do with the birds' nostrils. The kiwi is the only bird with nostrils at the tip of its bill. It has very poor eyesight and a highly developed sense of smell and finds its food by smell and touch. The nostrils of gannets open into the mouth, a useful adaptation for this bird which splash-dives from a considerable height. It avoids a problem known by most divers and swimmers — water up the nose. Another underwater expert, the shag, has nostrils when hatched but they close by the time the young bird leaves the nest, and adults breathe through the mouth. All marine birds, because they drink salt water, must be rid of excess salt. A gland exudes a concentrated salt solution through the nostrils (via the mouth in gannets and shags) and it may be seen dripping from the tip of the bill. Birds of the Procellariiformes order — albatrosses, petrels and shearwaters — have prominent nostrils in tubes along the top of the bill, and the group is often referred to as the tubenoses.

Vision is of paramount importance to birds, and their eyes are huge in proportion and extremely well developed. The two orbits of the eyes normally come close to meeting inside the skull, and the brain occupies the small space left behind them. Thus there is some justification for the derogatory term "bird brain". Being so large, the eye is able to move very little and this is compensated for by a very flexible neck. For example, an owl's neck can rotate almost 360°. Other birds have eyes placed high on the sides of their heads and they have a 360° field of vision without moving the head. There is a vision overlap to provide the important binocular zone at the front for judging distance, and another to the rear.

Birds have a nictitating membrane, a transparent third eyelid drawn across the eye horizontally. It protects the eye without shutting out all light. You can see it in some photographs of birds feeding their young, where the parent appears to be afraid of being hit by anxious nestlings.

The colour of the eye is often a feature of a bird's appearance. It is frequently brown or yellow, but can be almost any colour in the spectrum. Sometimes it changes with age, and sometimes there is a marked difference between the sexes of any given species. When making field notes for later identification you should always try to include the eye colour, where this can be seen.

Behaviour

Do all birds nest in spring? No, but there are few exceptions to the natural pattern of new life which in the temperate regions follows the return of warmth to the soil. Spur-winged plovers lay so early as to be nesting more in winter than in spring. There are eggs in their nests on the cold ground in Southland from June onwards. Delicately plumed spotted shags are at their nests on cliff edges from July, and wekas seem to nest through most of the year.

Some species of seabirds which breed around the coast of New Zealand nest in winter, but it is impossible to give any simple explanation why grey-faced petrels, Westland black petrels, and little (allied) shearwaters choose the long nights of winter to lay eggs while many other species nest alongside on the same islands in summer.

There is great variety in the sites where birds build their nests, or in some cases place their eggs without making one. Each species has its preferred site and consistently chooses this in all but rare exceptions. In most cases similar nest sites are chosen by all members of the same genus.

Most passerines (a term used to group small birds that perch or sing) nest in trees, building cup nests on the branches, but others are hole-nesters and these may use holes in trees, buildings, cliffs or clay banks. Of the tree-nesters you will learn that some, like the house sparrow, build high up (6 m) from the ground. Others, like the blackbird, are often quite content with a site no higher than 1.5 m. Kingfishers nest in holes in trees or banks; skylarks and pipits nest among the rough grasses of open ground. Kaka and kakariki and the introduced rosella parakeet choose holes in trees, as do owls. The welcome swallow attaches its nest to the wall of a building under a protective overhang or under a bridge or culvert, which gives the added protection of being over water. The buntings (cirl bunting and yellowhammer) nest close to the ground in tall grass or bracken, especially by ditches or banks. Harriers and falcons nest on the ground, the latter usually among the rocks of a bluff, the harrier among swamp reeds. All the gulls, terns and waders nest on the ground, mostly in colonies, and sometimes with no more than a shallow scrape to take the eggs.

The seabirds (petrels, shearwaters and storm petrels) nearly all lay their eggs in burrows, some being remarkably long and deep. Gannets nest on the ground of inshore islets or headlands, but some species of their relatives, the shags, prefer trees. Ducks, geese and swans naturally like to be beside or handy to water, but some ducks leave the ground for a hole in a tree.

After eggs are laid, they are incubated. Incubation is the process of applying warmth to the egg to allow the embryo to develop. Brooding — covering the eggs with the bird's body — achieves this, but not simply by insulating the nest and eggs with the body feathers. The parent bird develops "brood patches", areas which lose their feathers and receive an extra blood supply, so that a type of inflammation allows the easy transfer of body heat from bird to eggs. The size and location of the brood patch or patches varies from species to species. As the parent bird settles onto the nest it is usually easy to see the shuffling motions while the brood patch is brought into contact with the eggs.

The incubation period is the time from laying the last egg in a clutch to hatching of that egg. This can range from as little as 10–11 days for the white-eye to about 80 days for the royal albatross.

Almost all the possible arrangements for sharing the duties of incubation are found, from equal sharing between male and female to one parent being in sole charge. The female kiwi is an extreme example — she takes no further interest after she has laid her egg, and the male kiwi is left to carry out the long incubation of about 11 weeks entirely on his own.

The cuckoos have a different scheme. Our two species, shining and long-tailed, are nest parasites. They avoid the cares of nesting by laying eggs in the nests of other birds, one egg in each host nest, to be hatched and the young cuckoo reared by the host parents. For each species of cuckoo there is a short list of other species it uses in this way. Shining cuckoos nearly always choose grey warblers, and long-tailed cuckoos choose the nests of whiteheads in the North Island, yellowheads in the South. As an aid to having the egg accepted into the host's clutch, the colour of the cuckoo egg varies to match the ones already in the nest.

While the eggs are being kept warm, there are interesting differences in the behaviour of the brooding pair. Some species change over regularly during the day, the bird which has been away feeding sliding on to the nest the moment it is vacated. In other cases the sitting bird is called off from nearby. In many cases where the female performs most or all of the incubation she is brought food by the male and he feeds it to her on the nest.

The size of the clutch of eggs which each species lays is fairly constant but it varies widely between species. Kiwis and penguins lay one egg, sometimes two. Quail and pheasants, and some ducks, lay 14 or 15 in a clutch. Normally one egg is laid each day, early in the morning, but again this varies between species and some birds have a gap of two or three days between eggs. Incubation begins when the clutch is complete, so it follows that all young hatch out together. Some families, notably the birds of prey, are exceptions because they start incubating the first egg as soon as it is laid.

Nesting is normally timed for hatching to occur when the food requirements of the young are at their peak of supply — for insect eaters when insects are most numerous, for seed eaters when seeds are ripening. There have been cases where a species has not nested at all when natural disaster has caused a failure in the food supply. Loss of health in the adults is also likely to prevent them from reaching breeding condition at such a time.

Newly hatched young may be open-eyed, covered with down and able to leave the nest almost immediately. These are precocial or nidifugous young, such as those of ducks, quails, waders, rails. Others hatch blind, naked and unable to do more than lift a shaky head to be fed. These are the altricial or nidicolous young of passerines, petrels, parrots and several other families.

During the period when altricial young are in the nest it is important that food is available close by for the parents to gather quickly to keep the young supplied. The need varies greatly between different species. Some shearwaters and petrels feed 100 km from the nest burrow, and the young are fed each second or third night. Small passerines may need to produce food for their chicks every five minutes during daylight.

An incomplete understanding of a bird's requirements through the year has undoubtedly contributed to the decline of some of New Zealand's native species. Selective logging, which removes all the mature trees of one or two species, may remove one or two items from a bird's food supply which are a critical factor over a short period. Leaving birds in a large area of native forest may appear to be ensuring their survival, but the absence of, say, koromiko, eaten out by possums, or of totara could mean starvation for a species dependent on that fruit during certain times of the year.

Recent research has identified several passerine species where there are helpers at the nest. The nesting pair is assisted with feeding the brood by one or more others of the species. In some cases these have been the unattached offspring of a previous nest of the pair.

Precocial young follow their parents in search of food. Some such as banded rails eat what the parent finds them; others like the takahe take only what the parent gives them from its bill. One of the remarkable features of the kakapo, our unique nocturnal, flightless, ground-nesting parrot, is that its young are altricial, unlike the young of other flightless birds. So whereas the chicks of wekas and kiwis leave the nest to follow their parents in search of food, the kakapo parent must *walk* around its large territory gathering berries to take back to the nest. The only parallel would seem to be the penguins, but the penguin chick has evolved a capacity to absorb huge meals at long intervals.

The females of some species may share a nest in what is called communal breeding. Two or three pukekos sometimes lay in one nest, and the combined clutch of 12 or more eggs is hatched and the young reared in a co-operative system.

The majority of species raise only one brood each season, but there are many which regularly have two, even three. Many birds react to the loss of a brood early in the season by nesting again immediately, especially if the loss occurred at an early stage of incubation.

If you find that the nest of a territorial bird such as the blackbird has been attacked by predators, or is otherwise unsuccessful, watch for the building of a new nest within the territory soon afterwards.

Birds are often seen engaged in preening, which is the important process of maintaining feathers in top condition so that they can meet the requirements of flight and body protection. Feathers which are soiled or disarranged are usually attended to right away — they probably feel pretty uncomfortable. As well, regular preening sessions are devoted to reforming all the barbule links on each feather vane and oiling them.

The most usual time of moulting is the end of summer after the completion of nesting, which has more than likely caused some hard wear to plumage. Tail feathers, especially, get bent or broken when birds are sitting on a nest or struggling in and out of nest holes. All birds moult body feathers at least once a year, many twice or three times, but most study has been concentrated on the more easily identified moult of flight feathers. Each species has its own regimen of feather replacement but within a family a general pattern is followed.

Ducks and geese go into heavy moult towards the end of summer, and lose all flight feathers at the same time so that they are flightless. This makes them vulnerable to predators and it is harder for them to find food. To overcome this they move to large areas of water: a good example is seen in the paradise ducks which congregate on St Anne's Lagoon in North Canterbury. They feed on the grassy hillsides surrounding this lake but move quicky down to the water when danger threatens. By swimming to the middle of the lake they know they are out of range of trouble.

Birds of prey, being wholly dependent on flight to find and capture their food, moult primary and secondary flight feathers over a prolonged period. They are shed in pairs, one from each wing to maintain balance. Watch a harrier as it glides over you, and you will often be able to pick out the gaps in its wings. Tail feathers are shed randomly.

Penguins have a dense, thick covering of tiny feathers which have the sole function of protection — insulation from the cold seas in which they live. Obviously to lose a few patches of these would be disastrous, resulting in loss of insulation just as effectively as tears in a diver's wet-suit. So the penguin must come ashore to moult, retiring deep into a cave or dense vegetation where it remains for two to three weeks until the moult is completed. Since it cannot enter the water to feed, it survives on fat reserves built up in preceding weeks.

Our most common penguin, the little blue, moults in this way during the first two months of the year. Beach walkers, especially along the coasts of Cook Strait, should discourage their dogs from hunting through rocks and scrub as they will attack and possibly kill any moulting penguins they find.

Passerines moult once a year normally, in a general renewal of plumage after the end of the breeding season. Non-breeders will have started a little earlier. Although some scruffiness may be noticeable, they retain a good covering and the ability to fly. Flight is perhaps not as efficient as usual, but this is a time of abundant food so a good living is available without having to do too much flying in search of it.

Song

Bird song has always been attractive to people and far back in history there are records of birds being kept as pets for their song. This is in contrast to mammals. Even the voices of the closest domestic animals are endured rather than enjoyed. The explanation is that many birds produce pure tone which is pleasing to our ears, and most of this is in the frequency range (1–4 kilohertz) to which the human ear is particularly sensitive.

Birds use other means of communication, but with sound they have a signal which can carry much more information (in a given time) than any other medium. It goes fast and far, around corners and through trees, and is by far the most efficient signal in a forest. Whether bird vocalisations are similar to human language is extremely doubtful and we must be wary of making assumptions.

Birds produce song in the syrinx, an organ which does not operate the way our larynx does, because it has no vocal cords. The syrinx is a resonating chamber at the junction where the windpipe divides to go to each lung. The number and structure of the muscles which control the syrinx vary among the orders of birds, resulting in a great diversity of singing ability. The precise way in which the syrinx controls the flow of air is not fully understood.

All species with highly developed singing ability are grouped together in the sub-order Oscines of the Passeriformes (the perching birds). Studies of these show that many have a double sound-producing mechanism which allows two different sounds to be produced simultaneously, an amazing achievement.

Although the frequency range of bird song, and their hearing, is approximately the same as that of human hearing, some notes seem to be too high. The constant "zip, zip" of little riflemen, as they forage for insects around tree trunks, must be near the top of our normal range. It is not heard by older people or anyone with a slight hearing defect.

When the tui is singing you may have noticed that at times you hear nothing or no more than a whisper, some of this occurring while the bird hunches its back or stretches its neck as though putting great effort into the song. It is believed to be producing notes too high for our hearing and at the top of the bird's own range (about 21 kilohertz). Only the most elaborate equipment would be capable of recording this for analysis. However, this is a very unusual song. Most bird calls are within our range, which is helpful to us in analysing and understanding how they are employed. It contributes to our understanding of why gulls and terns have evolved short harsh calls which can be heard over a background of wind and waves, and why the clear high-pitched pipings of oystercatchers are so effective out on the estuary mudflats.

Birds' hearing differs from ours in their ability to discern exceedingly short time intervals. They hear each note of what sounds to us like a trill.

A bird starts using its voice before it hatches from the egg; in the last days of growth the chick in the shell hears its parent and signals to it with audible calls. In the case of ground-nesting birds such as pheasants, which may have 12–15 eggs, it is thought that communication among the chicks in the shells contributes to an almost simultaneous hatching. This has important survival value for these precocial chicks. If the hatching was spread over one or two days (as with most altricial tree-nesters) the parents would be unable to protect the actively wandering chicks while brooding the yet unhatched eggs. In experiments, the first few months of life have been shown to be the critical period for song learning in chaffinches. While they are still in the nest, the song they hear from surrounding males teaches them the song which they will use on reaching maturity. For them there is an innate "selective learning" which ensures that they imitate the songs of other chaffinches and not those of any nearby songster.

There is a difference between call-notes and song. Calls are one or two sounds which may be pure in tone or simply harsh cries. The term song is usually given to a series of notes which form a recognisable pattern. Some songs, such as the bellbird's, are of simple construction; the grey warbler and blackbird have much more complex songs. Normally only the male bird sings, but there are several species in which the female does too.

Full song has two main functions: territorial defence and mate attraction. In defence, singing can be a substitute for fighting and probably plays an important role in preventing physical combat, which is likely to injure both winner and loser. The male songbird commonly establishes a number of song posts around his territory and during the day delivers his song from each in turn. He also listens for his neighbours' songs to check they are not trespassing onto his territory. When two neighbouring males meet near their boundary the first reaction will be a challenge song and reply.

As proof of the importance of song for mate attraction, males of some species stop singing once pairs have been formed. Others continue to sing throughout the nesting period. In experiments female canaries were shown to be more active at nest-building when tapes of male songs were played to them. Some species maintain close pair-bond by singing in duet. One bird inserts notes with perfect precision into the song of its partner, sometimes to an amazingly complex pattern.

Many male birds defend their territories with displays of brilliant plumage, often enhanced with special breeding season adornments, but the skylark is both small and cryptic, that is, his colouring is concealing. He could be overlooked so he relies on song to proclaim his presence from high above his territory.

Within a species' song pattern there is considerable scope for individual variation. It is likely that every male songbird has at least one song which is unique. One study showed that four male yellowhammers in adjacent territories had distinctive songs which they maintained throughout the season, from year to year.

If you listen carefully to the same bird on several occasions you may get to know its special song. This is certainly possible with a song thrush which sings from the same perch every morning and evening. The repeated song of a chaffinch is also easily recognised, except that he complicates it by using variations. You need to know songs A, B, C, and D of the chaffinch in your garden to be able to recognise when a stranger has moved in. You can be sure that the resident male will recognise an intruder's song very quickly.

Some songbirds may use different songs at different seasons of the year, or have a repertoire of two or three songs, and give song A and song B during part of the year, but add song C in spring. The functions of alternative songs are not easy to understand. In territory defence you would think that one song would proclaim the owner, so why use another at certain times of the day? For mate attraction one song would seem to be enough to identify the male. So there is much still to be learned about this aspect of bird song.

Over five years of noting the songs heard from his house on the edge of Dunedin's town belt, B.J. Marples found that the bellbird has three easily recognised songs:

(1) A phrase of 7 notes. All year round.
(2) 2 notes, zizz, 2 notes, 6 notes. Autumn and winter.
(3) 3−5 descending notes. Autumn and winter.

If you learn to recognise the various songs, and notice when (and where) they are given, you could start an interesting study by marking them on a chart week by week. Rule a page out in a grid with squares for each song and each day. Tick the squares to show the days on which song A, song B, etc., were heard. Without any interruption to your daily routine you can build up a record which will soon indicate the pattern of each species' song in your area. In the process you can be sure that your appreciation and enjoyment of bird song will be doubled.

The full song is very often the only one which people learn to recognise. Tape recordings or records rarely carry anything other than territorial song when dealing with songbirds. Try to recognise other calls because they are important when identifying a bird in difficult conditions. Build up your knowledge of these minor calls from experience.

The white-eye is an example of a species which has a full song heard rarely in comparison to the familiar "creee, creee" communication call it uses continually. It has a rich fluting song similar to the blackbird's but with so little volume you have to be within 5 m to hear it, except that the bird is always perched within cover when singing. When white-eyes are common around your garden in winter, try to recognise the change in tone which distinguishes a warning (low-level alarm) from the communication call.

It has been shown that harsh alarm calls are composed of sounds hard to identify for direction. The alarm cry is given to warn everything within range, but the predator is unable to locate the individual giving the cry so the caller is not exposed to greater danger. On the other hand, it is important for the male's territorial song to advertise clearly the spot being proclaimed as its territory, and this is achieved with clear varied notes.

The few minutes immediately after first light each morning is a time when most birds engage in full song. When many birds, often of several species, sing at the same time, we call it the "dawn chorus". It is generally believed that the male is declaring he is still present on his territory, and will be defending it for another day. The chorus which results from the blending of songs from several different species in a rich forest habitat can create quite a moving experience. In other cases dozens or hundreds of birds of one species combine to produce a most impressive sound — and if you are in an area with a good population of bellbirds be sure to listen to their dawn chorus, an outstanding delight of the New Zealand forest. Captain Cook was obviously impressed in 1770 when he witnessed the dawn chorus of bellbirds in Queen Charlotte Sound, and was moved to write that often-quoted entry in his log.

A few species of birds incorporate mimicry into their songs, copying other species or frequently heard sounds. The starling is the best example of this but the value of mimicry remains a mystery.

The phenomenon of dialect is much the same in birds as in humans. Just as a person can be recognised as coming from a certain city or region, so can birds be placed. It is over 100 years since several European birds were introduced to New Zealand and we are beginning to recognise the development of a New Zealand dialect in their songs. The North Island kokako provides an example of strong regional dialects. This endangered species is being closely studied and its song is recorded for playback to locate birds. It is found that the populations of each forest (now isolated from each other) have a different song dialect. For instance the song of birds from Mamaku on the Volcanic Plateau brings little or no response when used in Northland's Puketi forest. About as useful as greeting the boys in a Sydney pub with "Hello you chaps, jolly decent day, isn't it"!

Scientific study of bird song becomes possible with use of the sound spectrograph. It writes each element of the song on to paper, indicating the frequency and length of every note. The spectrograph takes a short section of recorded sound and creates a tracing (a sonagram) which is a picture of every detail of the sound, spread out in time so as to include even minor elements so short in duration that our ears would not detect them. Here are examples of two New Zealand chaffinch songs:

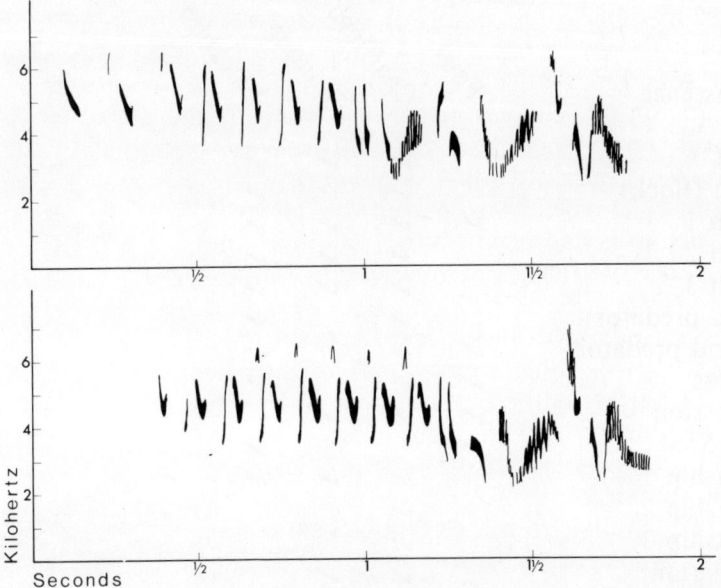

If you look closely at these two sonagrams it is not difficult to follow the familiar chaffinch song: a trill of about eight short sharp notes of middle range followed by a flourish. Close comparison of the two reveals that extra syllables are incorporated into the second song. They come between a trill which is similar to the first (fewer notes may give a slower-sounding start) and an almost identical ending flourish. These differences which the sonagram shows quite clearly would not be detected by the human ear in normal outdoor conditions.

All birds, including those which have highly developed songs, use a variety of simple calls. Three common ones are: a communication call used to keep in touch with other birds in a flock, an alarm to give warning of a predator, and a distress call given when seized by a predator. W.H. Thorpe, a British pioneer in the scientific study of bird song, made a list of the call vocabularies of many species, including the following ones which occur in New Zealand. You can see in this extract from his table that wide use is made of the sound signal.

Circumstance	Fowl	Chaffinch	Bunting	Blackbird
Flight		✓	✓	✓
Social (flock)		✓	✓	✓
Alarm 1	✓	✓	✓	✓
Alarm 2		✓	✓	✓
Alarm 3		✓	✓	✓
Flying predator		✓		✓
Ground predator	✓	✓		✓
Distress	✓	✓		✓
Aggression	✓	✓	✓	
Territorial	✓			✓
Courtship 1		✓	✓	✓
Courtship 2		✓		
Courtship 3		✓		
Copulation		✓	✓	
Nest site			✓	
Mate feeding			✓	
Food	✓			
Roosting				✓
Total number	6	13	10	11

Chapter 2

Identification

Names and classification

The scientific naming of birds, nomenclature, follows a logical and straightforward system which is very easy to understand, but unfortunately many people are scared off by the fact that scientific names are in Latin. The Swedish scientist Linné published his *Systema Naturae* (a system for nature) in 1758, using Latin, the international language of the time. His own name is usually quoted in the Latin form of Linnaeus. There have been no changes to his structure of a two-part name (binomial) for each form of life, or species, which goes on reproducing but remains distinct from all others. Related species are grouped into a genus, one or more of these into a family, families into an order, orders into a class, and classes into a phylum.

This is best illustrated by taking one bird as an example, the common house sparrow which Linné called *Passer* (the name the Romans had given it) and *domesticus* (meaning "belonging to the house"):

Sub-phylum	VERTEBRATA	Vertebrates (animals with backbones)
Class	AVES	Birds
Order	PASSERIFORMES	Sparrowlike, perching birds
Family	Ploceidae	Weavers
Genus	*Passer*	Sparrows
Species	*domesticus*	of the house

It will help you to become familiar with scientific names if you think of the genus as the surname and the species as the given name: *Passer*, Smith, *domesticus*, John. Another bird with the generic name *Passer* must be closely related to the sparrow, but another species called *domesticus* is no more connected than another person called John.

Below the level of species there may be subspecies or races which are geographically separated, hence not interbreeding so as to merge back to the common species. In New Zealand there are many cases of North Island and South Island subspecies. For these a subspecific name is added to give a three-part name (trinomial). For instance, *Rhipidura fuliginosa*, pied fantail, becomes *Rhipidura fuliginosa placabilis* for North Island fantail.

Any person who describes and names a new species (or subspecies) must comply with the rules of an international body. Descriptive names are usually chosen, or a name in honour of some person such as the discoverer, then these are Latinised. Some strange Latin results from the practice of simply adding an i to the surname, e.g. *cooki, banksi* and *macgillivrayi*. Descriptive names are more useful and *chathamensis* for Chatham Islands' species is one which is readily understood. The specific name *rufopectus* is a reminder that the New Zealand dabchick is the one with a reddish breast (or rufous pectoral feathers).

When a specific name has been accepted it cannot be changed unless it is proved that an earlier name was given to that bird. Priority always belongs to the first published description, and there have been lengthy disputes over priority. Spelling is not altered, with the results that you will find three different Latin spellings for New Zealand, according to the custom or fashion of the time or the person describing the species.

In Appendix 1 the scientific names of New Zealand birds are listed showing the families into which they are classified. Note the sequence of families – all good books on birds use this system, which ranks the families in the supposed sequence of their evolution. The most primitive birds are at the beginning and the highly developed ones at the end. For New Zealand this means starting with the kiwi and ending with the introduced rook. A schedule of the birds of a region giving full information on the taxonomy (scientific classification) of each, is called a checklist. (This name deceives some people who expect to find one of those checking-off lists of birds to look for.) To have any validity a checklist must be prepared by a reliable authority, and the international rules must be followed. The *Annotated Checklist of the Birds of New Zealand* was prepared by a committee of the Ornithological Society of New Zealand in 1970. Amendments and additions were issued in 1980, and the book is now being revised for reprinting. This checklist has every bird recorded in New Zealand, including those which have become extinct since about 1800. Each entry is annotated with references to important published articles on the species or subspecies. Another source of taxonomic and historical data is *New Zealand Birds* (2nd edition, 1955) by W.R.B. Oliver. It is out of print but available in many libraries.

The custom in biological writing when mentioning a second species of the same genus is not to repeat the generic name but use only the first letter. A paper dealing with the song thrush (*Turdus philomelos*) and then mentioning the blackbird would refer to it as *T. merula*. Similarly, names of subspecies can have the genus and the species abbreviated to initials, remembering that genus always has a capital letter, species and subspecies lower case.

Common or vernacular names need standardising as far as possible, so that we know what bird is being talked about, but there is no need to be rigid when there is the scientific name to fall back on. North Otago farmers are more likely to know what you mean if you talk of German owls rather than little owls. The duck which we call grey duck is the same species Australians call black duck, so a trans-Tasman birdwatcher should remember to use the name understood by the locals.

Common names can be misleading. The hedge sparrow is not a sparrow, and sea swallow is another name for the white-fronted tern. There are birds called robins in every English-speaking country, but they vary widely in their relationship (if any) to the robin of Britain. Learn the scientific names to avoid these confusions.

Maori names are almost entirely representations of the bird's call, from kiwi to piwakawaka and tieke. They are appropriate for endemic species such as the kiwi and tui, but can cause confusion when applied to a bird that occurs also in many other countries.

Sometimes the names of orders (or occasionally of families) are adapted when it is necessary to have a name to cover a group of species. The commonest case is the use of passerines for the Passeriformes, when "perching birds" is not considered precise enough. Aviculturists, the people who keep and breed birds (in many cases achieving a deep knowledge of their breeding behaviour), have their own terms, such as hookbeaks for the parrot family (but not including birds of prey).

Waders is a term covering the birds of the sub-order Charadriidae — plovers, dotterels, oyster-catchers, sandpipers, etc. — but sometimes it may include others which share their habitat. North Americans use the term "shorebird", which can usefully include herons and similar birds without argument. Birds of prey are eagles, hawks, falcons, vultures, etc., and sometimes include owls, the other group of predators. Raptors means the same. Ducks, geese and swans are waterfowl, a term normally excluding other aquatic birds such as shags or grebes. What are shags in New Zealand are cormorants to the rest of the world, but Britain has one species known as the shag. (Twelve of the world's 39 species are in the New Zealand region.) Pelagic birds are those which live at sea, such as petrels and alba-trosses, coming ashore only to lay eggs and rear young.

An endemic species is one which lives and breeds only in the area being discussed. The tui is endemic to New Zealand; the kea is an endemic South Island species. Some of our well-known native birds such as the white heron are not endemic because there are breeding populations of them in other parts of the world. Native (or indigenous) simply means occurring naturally. Introduced species are those brought to the area by humans, either purposefully as with the finches, or accidentally as in the case of cage escapees such as the rosella parakeets. You may sometimes meet the strange term "self-introduced" applied to birds such as the white-eye, which flew from Australia to become established here from about 1861, and the white-faced heron, first breeding here in the 1930s. Both these species, and others like them which cross the Tasman entirely on their own, become native to New Zealand. To state it more scientifically, they extend their range to include New Zealand. This is called colonising.

Feral birds are those living and breeding in the wild without dependence on humans. The pigeons of the countryside cliffs and quarries are a domestic species which has reverted to the wild state. Sometimes it is difficult to judge whether a bird has achieved a return to the wild state, or whether it still relies on handouts, as city pigeons do. Many cage-birds escape each year, but few survive to become feral. There are no feral canaries or budgies in New Zealand, though many hundreds (or thousands) must have escaped in the last fifty years. New Zealand obviously does not have the required habitat.

Identifying birds

Much of the enjoyment of birdwatching is in being able to put a name to the birds you see. Each observation of that particular species adds to what you knew of it before. Identification is really the foundation for any continuing observation of birds, whether for enjoyment or scientific study. Beginners pass through phases of despair at never being able to identify birds they see. They wonder at those people who can recognise a bird at first glance. There is no quick and easy way to identify every bird. Those who can have learned a lot more than identification points. Structure and behaviour, how birds are classified, how various habitats contain different species — a knowledge of all of these is the basis for easy identification.

Which comes first — identify a bird to learn about its behaviour, or learn about its habits and where it is found in order to identify it? A compromise is called for: know something about behaviour so you can identify, and this will allow you to learn more about behaviour.

To be successful at identification you must get into the habit of making notes in the field, and referring to books later. A field guide aims to give the field characteristics of a bird, and it is intended to be kept handy. It is sad to see a beginner, book in one hand and binoculars in the other, thinking that once seen the bird can be matched with a picture and instantly named. The result of that method is almost always failure, and many give up, thinking they will never learn the secret. To avoid this, first learn a few key features to look for, make some rough notes while looking at the bird, then go back to the field guide to consider the finer points which will decide the identification.

The key features for each group of birds distinguish them from others in the same order or family. With gulls it is the colour of the bill and amount of black on the wings. (Ignore the white head, white underside and tail — they *all* have that.) For terns, note bill colour and exact extent of the black cap; with ducks, colour of head and colour in the wings are probably the most important. Migrant waders always need close examination, but bill size and shape allow you to make a preliminary classification. In preparation for this, browse over the illustrations in a field guide, restricting yourself to just one family of birds in each session. Establish in your own mind the one or two key points distinguishing each species.

The next secret in quick identification is to anticipate. Know what birds to expect in the habitat you are moving through. This has the effect of narrowing down the number of species to which a suddenly appearing bird could belong. Suppose you are walking along a track in native forest in the North Island and a sparrow-sized bird flies across the track a few metres in front of you. Even without knowing which species occur in this particular forest, you have only to consider robin, tomtit, whitehead, chaffinch, plus shining cuckoo in summer. The few seconds the bird is in view may be long enough to note a key feature that allows the species to be confidently named.

It is a good idea to go out with the aim of seeing one particular bird known to be in the area. Before you start, know what points to look for and be prepared to write notes for your own future use. When you find the bird, watch carefully until you feel you will know it wherever you see it in the future. It doesn't take very long to cover all the commonly seen birds this way. Then you are in the happy position of being able to spend your time on those birds which look different.

Give each bird a quick look as it appears, mentally labelling each until you spot one you don't know, and then another challenge arises. Apply the same technique to this newcomer — identify it, get to know it, add it to your growing list of "birds that I will know anywhere".

You will find that the birds that are around are different every time you go out, even to the same place, so there is a challenge every time. In this way you will pass through the stage of just "bird spotting" to a deeper interest in them and their behaviour. Get to know all your local birds first. By recognising the common birds of your garden you will have a base to build on. These ones will be comparatively tame, allowing you to get really good views of them.

Strict honesty with yourself is essential when recording identifications. Every time you are out birdwatching there will be cases where you do not get a good enough look at the bird to identify it. After it's gone you realise you are not sure of some important feature. Bad luck, and a simple case for admitting you don't know that one. As you get better at identifying the commoner birds quickly, there is a temptation to make a quick decision on the briefest look at a bird. It is wiser to spend some time making quite sure; it is never safe to make assumptions and a mistake can be embarrassing later.

Appearance

Careful note of a bird's shape is likely to lead to a correct identification, though you will probably need some other detail to make the final decision. Birds come in a great variety of shapes and the members of any one family have a distinct similarity. All parakeets are streamlined with long tails; our parrots have much heavier bodies and the tail is shorter and square. Some individual species have such a distinctive shape that it is the simplest way to identify them. Wader watchers know the turnstone by its short neck and hunched shape long before its colour can be seen. In the garden in winter female greenfinches can look extremely like female house sparrows but for their heavier build.

Size is often difficult to estimate, so try to compare an unknown bird with one you know nearby. If you can wait until they come close together, you have an ideal comparison for your notes, and you can record points such as tail longer, legs shorter, stands more upright. Comparing the size of a strange bird with a familiar one not present is less reliable, because your judgment is affected by the conditions in which you see the birds. "Same size as a blackbird" when applied to a bird on an estuary cannot be reliable when the blackbird you have in mind is one in the shrubs of the home garden. Field guides always give the length of the bird in centimetres or inches, so make an estimate of total length and check it with the book.

Colour is only one point of recognition, and identification can often be made without considering it. Colour can be unreliable — wet plumage, reflection of bright sunlight, and so on, can make colours appear quite different and sometimes very confusing. Get to know what *the bird* looks like, and you will never mistake a starling for a blackbird even if they were both painted with yellow stripes! Jokes aside, blackbirds sometimes have partial albinism, a few white feathers amongst the black. So if such a black and white bird appeared on your lawn you should be able to say, "There's a blackbird with some white feathers in its wings," instead of spending hours searching through books for a species which doesn't exist.

The distinctive look of a bird, the general impression of it, is what is called its "jizz" — a silly word, but a very useful one to sum up all the things which give that species its individual character. Many birds in the moult or juveniles in the process of assuming adult plumage can have colour patterns that seem "all wrong". If the jizz of the bird is familiar you will be able to identify it in spite of some unfamiliar plumage.

Although there are good reasons why characteristics other than colour are used to identify birds in the field, plumage colouration is bound to be important. The variations in feather shape, size and colour have been discussed in Chapter 1. You will need to be familiar with the terms given there if you are to compile precise descriptions or refer to books to distinguish one species or subspecies from another.

A useful exercise in interpreting detailed descriptions is to spend some time comparing a description with a good photograph of the bird, or better still, with a museum specimen. Be prepared to assess the descriptions critically because a field guide may overlook an important feature.

Keen ornithologists usually own two or three field guides — Australian guides are useful too, since most of the rarities which turn up here have crossed the Tasman. For guidance on which books to consult, refer to the annotated bibliography on page 239.

Behaviour

Birds are so specialised, each so devoted to its own ecological niche, that their actions identify them just as surely as their appearance. When too far away to see the shape of a bird's bill, you can get a good idea of whether it is a thin probing bill, a strong seed-crushing bill or a hooked tearing bill by watching how the bird feeds. You then have a strong lead as to which family it belongs to.

Being so colourful, birds are often described by colour alone. It is not uncommon for a person to say something like "I saw a strange black and white bird on Sunday. What would it have been?" (Birdwatcher thinks . . . magpie? albatross? pied tit? black-backed gull? oystercatcher? . . .) The first question to ask is "Where did you see it?" If it was in a farming area, all but two or three black and white birds have been eliminated. The next question is "What was it doing?" If the answer is that it flew up from the ground and perched on the tip of a shelterbelt tree, you can be pretty sure that it was a magpie. Try to confirm this by asking about size and any other points that were noticed.

Maybe there is a lot more to know before you can name a species. In many cases that is simply because you are not familiar enough with the habits of the one which was observed. As you become more and more familiar with the way birds feed and move about, you will identify them by their movements, especially in difficult light or when they are at a distance. This is one reason why it will pay you to look carefully at every common bird whenever you have the opportunity.

Starlings and blackbirds are both common birds which are black and roughly the same size. Yet they are very easily distinguished on the ground, in a tree, or flying, because each of them has some special characteristics.

When a starling is searching for grubs or cleaning up the scraps, take a few minutes to observe it closely and see how it moves in definite strides, how it stands quite upright, how its shortish tail is no more than a completion of its trim, sleek body, and projects only a little beyond its wing-tips. When it flies off, see the rapid, regular wing-beats. Its wings are triangular, quite short and sharply pointed, and are often held straight out for long glides, especially when circling in to land. It probes for food, feeling down into the turf to grasp a grub rather than digging it out.

When the blackbird searches for worms in the lawn it moves in quick little shuffles with occasional hops — very different from the starling's strides. The body is held almost parallel to the ground, and a long tail stretches well past the wing-tips. A sudden stop on the ground or the balancing needed when it lands brings the tail right up to the vertical. The blackbird finds its food by digging with a powerful bill, tossing aside fallen leaves and often making quite a hole in soft ground. It will fly off swiftly, at first low over the ground, with powerful but relatively slow wing-beats.

Note how goldfinch flocks feeding on weeds fly up suddenly, dropping down again just a few metres away; how white-eyes move in tight little flocks of a dozen or so, pouring out of one patch of cover and into another.

Even in the same tree each species has its own way of feeding. Consider three small native species which feed on insects in the bush. In a beech tree a rifleman will search trunk and branches for insects hiding in the bark; a grey warbler will work through the leaves and twigs at branch end, fluttering around to pick off the insects at the tips; a fantail will concentrate on insects flying around the tree. So if a small bird is seen engaged in one of these activities you are already most of the way towards identifying it.

Song

If you learn to identify bird songs and calls you will have a wonderful short-cut to knowing which birds are around, even when the cover is so thick you see very few of them. Always be alert to note a call or song, being very careful that you attach it to the correct bird, which is not always easy in the bush. In one or two cases a sound other than a call can be used to identify the bird. Many New Zealand pigeons in heavy bush are recorded only from the unmistakable swish of their wings.

Start to learn bird songs in a garden where the birds are easily seen and each voice can be identified in turn. (For more information on bird song, refer to Chapter 3.)

Radio New Zealand has made a very useful contribution to our knowledge of New Zealand bird songs by playing one call each morning on the National Programme at 6 a.m., 7 a.m. and 9 a.m. (also 8 a.m. on Sundays). A change is made each Saturday, drawing from a library of over 40 calls. This gives you the opportunity to get to know a song by listening to it several times during a week, and in the course of a year there is a wide selection from native and introduced species.

Nests and eggs

The identification of nests and eggs is an interesting study in itself. The surest way to know what you have found is to see the bird, then take a good look at the shape and construction of the nest and the materials used. How and where the nest is placed helps to identify it too. Each tree-nesting species consistently applies its own method of placing the nest on branch or outer twigs, high up or low. Each species of duck conceals its nest in a different way, and you will be able to learn from photographs that there are small differences in the nests of ground-nesting gulls, terns and waders. Even the nests of congeneric blackbirds and song thrushes are finished off so differently one would not guess that they are so closely related. Somewhere in the process of evolution a nest with a hard lining of dried mud became established as a survival advantage to the thrush, while to the blackbird a lining of fine grasses was the right thing to do.

Chapter 3

Fieldwork

Equipment

As a hobby, birdwatching has one strong point in its
favour — it is not expensive. It is usual to start with
no equipment, but two things are necessary —
binoculars and an identification guide. Although you
continue birdwatching for a lifetime, these will
remain the only items you need to invest in. Because
of their importance, they must be chosen carefully.
The annotated bibliography on page 239 will help
you choose the books.

Binoculars

Binoculars are available in a great range of sizes, and
types, and prices. Generally speaking, quality
increases with price, so stretch your budget to get the
best quality. The choice is personal to some extent.
Try a wide range before you make a decision.

A magnification from 7 to 10 is considered the
most suitable for birdwatching. Binoculars are
described by two figures, e.g. 8 × 30. The first
figure refers to the magnification, the second one
gives the diameter in millimetres of the objective lens.
The size of this objective lens is important because it
controls how well you will see in poor light. Ideally
the diameter should be at least five times the magnification: 8 × 40 is good, 7 × 50 even better for
light-gathering power. Light-gathering is the more
important factor of the two. If you take the time to
compare binoculars you will find that you see a bird
better with good light admission but smaller

magnification. The bird may even look bigger! For this reason models such as 12 × 40 should be avoided.

The field of view is also important. Most birds will be moving about while you are watching them. It is most frustrating if the binoculars give such a small field of view that you are continually losing sight of the birds. For this reason telescopes are unsatisfactory for moving birds, and for the really active ones like swallows, binoculars have to be put down too. Manufacturers express the field of view in two different and confusing ways:

• As the area seen at a certain distance, e.g. 350 ft at 1000 yds. This means that a space 350 ft wide can be seen through these glasses by a viewer 1000 yds distant. (Sometimes the figures are metric.)

• As the angle of view, e.g. 6.9°. This is the angle of the wedge of vision you see through the lens. As a guide, 6.7° is the equivalent of 352 ft at 1000 yds.

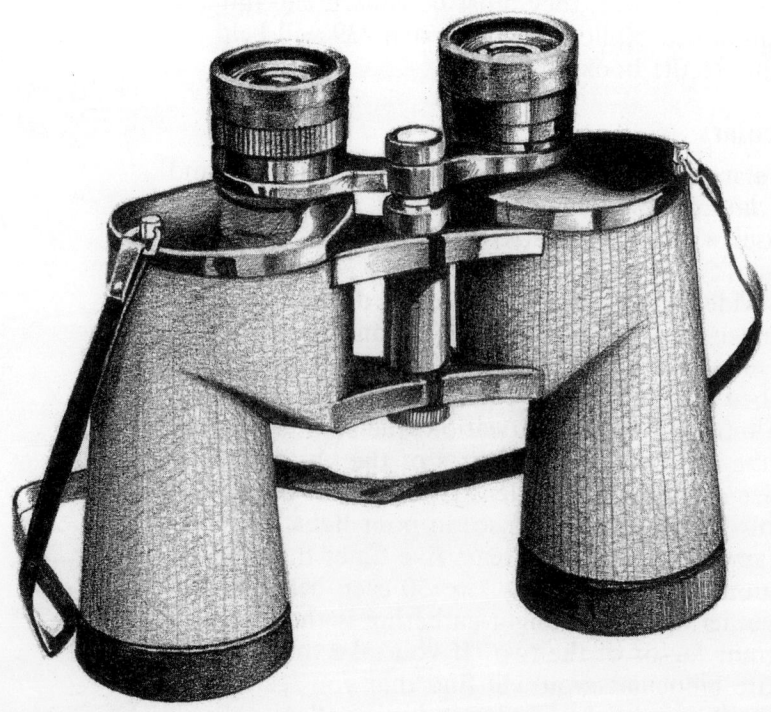

On this scale one tenth of a degree is significant, and anything less than about 6.5° is not useful. Some binoculars are sold as "wide angle". Note the field of view to make sure this is the case. (Although the question is sometimes asked, it is difficult to say how far you can see with good binoculars. Of course if you look at the moon through them, you will know they are good for 360,000 km!)

Heavy binoculars may be more sturdy, but you will not love them hanging around your neck all day. The size which is ideal for light gathering (7 × 50) is not suitable for birdwatchers for this reason. It is more suited to a boat or lookout post where it rests on a shelf until required.

Quick focus is a necessity for the birdwatcher in order to have a sharp image of a bird moving from branch to branch at changing distances. Central focusing is essential, and the press-bar fitted to some binoculars is a good device for rapid focus. Apart from the central focusing wheel, binoculars should have a separate adjustment on one eyepiece to allow for the normal difference between the left and right eyes.

Adjustment is made by focusing with the central wheel using your left eye only, right eye closed (supposing the right eyepiece is the adjustable one). Then close the left eye and focus on the same object with your right eye, this time using the eyepiece adjustment. Note the adjustment which suits you on the small scale marked on the eyepiece (usually 3 + across to 3 −). This will be your setting for ever more, and later focusing will be done with the central wheel.

Beware of binoculars which meet all the requirements until you try to focus on something close and find that it is hopelessly blurred, even at maximum adjustment. The very best binoculars will focus down to 2 m, some to 4 m or 5 m, many only to 10 m. It is quite common to want to see plumage details of a bird closer than 10 m. Depending on the price you can pay, you may need to compromise with other features.

A zoom lens gives you the ability to search with a

lower magnification and then bring in the subject on full power. The birdwatcher normally wants to use maximum magnification at all times, so this is a less attractive feature, and you would need to be wary of losing other advantages to provide this one.

Always try binoculars into the light, looking at some sharp-edged object against the sky. Poor optics create a "rainbow" spectrum around the object and the true colours are completely lost.

Most modern lenses are coated to prevent glare.

Permanent eye-cups can be a problem for spectacle wearers, but rubber roll-back cups are available as standard or extra for many makes. Rainguards and soft cases are often offered and these are worth having to protect the lenses during the hard wear which the average birdwatcher's binoculars get. Hard carrying cases protect the glasses in a pack or a car, but are too awkward to carry about in the field when you need instant access.

Other features include rubber coating over all external surfaces, which gives useful protection but adds to the weight, and watertight bodies, some nitrogen filled, which are the choice for marine conditions. Roof prism binoculars are ideal because they are smaller and lighter, but you may have to settle for a smaller field of view. There are models not much more expensive than conventional prisms.

Secondhand binoculars are worth looking at in the hope of getting what you want at less cost. Make sure you test them really well. The most common serious fault is prism mis-alignment. The result is your eyes are no longer looking along parallel lines and although eye muscles compensate for some of this, the user soon gets eyestrain and a headache. The test is to hold the binoculars quite steady while focusing on a prominent object in the distance. Close one eye, then the other. If the object jumps when you change from one eye to the other, the lenses are not in line. The cure is "re-collimating" by a repairer, which can be quite expensive. Choose your repairer carefully and always get an estimate of cost first.

Clothing

There are one or two things to consider when you are choosing clothing for a birdwatching trip. Colours should be inconspicuous — browns, greens or greys. Unfortunately some good-quality waterproof gear is brilliant yellow, which may be an excellent safety feature, but it will scare away birds long before you get near them. Wear plenty of clothes, it is better to be too warm when you are moving along than too cold when forced to sit still for long periods when you are in sight of the birds.

Telescope

A telescope is not something a beginner should buy. However after some experience you will know whether a telescope is likely to be of use. When choosing a telescope do not go for very high magnification. The advantage is outweighed by lack of definition, loss of colour and heat haze distortions. Most bird work is done with nothing above 25×, and 20× is recommended. Light-gathering is not a problem because telescopes are most used at estuaries or lakes where there is ample light. Most telescopes are offered with a selection of eyepieces ranging from about 15× up to 60× or higher. If you need high power for sea watching get the high-magnification eyepiece but don't rely on it for detailed work. Focusing distance must be considered, because wader watching sometimes calls for use of the scope down to about 25 or 30 metres. Some allow an adaptor for a 35 mm camera to take photographs through the scope. These photographs can be valuable for identifying rare species, but the slides are not the same quality as those taken with a telephoto lens.

Notes and written records

Once you have started to identify birds and take notice of their habits you will realise the importance of keeping notes. Get a hardcovered notebook which fits into your pocket, preferably one with a place for carrying a pen or pencil. Have a rubber band around half of it so it easily falls open at the page to be used next. It must be ready for instant use so that you can jot down a note while still following the action.

A beginner's first notes are likely to be a simple "bird list", that is, a list of species and numbers. This is a good way to start and is the basis of our knowledge of birds in an area: which species were present at what time. Recorded faithfully over a long period, these bird lists can provide very valuable data. In the case of rarities and vagrants the simple note of presence at a certain date is important, but of course when a note is made the birdwatcher might not realise that this bird is rarely seen in this particular habitat.

The next logical step is to state the breeding status. "Breeding confirmed" can be recorded when you have found eggs or young in the nest, or young just out of the nest, adults repeatedly carrying food to a probable nest site (such as one which you are unable to see into) or a recently used nest which you can identify with certainty. "Breeding presumed" means that you have seen one of the following: an adult carrying nesting material or food, or a male singing regularly or strongly defending a territory in the breeding season.

It is a good idea to make your notes include impressions and questions which come to mind — these are clues which might turn out to be very useful when you come to solve a puzzle of identification. "They landed on the sea as if they didn't know how to use their wings to slow down." That could be a good indication that you had seen diving petrels. "Why didn't it fly at once instead of running along the track in front of me?" That sounds like pipit behaviour and a strong clue towards separating it from the skylark, which looks so similar.

The very best place to start recording birds systematically is in your own garden. Rule up a page for each month, with a wide column for species names down the left, then 31 narrow columns for the days of the month. The common species (which you know will be seen on at least one day of each month) can be written in, with spaces left below for other birds as they turn up. Pages like this can be photo-copied to save ruling up each month. Keep the sheet in a handy place so you can tick off each species as you see it. Take the opportunity to train yourself in a little scientific discipline: *never* tick off any bird until you have seen it that day.

Even a common bird like the blackbird may not be seen some days, although you know that it will be in the neighbourhood. When you have completed a month which has several gaps opposite blackbird you have a simple indication that it is less common in that month. This chart will soon begin to give you some information, such as which months chaffinches or fantails are in the garden, when red-billed gulls are around, and so on. Recording everything seen or heard from your property can add quite a few unusual species like pied stilts flying over at night, passing flocks of ducks, etc.

The next step can be to distinguish between birds seen and heard. On this chart H instead of a tick would be sufficient, but in census work the numbers are separated by an oblique slash so that 8/2 means eight seen and another two heard but not seen. Another advance is to record when full song is heard by putting S in the square. After the first year's cycle has been completed, you will find that knowing when to expect the first song of, say the song thrush, adds real interest to your home garden birdwatching.

This daily record sheet is something which anyone can get going at any time, and it can be done without interruption to normal routines. If you go out to work, any odd minute in the morning and some time after you get home in the evening is all that's needed. If you are away for all daylight hours in winter, record on Saturdays and Sundays only. The results from keeping this going for two years or more will fascinate you.

Wherever possible note down comparisons on size and other points. "Darker brown . . . longer legs . . . flight was much slower . . . wings more pointed than . . ." are all ways of defining small differences which will be useful later. An exact description of a bird will also try to take note of relationships which are not easy to get into a sketch or even to show up in a photograph, for example, "bill about 1½ times as long as the head; folded wings project 2 cm beyond tail."

It is often important to be able to find old records in your notebooks promptly (essential, if you want to write something for publication). There are so many methods that it is best to devise your own system and set it up in a way that best suits you. The easiest is simply to keep notes in date order, but you might like to have a cross reference to species, or to locations. Some people keep card files, and many field notes are now going on to computer files. One word of warning — be careful not to have a system which involves more time organising the notes than out making observations.

Suppose, on a birdwatching expedition, you find a bird which seems to be a rarity and you feel that good notes must be made. The ideal record would be compiled in three parts: (1) field notes written while observing the bird, (2) field notes written immediately afterwards, (3) points added later when writing up the record.

(1) While watching the bird note:

• its size, shape and structure; length of tail and legs, size and shape of bill,
• exact description of the plumage as far as possible; colours and feather patterns,
• how it was feeding, its movements and flight pattern; comparisons with other species you know,
• any song or calls heard.
(2) A description of the habitat, the weather conditions, how long you watched the bird, what power binoculars you were using.
(3) List other species you could possibly have confused it with, and why you discarded these choices. A confirmation received from other observers who saw the bird later, etc.

The most important notes are those made on the spot — that is, when you try to record everything with an open mind. Establish a system of your own for bird descriptions and always work to it. This might be: bill, legs, plumage (working from head to tail), wings, then underside. If you have friends with you it is a good idea to agree on each description. For instance, before writing it down, agree on whether leg colour is dark brown, medium brown, or greenish brown. That way you will end up with a reliable description.

Bird song

Writing down bird songs in your notebook is not easy, but it is often necessary to have something to remind you of the sound at least. Most books use the traditional method of writing phonetically or syllabically. This conveys some idea of the song but cannot say much about pitch, tempo or duration. The words can remind us of the call, such as "to-bac-co" for the crowing of a California quail, but working the other way, it's almost impossible to know the call from reading this.

The first reaction of many people to this phonetic representation of bird songs is to treat it as a big joke. We have all been influenced by childhood story books in which the wise old owl said, "Too-wit-to-woo"! It is hard to overcome this handicap and to appreciate the usefulness of the phonetic writing which has been used for the yellowhammer's song for many, many years: "a little bit of bread and no cheeeese". This gives the rhythm of the song and if you have heard the bird sing, the phrase is a useful reminder.

People with musical ability have written bird songs in musical notation but this is difficult, and the recent trend in books is to use sonagrams (described in Chapter 1). It is not too difficult to draw a rough sonagram of the call when you are familiar with the technique.

Choose your own system and practise with it so that you can write all sorts of bird songs and calls for your own purposes, even if they might convey little to anyone else. In addition, describe the structure of the call with such terms as chatter, warble, screech, and the quality of the sound as fluting, shrill, whistling, etc. In one way or another it is certainly possible to get a bird song written into your notebook.

Weighing and measuring

Recording data from a bird in the hand includes weighing and measuring. Weighing can be done most easily with a spring balance. The bird is put into a lightweight plastic bag (head downwards) where it will lie still long enough for the weight to be read. Of course the weight of the bag must be known so that it can be deducted.

Usually measurements are taken of the wing, leg, tail and bill, and sometimes the overall length. Wing length is measured with the wing bent, and is the distance from the carpal joint (the "shoulder") to the end of the longest primary. Holding the bird in one hand, its wing is laid on a rule and the primary feathers flattened and straightened along the rule. There are different schools of thought about this primary feather straightening, which is unfortunate since it is a very important measure. Some say flatten out the cup of the wing only, others say that the normal curve in the long primary feathers should be straightened also; others say neither, measure as is.

Therefore in every case it is wise to note next to your measurements what has been done — "straightened and flattened" or whatever.

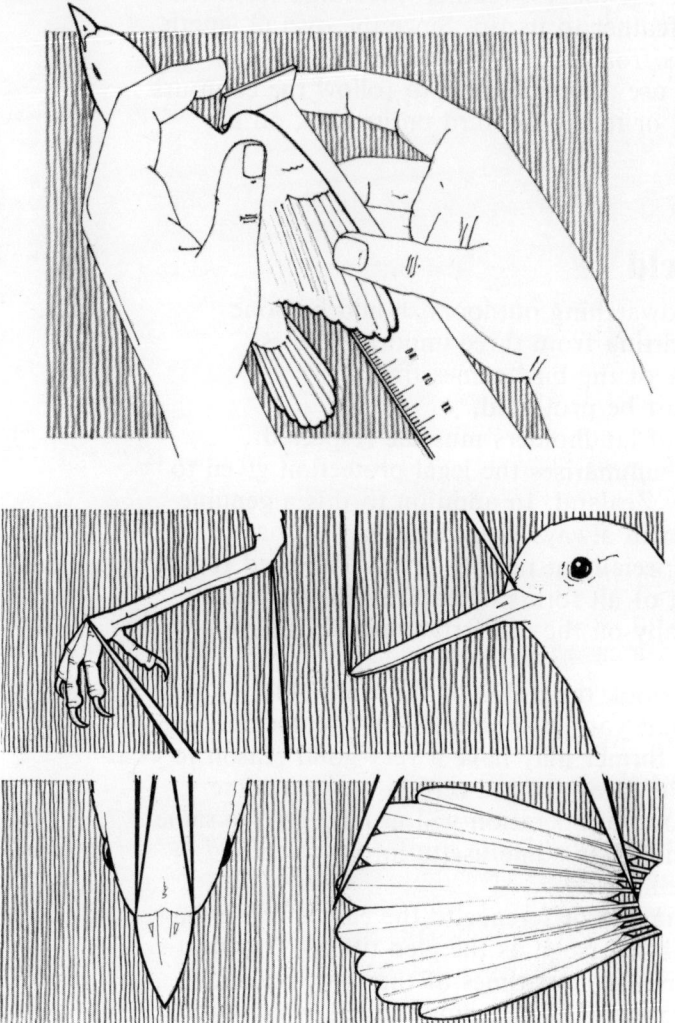

The length of the tarsus bone is measured from the joint above the middle toe (in front) to the notch behind the upper end. Vernier callipers do this best. Bill length and width are also taken with vernier callipers which can give decimals of a millimetre. Length is taken from the tip of the upper mandible to the edge of the feathering on the forehead, in a straight line, not attempting to follow a curve in the bill. Width is taken at its widest point. Tail length is the length of the longest feather, measured from the base of the feather to its tip. Since the overall length of the bird is from bill tip to end of tail, it is necessary to use a flexible tape to follow the contours of the body, or to lay the bird on its back on a bench.

In the field

All your birdwatching outdoors should be done without departing from three important rules:
• the welfare of the bird comes first,
• habitat must be protected,
• the rights of landholders must be respected.
Appendix 3 summarises the legal protection given to birds in New Zealand. In addition to this a genuine birdwatcher will always keep disturbance to a minimum especially at nesting times. The need for conservation of all forms of nature will be seen to follow logically on the understanding of the life of birds.

Never overlook the rights of the landholder and make sure that you have permission to enter on every occasion. A farmer may have a very good reason to keep everyone away from a certain area on some days, and your co-operation will usually get the same in return, and often some useful information and advice as well.

Seasons make a difference to the ease of observing birds. Bush birds (such as the pied tit) are friendly and inquisitive at most times of the year, but may become secretive when breeding. Others which are normally not easy to see may follow you with loud alarm calls if you are in their territory in the breeding season. Prominent trees in flower or with ripe fruit bring birds from a large area. The hard times of late winter and early spring bring seldom-seen birds into parks and city gardens looking for food.

Many bush birds can be attracted with a squeaker, and in dense bush or scrub you will see more than you would without one. The most effective squeaker is a piece of white foam polystyrene on wet glass. You could carry a small bottle of water, but any clean piece of glass can be wet with spit and the plastic rubbed on it to produce the squeaking which has a fascination for many birds (and some small mammals). With practice polystyrene and glass can be made to produce very realistic imitations of bird calls, from the soft quacking of grey ducks to the "stitch" of stitchbirds. Sucking through moistened lips (or on the forefinger) can produce the squeaking also, and some people can imitate several bird calls sufficiently to bring them around or at least slow them down, which can make all the difference when you're trying to identify something moving through the undergrowth.

The right whistled note will always get a response from a fernbird hiding in the dense cover of fern, bracken or rushes in wet places. The fernbird is the one bird easier to find the more noise you make! Crash a few metres into its territory then stop still. The fernbird will appear in no time right beside you. Listen to the fernbird laughing when you sink slowly into knee-deep swamp water, through not checking what was under the vegetation!

In fieldwork a tape recorder may be used to record bird calls to identify later, but it is even more useful as a means of attracting birds. The song of a stranger brings an immediate response when played to a territory-holding species. The male sings in response and comes immediately to investigate. Our knowledge of the distribution of some shy and inconspicuous species is almost entirely dependent on the use of tapes of their song or calls. The North Island kokako is a good example. This species is found only in unmodified native forest, spending much of its time in the canopy where it is difficult to see. When tapes of its song were played in North Island forests an unexpected number were found.

When using a tape, find the right habitat, then settle down quietly out of sight and play the call, moving the speaker around. It doesn't matter if the volume is louder than a natural call. Amazingly, birds seem to ignore distortions in a recording unable to cope with all the frequencies of a bird's song, but a song played out of season will be ignored.

Birds of prey are well known for the habit of casting pellets. These are formed from indigestible matter eaten with food: bones, feathers, fur, etc. are formed into a ball and ejected via the mouth. The ground under customary roosting or sleeping places of hawks and owls can be searched for pellets which provide evidence of the food taken, by way of identifiable feather or fur fragments, beaks, or insect wing-cases. The habit is not confined to birds of prey, and nearly all species seem to have the ability to eject undigestible matter from the gizzard.

Locating the nest

A field guide often gives brief information on nest location. Other books in the bibliography will give you detailed information and photographs of the nest sites of many common species.

Finding nests, even when you know where to look, can call for much skill and experience. Some birds conceal their nests. Others with conspicuous nests rely on inaccessability for safety. Getting into a position where you can watch satisfactorily is often difficult. But as well as looking for the nest itself make use of other clues such as odd straws dropped below a nest, or chips of wood below a hole in a tree — a good indication that kingfishers are at work. Some but not all birds create a mess of droppings below the nest as the brood grows. The very strict hygiene of some small passerines leaves the area just as clean as when they arrived.

Broken eggshell tells you that young have hatched. You will be able to work out which species from the colour and pattern of the shell. Parent birds of most species carry the eggshell from the nest as soon as the young hatch, dropping it well away from the nest to avoid attracting predators. If you find a half shell you have a clue that there is a nest nearby (10 m–30 m) with newly hatched chicks. An emerging chick chips its way out through the shell and then bursts it open by stretching its neck and legs in a way that normally leaves the empty shell roughly in two halves. An egg attacked by a predator can be recognised by the way it has been bitten or pecked into from one side. Some shy species cannot be approached closely without fear of causing desertion. Look for their eggshells to know when hatching has occurred.

Probably the most successful method of locating a nest is to follow a bird which is carrying nesting material or food. This is called "watching back to the nest". The bird will probably not fly directly to the nest, so the first trip may give you only the general locality. Then get behind some cover and wait for its return. If the bird is unsuspecting, it will not be long before it is moving along the same route. By advancing in easy stages you will get to a position where you can see the nest site or the tree or bush it is in. At this point plan an approach which will least disturb the nesting birds. Whenever possible, wait for both birds to be absent before you go to the nest. If you must put a sitting bird off, do so as gently as possible. A bit of noise a few yards away will often get the sitting bird to slip off quietly. If you blunder in, pushing the vegetation aside quickly, a brooding bird will rush off in panic, sometimes kicking an egg out of the nest as it goes, and quite often deserting permanently. That brood is then destroyed and you will have lost the chance to watch it through to fledging of the young.

"Dive bombing" is the only way that nesting birds can hope to drive off intruders. By making repeated swoops, usually with angry or distressed cries, they often succeed in frightening off humans who don't understand what the commotion is about. If you feel you have good reason for visiting ground-nesting gulls, terns or waders, remember these points:
• Be very careful where you step. Nests and eggs are cleverly camouflaged. You may not be able to distinguish them from sand or stones until you are within one or two metres. If birds are screeching around your head, the tendency is to watch them

instead of where you are stepping. Don't let that be the cause of your crushing a nest or chick.

• If you are scared of being pecked or scratched, carry a stick or a twiggy branch over your head. Birds will keep clear of them.

• The chaos caused by your visit to the area may have serious effects not obvious to you at the time. A tightly packed nesting colony is a complex social organisation. In a disturbance running chicks often finish up outside their "legal boundaries". After you have gone, returning adults drive these strange chicks away. They wander into other places where they are just as unwelcome. They are pecked and bullied until many die before finding their parents. Make your observations from the edges of a colony. Choose a nest on the perimeter for study or photography.

Counting birds

Bird counts are an important part of birdwatching. To know how many of which species were at a certain place at a certain time can be a useful piece in the jigsaw puzzle which makes up the life of a bird. Some people think that birdwatchers just count birds, but if there were no more in it than that it would be a pretty unexciting occupation. There are techniques which allow you to produce more accurate counts than just noting down what you see. Particularly in the bush, birds are very mobile, and it is very difficult to end up with an accurate total when you are never sure how many birds you have seen, as ones which look the same appear and disappear all around.

A census technique, following scientific principles, gives a reliable estimate of the number of birds present with the most economic use of time and effort. A widely accepted census method is the five minute count at 200 m intervals. The observer moves through the bush, preferably on a marked line or track, stopping every 200 m to record all the birds seen or heard in exactly five minutes. Notes differentiate between those seen and those heard, and include only the birds within 50 m of the counting point. In dense bush or steep country the distance between count stations may be varied from 200 m.

The aim of such a census is to produce data for comparison with other counts in the same place, over many seasons. It will be valid for comparison with similar habitat in another part of the country counted by the same method. This is never possible with simple counts of the species recorded in a certain place, even if the observer makes comments like "common, very few", etc.

If you have an interest in the bird population of an area of bush, you should decide on a census method and stick to it over regular counts. Mark the tracks to be followed, measure out the count stations and mark them. Counting is an activity where the single observer working alone can do valuable work, particularly if the counts are repeated for several years.

Practice will help you develop skills in counting flocks of birds. Before starting to count a resting flock plan how you will go about it and at which end you will start. Flocks are usually spread irregularly. Note how they are standing or lying so you won't make the mistake of double counting or missing some. Identify one or two markers which will allow you to divide the flock into sections. Birds in large flocks are best counted in twos, threes or fives, because your eyes tire as you struggle on counting one at a time. If you need to be quick because the flock is likely to fly off, count one block of 100, then use this as a measure to count off the rest in hundreds. If they fly before you have finished, make an estimate of them in the air rather than giving up altogether.

Groups of birds feeding on the ground can be very difficult to count. You are more likely to get an accurate figure if you count quickly before the movements to and fro confuse you. Welcome swallows feeding over a pond or stream are almost impossible, every bird flying in a different direction, twisting and backtracking this way and that. Extra care must be taken with shags, dabchicks and diving ducks which stay under the water on long dives. Your best chance of a correct total is to take the highest number you get after several counts. Even then there is the likelihood of missing one or two under the water. Record the number with a plus mark after it, meaning that you are certain of that number but there were also some others.

A count of a special kind was carried out by members of the Ornithological Society of New Zealand during the ten years 1969–1979. This Bird Distribution Mapping Scheme set out to record the species present in each 10,000 yard square of the national map grid for the mainland and offshore islands — and that includes some remote and rugged parts of New Zealand. The result was 96% coverage, and an *Atlas of Bird Distribution in New Zealand*. It is a very valuable source of information.

Banding

Bird banding or bird ringing mean the same thing. In New Zealand we usually call it banding and say it is a band, not a ring, which is put on a bird's leg.

The only practical way to be sure you are dealing with an individual bird is to give it a unique and permanent number — like a car registration plate. Without this it is easy to make misleading assumptions. Reports that the same bird has been visiting a garden or nesting in a certain place for ten years cannot be accepted if the bird was not identified by a band number. The report might be correct, but it could also be wrong. When a bird dies it is usual for another of the same species to take up the vacated territory or nesting place. Secondly, birds are banded so that they can be identified if they turn up somewhere far from the study area where they were banded.

Bands always carry two items of information: a number, and an address the band can be returned to. Bands on New Zealand birds have a number (with one or two letters) and "Send Dominion Museum, N.Z." or "Send National Museum, N.Z." or "Send Wildlife Service, Wellington, N.Z." either in full or abbreviated according to the size of the band. The museum addresses date from the time when banding records were kept there.

Does a band hurt or hinder the bird? The first aim is to fit the band so the bird is not harmed. A properly banded bird does not seem to be inconvenienced once it has got used to the bracelet. The lightest, strongest and most durable materials are used for bands; aluminium alloy for the small sizes, monel metal or stainless steel for the larger ones. Bands for small birds are very light (25 bands weigh 1 gram). Another important consideration is that birds go through rapid weight changes. The equivalent of about 6 kg in human weight is lost in one night's sleep to be put on again the next day. The equivalent of 15–25 kg is put on in cold weather. A female bird carrying developing eggs has as much extra weight as several hundred bands. So a bird will not be handicapped by the weight of a band any more than you would be by an extra sock or a watch.

Reading the numbers on a band normally means the bird must be captured, although some records are obtained by watching patiently through binoculars. Coloured bands allow the individual to be recognised without handling, and are used in any study where instant recognition is needed. They are usually plastic and may not last very long, so a numbered metal band is put on the bird as well. Using just three colours (plus the metal one), 400 combinations are possible by changing the position of the colours on the right and left legs.

Always keep a lookout for banded birds, and make a note of coloured bands whenever you are able to list them with certainty. A few enquiries to a local museum or wildlife officer should locate the person who is studying the banded bird. He or she will want to know exactly where the bird was, on what day. Every dead bird seen on the roadside or beach should be turned over to look for a metal band. If you find one, the band should be removed, flattened, and sent to the address stamped on it, with your own name and address, the place and date the band was found, and any information on the apparent cause of death. You will receive an acknowledgement to tell you where and when the bird was banded, which often proves to be very interesting. It is surprising how far even the commonest birds wander. A band should not be removed from a live bird, simply record the details and advise the organisation responsible.

Chapter 4

A study project

When a close study is made of one bird, not only do you find out about that bird, you also gain basic information about birds in general which allows you to compare the activities of other species. Any study project is a matter of answering questions which arise at each step. Here, questions are posed on the life of the starling. They are intended to give you a start, but do not cover the whole subject. Some questions can be answered simply, some take years, or may never be answered. That is what science is all about. There is no need to go into all the studies suggested here to get a lot of enjoyment — just go as far as your time and curiosity allow you.

It's a good idea to start by recording easily observed starling behaviour. As you do this, something might interest you and lead you to follow it more closely. The vital thing is to keep notes. Make sure you write down what you see and the date it happens. You will get a lot of pleasure from following the annual cycle of the bird's life, and later, predicting what will happen next. Without notes records become uncertain, important information gets forgotten and it is easy to lose interest and give up.

The starling has been chosen because it is common throughout the developed parts of the country. Its ideal habitat has many potential nest sites in buildings or mature trees and large areas of short grass for feeding. Nearly all farmland carries a good population. In cities the lawns, parks and playing fields provide feeding areas for the starlings which

nest under the roofs of buildings and supplement
their diet with scraps of garbage. Starlings are absent
from heavily forested areas and high country.

As an introduced bird, it is not protected and may
be trapped, handled for measurement or studies of
feather moult etc., and banded without a permit.

While this makes the starling convenient to study,
more important, it is a surprisingly interesting bird,
providing plenty of challenge for intensive study.

Much of the starling's life is spent in flocks and
numbers of birds nest close together. Social stimulus
is probably an important factor in much of their
breeding behaviour, causing egg-laying dates to be
synchronised to some degree. Your study will prove
to what extent this is true in the conditions prevailing
in your district.

The starling

The starling (common starling, European starling),
Sturnus vulgaris, is a native of Britain and Europe,
and was first introduced to New Zealand in 1862. It
soon became established and spread rapidly
throughout the country, finding its own way to the
Kermadec and Chatham Islands. It is a successful
species, thriving in its original habitat and adapting
quickly to conditions in all countries where it has
been introduced.

It belongs to the order Passeriformes, family
Sturnidae, a large group of 100 species of starlings
and mynas. The Indian myna (*Acridotheres tristis*)
found in northern New Zealand is a close relative.

The starling is glossy black, with green and purple
iridescence in sunlight, speckled with whitish spots
prominent in winter. It is 20 cm long, stockily built
with a short tail. The yellow bill turns dark grey in
autumn and winter. Its legs and feet are dark brown.
The sexes look alike, but in the breeding season the

North Island brown kiwi
(Rod Morris)

Fiordland crested penguins
(Rod Morris)

Yellow-eyed penguin
(Rod Morris)

Australasian gannets
(Rod Morris)

Little blue penguin
(Rod Morris)

Royal albatross
(Rod Morris)

Pied shags
(Geoff Moon)

N.Z. scaup (Black teal)
(Don Hadden)

White-faced heron
(David Stonex)

base of the bill is blue in males, pink in females. The eye colour is different, the iris of the male is all dark brown, whereas in the female it has a paler ring. The young have pale chocolate-brown plumage with white throat.

The starling is a hole-nester. Its natural choice is holes in trees, cliffs or banks and, like most hole-nesters, it readily takes to artificial nestboxes. Close observation of the breeding cycle is a major part of the project so you will need to put up some nestboxes.

The nestbox

A suitable place for a nestbox needs to be:
• Safe from predators. It is best about 2.5 m (8 or 9 ft) off the ground, and inaccessible to cats. If a cat can climb to the box it will reach for the chicks, or sit for hours keeping parents off the nest or waiting to catch a sitting bird as it tries to leave.
• Easily watched. Have it handy to a window but not so close the birds are scared to enter it, or come and go nervously at high speed, which makes it difficult for the observer.
• At least partly sheltered from the weather.
• Away from high levels of human activity. For instance, a nestbox over the back door would mean the birds were disturbed every time someone came in or out. To avoid mess made by bird droppings have the flight path over lawn or garden.
• Accessible. As you will regularly inspect the nest, have the box in a place that makes your task easy and causes least disturbance to the birds.
• Higher than nearby objects. Song perches near the nest are important to the starling, but you won't want it to use yours or your neighbour's clothesline. Keep the box a little higher and the male will use the nest box as his singing perch.

Wood is the best material for the nestbox. Any scrap boards can be used but 15 mm pine is probably best. Put it together snugly to make it dry and draughtproof, and when you have chosen a place, make sure it is attached firmly. The most practical size and shape is 30 cm (12 in) high, 15 cm (6 in) wide and 15 cm deep. These are minimum inside measurements; a little extra is welcome. The top should have a small overhang at the front to act as a veranda over the entrance hole, and must slope to the back to shed rain. It should be hinged at the back edge so that you can inspect the nest. Make a round entrance hole, 45 mm (1¾ in) in diameter if you are using timber up to about 15 mm thick, but a shade larger in thicker timber. If the birds can't get in without a struggle, file it back a little. Have the bottom of the entrance hole 20 cm (8 in) from the base of the box. A small perch about 45 mm (1¾ in) below the entrance will make it easier for the birds to get in and out.

The small entrance hole keeps out mynas which could kill the nestlings..In regions free of mynas the hole size could be a little larger. Starlings are able to handle mynas in most situations and they are sure to rear some young even if others are lost in raids. By making nestboxes inaccessible to mynas you will have more successful nests to study.

Many observations can be made with a single nestbox but three or more are recommended to increase the possibility of interactions between the different pairs. When the boxes are up, stop starlings from nesting under the roof of your house. This will bring them to the nestboxes. In any case they should be kept out of the roof. In an unlimited space they make a large heap of straw, added to in successive seasons, thus creating a fire risk.

Banding

If the starling's behaviour is to be accurately recorded it is necessary to colour band birds so an individual can be identified with certainty. As you are likely to be dealing with a small number of birds, one colour band per bird is enough. Choose six plain colours and you can identify 12 birds using either leg for each colour. An alternative is to use two bands, the same colour on each leg. This is helpful when you can see one leg only. Or you could band females on the left leg, males on the right, so the sex of the bird (shown in the eye colour) is easily distinguished at any time. Coloured plastic bands can be purchased from the larger pet shops. Make sure you get a size which fits the leg loosely but without a space to catch on something.

If your study is extended you will need two-colour combinations which will identify up to 72 birds (6 x 6 on left leg, 6 x 6 on right), or three bands for 432 combinations using six colours. A simple colour banding system is of great value but colour bands on their own have limitations. They cannot identify a bird away from its "normal" area, and they never give the positive identification of an individual achieved with a numbered band. If you decide to pursue aspects of the life of the starling and need numbered bands, advice will be gladly given by the Banding Officer, N.Z. Wildlife Service, Wellington.

Catching birds to band and later to handle for the study of moult, etc., requires knowledge of the equipment. Your aim must be to capture the bird while causing the least distress. A hand net over the hole of the nestbox is effective but not recommended when there are eggs or young. Mist nets used by professionals are not available to everybody. A simple trap is suitable for the inquisitive starling.

Traps can be portable or permanent, attended or automatic. A drop trap can be put almost anywhere. It is a box shape in wire netting, bottomless and with one side propped up with a stick. A line attached to the prop pulls it out when a bird enters to get bait and the trap drops over the bird or birds.

Waiting for birds is a time-consuming exercise, but there are advantages. You can choose your bird, letting the unwanted ones go free. As well, you are there to attend to the trapped bird immediately.

For the trapped bird, the most traumatic part is when your hand is placed on it and this is when it makes the most effort to escape. For this reason the trap should be made so that it cannot damage the bird. When bashing against wire netting birds can be hurt around the bill, the forehead or the eyes through trying to push through the mesh. They suffer less if the mesh is large enough for the head and neck to go through. For starlings this would be 2 centimetres. The green plastic-covered netting sold in garden shops has the advantage of "padding" over the hard wire.

Funnel traps are designed on the principle of the crayfish pot — the bird enters to get bait but is unable to find its way out. An effective trap must have a second compartment joined by a funnel to the first. It is a good idea if this holding compartment has a small catching pen off it so the birds can be lifted out without trouble. A funnel trap does not have to be watched continuously but should be checked frequently, especially if it is on the ground or any other place where cats can get at it. When not in use the trap should be baited but left open so that birds can pass in and out freely and so become used to it.

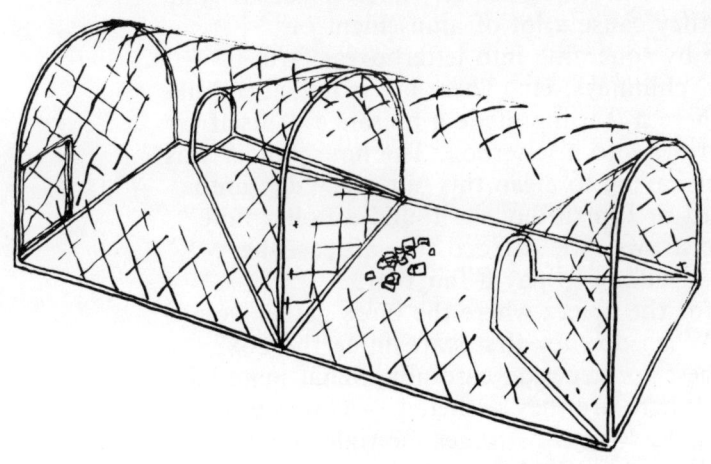

Observation

Nesting

The nest site is the centre of starling life through most of the year. When is it first taken over, and is it by a male or a female? How closely is it defended? Starlings are known to change from one nestbox to another — under what conditions does this occur? Is it only when the previous occupants disappear, or when only one of them goes? If one, this may indicate which bird of the pair is the main occupier. We know that in some species of birds the female chooses the site; in others it is the male, and he then attracts a mate, sometimes leading her to the exact position which he has chosen for the nest. What situation applies to your starlings? One obvious sign of occupation by a male is that every morning (except in summer) he sits on the nestbox and sings.

Watch for any activity near the nestboxes which looks like searching for an alternative nest site. Outside the breeding season there may be starlings on the lookout for nest holes in any likely place. It is at this stage they cause a lot of amusement or annoyance by squeezing into letterboxes, farm machinery, chimneys, etc. There are many stories like the one where a starling made a nuisance of itself by stuffing straws into a letterbox. The householder was annoyed at having to clean this out every day until on the third or fourth day she found a dollar note among the straws. She decided that at least the starling was willing to pay a fair rent.

Watch for the places where the birds gather nest material. When do they first start lining the box? Note the nest construction carefully. What materials are used? Where are they gathered — close by, or do the birds make long trips to get the right materials? Note the date when the first material goes into the box and when later bouts of activity occur. Do both sexes do this work? Since the same nestbox is used year after year, what is done by the birds to clean out or renew the nest material?

Watch for attempts to steal nest material from other starlings. Is it males or females that do this?

You will see the resulting nest defence fights and be able to establish the part played by each bird. Are fights male to male and female to female, or is it a free-for-all?

Starlings clearly do not defend large territories because they can be seen feeding in flocks at all times of the year. Find out what size "nest territory" they defend apart from the actual interior of the box. For what part of the breeding season is this territory held?

As you inspect the nest regularly the birds will become used to you, but they will never be happy to have you go to the nestbox. Organise well and get your work done promptly to cause as little disturbance as possible. During incubation give the sitting bird time to get off the nest without panic. A little noise nearby will get it out of the box before you are too close. Please note that starling nestboxes should not be opened up later than 17 days after hatching, or the chicks will escape in fright and perish because at that age they are not old enough to survive.

When the nest is completed or nearly so, you may see the pair mating, and you will know that egg laying is about to start. Are there any display rituals before mating? Does mating take place at the nestbox, within the nest-territory, or somewhere nearby?

Eggs

Accurate recording of the dates eggs are laid is crucial to the study of the breeding cycle. Many other activities will be calculated from these dates. After the first egg, what is the interval until the next and subsequent eggs? If daily, is it always the same time of day? A common practice when studying nesting is to mark a number on each egg. This is not recommended because starlings throw out any egg which is marked. When the full clutch has been laid, incubation will begin. Pinpoint this, bearing in mind that it is now very important not to disturb the breeding pair. In the early stages they are prone to desert the nest. Later there is an obvious commitment to the growing chicks.

As incubation proceeds, find out how this task is shared between the two birds. When one bird is on the nest what does the other bird do? Does it stay close by, on guard, or keep right away? If they share, how often do they change over? Note the length of time the eggs are left unbrooded. (This seems to vary a lot between species.) The field guide says that hatching occurs after about 13 days. Check carefully around that time. Do all eggs hatch on the same day?

Chicks

Young starlings are nidicolous — they emerge from the egg helpless, bald, blind and unbeautiful. When do their eyes open? What down covering do they acquire? At what stage do the first feathers emerge? Which feathers are these, and how much longer is it before other feathers follow? Note the distinctive pattern of feather tracts on body and wings. Is the progress of all chicks in the brood identical? At what age do they cease producing faecal sacs which allow droppings to be removed by the parents? How is nest hygiene maintained after this?

Once there are chicks in the nest, the quiet fortnight of incubation gives way to a constant struggle by the parents to keep the chicks full enough to stop their noisy begging. You could estimate the daily feeding rate by taking a sample count of the visits the parents make to the nest in one hour of one day, but this tells only part of the story. Feeding rates vary at different times of the day. One complete day of recording every visit is needed. Perhaps you could encourage a friend to help so each of you could get meals and a bit of exercise.

Get a clipboard or pad with lined sheets ruled in three columns: column 1 headed "Visits by female", column 2 headed "Visits by male", and column 3, "Sex not noted". The speed at which the parents come and go will mean you aren't always able to distinguish between them so the third column is necessary. Attach a digital watch at the top of the board, and write the time (hour, minute and second) in the appropriate column as each starling goes into the nestbox — 9.21.06, 9.24.34, 9.25.17, etc. At the end of the day an analysis of this data will give you:
• Total number of visits made by the parent birds. (Count the total number of entries on the sheets.)
• The proportion of visits made by the male.
• The proportion of visits made by the female.

• Peak times for feeding. (Rule off the sheets at each hour and count the visits in each period.)
• The greatest interval that chicks are left without feeding.

A compromise method would be to take an exact hour four times during the day, say after dawn, mid-morning, early afternoon and an hour before sunset. A mechanical or electronic device could be built to record each visit. This is not easy because it must be in a position where *every* visit triggers it, without scaring the birds off. The parents enter the hole from a dozen different angles when they are busy feeding a growing brood.

Compared to other species of passerines young starlings are slow to leave the nest, although they appear developed enough to do so. Do you have any explanations for this? Record the date of fledging, as well as the number of days since hatching. How do parents look after the fledglings? Does each parent care for half the family or do they stay in one group? Are both parents equally involved and for how long? Do the young follow the parents, or wait for food to be brought to them? Do the fledglings return to sleep in the nest?

It is not easy to keep track of a family group as it moves about, but you may be able to answer some of these questions. The starlings will not be far from the nest in the first few days. This is a time when the young are vulnerable to predators, and household cats take a heavy toll.

Physical changes

In February you will notice the first signs of moulting. Prominent whitish spots appear on the birds' bodies, although head and neck may be unchanged. New contour feathers are growing to replace the old ones which are by now well worn from climbing in and out of nestboxes. This is the month for closest study of the moult sequence if you decide to get involved in it. Your banded birds will need to be caught and examined frequently to note the progress of the moult, recording exact dates for each step. Starlings have 10 primaries, the tenth being very small.

Take special note of the immature birds which left the nest in November or December. Replacement of their light brown plumage with glossy black produces some unusual birds for a week or two. Is the sequence of moult the same for both adults and young? Do the immature birds all moult at the same time regardless of the date they left the nest? Watch for differences between males and females. Having observed this main moult occurring in late summer, you will have to watch for any other periods of moult in the starling. Occasional handling of the banded birds will allow you to determine this by careful counting of the primaries, secondaries and tail feathers, noting the stage of growth of each one of them. Examine the contour feathers at the same time. This may give you the answer to that little mystery of the starling's disappearing white spots.

Every year someone gets excited about some rare birds appearing in suburban gardens — black with orange crowns. Starlings are just as fond of the nectar in flax flowers as tui are and the pollen stains from the flax flowers make them look quite smart!

The twice-yearly change in the colour of the bill is another interesting thing to watch for. In some ways it seems more strange for subtle hormonal changes in the bird's body to cause this quite striking change in the hard plates of the bill, than the dropping out and replacement of worn feathers. Record the dates and relate them to the breeding activity of the individual. Are male and female bill colour changes synchronised or independent? There may be a timing difference between those birds which have reared young and those which have remained unattached.

Behaviour

Some species of birds pair for life. Some pair-bonds last during only one breeding season, and others separate during autumn and winter and take up again with their old mates the following spring. The starling pair-bond has been described as "flexible", so keep a close watch on pair behaviour.

When does a pair-bond seem to form? In winter flocks or at the nestbox? Is there any evidence of it being maintained through the winter? Are there any "divorces" — one bird leaving to pair up with another? Was the new mate paired or free before the change? At what stage of the breeding cycle did this occur? Record which one of a pair moves to another nestbox. This is evidence on which sex is the chief occupier of the nest site. What is the recent nesting history of the divorced pair? Does success or failure have any bearing on pair changes?

Watch for cases of polygamy where one male has two females. If each has a clutch of eggs, watch them carefully for results. Your observations should show that starlings react to circumstances in certain predictable ways. Is the statement that pair-bonds are flexible accurate or an oversimplification? This aspect of behaviour could be an entertaining study on its own.

The colony-nesting aspect of starling behaviour is said to influence the synchronisation of laying dates. Does it influence the ending of the nesting period? What is the situation when a second clutch is laid?

Survival in the hard climate of northern Europe requires birds to spend much of the summer building up fat reserves before the onset of winter. Adults need to be free of the demands of feeding young and the young of the season old enough to feed themselves efficiently. The survival of the species would be in danger if birds did not start the winter in peak condition. Nesting must not encroach on this vital build-up period. This requirement is hardly necessary in the milder climate of New Zealand but the starling is unlikely to have made a complete adjustment to its new habitat. You will find it interesting to record how starlings in your study group finish the nesting season.

Record all cases of nest failure and the cause. The date on which a pair abandon a first clutch will be an important influence on whether or not the pair (or the survivor if one is lost) have another clutch of eggs. If another clutch is laid, is there the same number of eggs? How do other details compare with the first clutch? What about second broods after the successful rearing of the first? Does there appear to be a latest allowable time, a "closing date" for rearing a second brood before the season ends? Nestboxes occupied by pairs with second clutches must be watched very closely around the middle of December.

The male starling makes such an amusing variety of sounds that many people would hardly classify the result as song. However, if you listen carefully you will realise that this is a complex song that incorporates mimicry of other birds and local sounds. It has a pattern of whistles and clicks, which sounds like bill clacking but isn't. You can soon identify the source of sounds, such as factory whistles, barking dogs or ambulance sirens. It is an interesting exercise to list the bird calls mimicked by each starling. Quite likely you will get a list of five or six species, maybe more, mimicked by one bird. Can you guess where these calls were heard? Do all the males in your study group mimic the same species? If there are differences you would have a fascinating puzzle to solve — where did one bird pick them up, but not the other?

Note the times of the day at which the male sings, and where his song perches are. What is the duration of each song period? Is there variation during the seasons? There may be a part of the year when he does not sing at all — record this carefully. Does the female ever sing?

You will soon get to know the alarm call, "queerk". Also learn to recognise the high level alarm call, "chip, chip" and what circumstances cause it. What is the reaction of other starlings, the bird's mate and then others in the area, to each of these calls? Do you have an explanation for the postures and wing-waving which the male engages in while singing?

You may be lucky enough to see a starling engaged in the strange process of "anting". A bird on the ground (near an ants' nest) will pick up an ant in its bill then wipe it along its primary feathers. After one such movement the ant is discarded and another picked up and used the same way. It is believed that this is a feather-maintenance activity and the formic acid produced by ants is wiped along the feathers to clean them. Bathing and preening always follow an anting session. Starlings are one of the birds most often displaying this odd behaviour, but it has rarely been recorded in New Zealand.

Starlings were introduced to New Zealand to combat pasture pests. To what extent are they doing this? In Europe ground invertebrates are said to be the major item of their diet but is this the case in New Zealand? Note where you see starlings feeding and when, so that you may be able to build up a picture of their feeding habits through the seasons. They often feed in flocks — does this habit continue right through the year including the breeding season, when most birds are strictly individualistic? Take note of the size of flocks in each month of the year. This probably varies in different parts of the country and different habitats. To find out the feeding range of a pair — how far they forage from the nest — you would probably need colour marking, but you may be able to make conclusions without that. The feeding range is said to be no more than 500 m, mostly around 200 m.

You are probably aware that starlings roost together overnight in large numbers, sometimes tens of thousands, in places chosen for the safety they provide. Some variations to this habit have been recorded in various parts of the world. You could set about discovering how local starling populations roost.

Firstly, it might be best to locate the main roost in the area. This is most easily done in winter when the feeding flocks are larger and the evening return to roosts is earlier. In the hour or so before sunset small and large flocks take a straight-line flight to their roost, so it is not too difficult to "home in" on its location. Pine plantations are popular places. Wellington city birds roost in pines on the slopes of Mt Victoria; the pine plantations around Pleasant

Point Domain on New Brighton spit hold Christchurch starlings. Inshore islands are often chosen, no doubt because of the absence of most or all predators. Many Auckland birds cross each night to Rangitoto Island. Tokomapuna islet by Kapiti Island takes birds from the Paraparaumu–Waikanae coastal area.

There are frequent unexplained changes of roost: some are used for decades, others don't last a season. "Staging posts" where the birds gather, are moved regularly, but it will not take you long to find the places which are currently in use in your area. The changes are not made without some reason. It would be worth keeping a record of the use of staging posts in your area with the hope of coming up with some answer on this.

The advantages of the roosting habit are said to include safety in numbers and flying with other birds in the morning to known sources of food, rather than spending each day searching. There must be some survival advantages for the habit to continue because it costs the birds energy and time to fly 10 or 20 km (or more) each night and morning between feeding place and roost.

When you know where the main roost is, find out whether the birds go straight there from your garden. Is there an assembly area where birds gather before moving to the main roost? A small group of trees, or just one tree of a line may be full of chattering, singing starlings late on winter afternoons. Are these assembly points for birds feeding locally? Watch one evening to see where the birds come from and whether or not they stay to sleep there. Do all birds go to the roost? What happens in the breeding season? When one bird is brooding eggs or chicks, does the other sleep in the nest, stay on guard nearby, or go to a roost?

Starlings are unpopular when they foul window ledges or pavements below trees where they roost in the central city in winter. Escaped heating from buildings combined with car exhaust fumes keep the air temperature in the city about 2°C higher than the countryside during the night. This is as attractive to starlings as the beaches of Fiji and Hawaii are to us in July.

To estimate the number of birds using a roost settle yourself into a vantage point well before sunset, and count the birds as they come in. It won't be easy because they may be arriving from all directions and flying fast. Some small flocks enter the roost with the spectacular tumbling flight which is a device to confuse predators. Small flocks fly quite low, often along the same route each night. Locate one of these flight lines and you will be able to note the time relative to sunset, the number of birds passing through and how this varies during the seasons. In stormy weather starlings fly as low as half a metre above the ground over open spaces to avoid the wind as much as possible.

Once they arrive at the roost they take up positions according to their status. The arguing and jostling accounts for the noise which can be heard a long way off. The safest positions in the centre of the roost go to adult males which have won this right perhaps after years of coming to the same roost. Young birds will be around the edges.

Morning departures are made in waves of birds which scatter to feeding areas, flying as directly and as fast as they came in the night before.

Survival and longevity

The survival of a ground-feeding species is very dependent on the availability of food through the critical winter months. Cold ground means fewer insects and hard frosts make the ground almost inpenetrable. New Zealand pasture land has a much milder winter than the one experienced by the starling in Europe. We would expect them to be able to survive much more successfully here.

To find out how long starlings live you would need to use numbered bands to follow individual birds throughout their lives. A large-scale banding project would be necessary to get enough data to provide reliable answers to all the questions of survival and longevity. This is probably outside the scope of an amateur working on his or her own. It is thought that the average life of a starling is only 12 to 18 months, as a result of large numbers of immature birds not surviving the first winter. Those which learn to survive through those early months have a much longer life expectancy. The oldest recorded starlings are a 17-year-old in Britain, and a German bird over 21 years old. The New Zealand situation is interesting: if there are fewer predators here and winters are much milder, what is it that keeps starlings from increasing rapidly?

Record the apparent cause of death of any bird you find dead. In the case of your banded birds, record as much data as possible: age, sex, state of moult, whether breeding or not (and at what stage) as well as the date and cause, if known. It may take a long time to get a picture of the common causes of bird deaths in your area, because we find only a very small proportion of wild birds that die.

Starlings spend much time feeding on the ground, so cats must get many of them. Some become easy prey when a desperate fight over a nest site brings two birds rolling on the ground, locked together bill and claw. The communal nesting habit is a mechanism of defence against predators. Birds of prey are not a major threat. A starling would probably be too big for a morepork to attack, and New Zealand falcons are so uncommon in developed areas that their total take of starlings could be no more than a few hundred in a year. The sight of a harrier usually puts ground-feeding flocks of starlings into the air to fly in tight flocks which twist and turn in defensive movement. Sometimes they will harass the harrier, sending it quickly on its way. Such excitement is unnecessary as the harrier is most unlikely to attack a healthy starling. However, we must acknowledge that some inherent fear of a bird of prey is sure to be retained by a species native to Europe where falcons and hawks are active predators. Record any predator attack you witness, whether successful or not.

Try to build up a record of the starling's relationships with other species, especially natives.

Observe reactions when feeding and when nesting, and try to assess whether the starling is aggressive beyond "holding its own". It has been accused of driving out other hole-nesting species, even the kingfisher. Look for hard evidence of this. Try to assess whether it occurs when there is a real shortage of nesting cavities or through aggressiveness.

Part II
Habitats

Chapter 5

Gardens and parks

The typical New Zealand garden of town or city suburb is still the quarter acre. Some would make it the butt of all sorts of jokes and others blame it for suburban neurosis. We can be very glad that the unwritten law of "flowers in front, lawn, vegetables and a couple of fruit trees at the back" has preserved enough open space to support some birds around our houses over all seasons. Without a doubt, watching birds in a suburban garden could provide enough interest for a lifetime of enjoyment, or enough data to complete a thesis for a university doctorate. So there is no better place to start, and if you have few chances to go on trips to exciting bird places, it does not matter. There will be plenty going on around home.

Does anyone know exactly what house sparrows live on apart from household scraps? Seeds, of what? Cock sparrow develops his black bib slowly through the winter. How long does it take in your district — and is it the same in all New Zealand climates? Probably not. It does not take long to think of plenty of questions remaining to be answered.

The suburban garden is an environment severely modified for people and the house sparrow is the

only bird which seeks out human buildings. However, several others take advantage of the side effects or useful features of our homes and their garden surroundings. These are the ones which we can encourage with large trees for safe cover and nest sites well away from disturbance, and shrubs for berries and for cover close to the ground.

New Zealand's temperate climate means that there is growth in plant and insect life at all times of the year, and these will always be able to provide at least some food to some species of bird. Just how much attention the local bird life gives to your garden on any day will depend largely on what other food is available in the area. A good expanse of lawn among closely packed housing will be popular with blackbirds and song thrushes unless it becomes hard and dry. Flowering or berry-carrying shrubs in winter seldom fail to attract birds because this is a time of general shortage of food. At other times a food source in the garden may not get the attention you expect. You have probably noticed that damage to precious orchard fruit varies from year to year for no apparent reason, or a certain fruit tree will be left alone during the first week the fruit is ripe, but attacked from dawn till dusk in the following days. The explanation will probably be that somewhere nearby there is another source of food which the birds preferred. One year while your crop of ripe cherries is being demolished someone in the next street is rejoicing that his apricots are being left alone. A temporary shortage of food will often cause birds to eat fruit or vegetables which they normally ignore (such as tomatoes) or to attack fruit before it is ripe.

In recent years there has been quite a lot of thought given to planning gardens so that they attract birds and most garden shops will gladly give advice on the selection of plants. The New Zealand Wildlife Service has produced a pamphlet on *Tree Planting for Native Birds*. So help is available if you want to improve the habitat which your garden presents, and if your neighbourhood has a reasonable number of trees, you should never be without the company of birds. The other factor which influences the type of birds in the garden is the district which you are in. Obviously, to be close to an area of native forest greatly increases the chance of having visits from New Zealand pigeons and tuis.

Blackbirds are resident throughout the year, and normally the more shy song thrush is there too. Thrushes have disappeared from some suburban gardens in recent years, leaving them without the beautiful song which enriches cold winter mornings from the month of May and continues until December. The blackbird's rich fluting song does not start until about August. If you have any difficulty distinguishing these songs remember that when the thrush has produced a phrase of pure, clear notes it often repeats it, perhaps more than once. The poet Robert Browning recognised this when he wrote:

That's the wise thrush; he sings each song twice over,
Lest you should think he never could recapture
The first fine careless rapture!

Both blackbird and song thrush are strongly territorial in the breeding season, and the choice of a prominent song perch within the territory helps to define the boundaries. The singing male gives both audible and visual signals that this territory is occupied and will be defended. With no knowledge at all of these species, we can enjoy the rich melody of their songs. An understanding of the place of the song in the life of the bird can add another dimension to our enjoyment.

The house sparrow is in every street every day of the year but it would be a pity if you took no interest in it merely because it is so common. If you are a beginner, use it to practise on; if experienced birdwatchers were all asked to describe the male sparrow's plumage exactly, there would be some worried people and a fairly low "pass rate". The plumage changes through the seasons and it is made up of quite a complex feather pattern. The slow emergence of the familiar black bib from under the grey breast feathers as winter progresses is very interesting to follow. You could also try keeping a record of the daily movements of sparrows, which may show that they leave the surrounds of the house at certain times of the day to feed on paddocks or roadsides when grass or weed seeds are ripe.

The other common birds of New Zealand town gardens are also nearly all introduced species. Starlings are around right through the year but they go to a communal roost, several kilometres away perhaps, in winter and they join daytime feeding flocks in open country. The seasonal movements of blackbirds and song thrushes will require to be learned for each particular locality. Could you state with any certainty whether there are song thrushes in your garden in April, or blackbirds in February? The only way to understand the local movement pattern is to make a record of whether or not each species is present each day. Interesting patterns then emerge.

Some local movements are known at least to a limited extent. For instance, chaffinches move to the coasts in the autumn, with the males returning to territories in June or July and females joining them there in the first few days of August. But this generalisation may not be accurate for your district and we have yet to learn what variations apply from north to south, dry areas compared to high rainfall areas, etc. If you keep a simple record over two or three years of whether or not the chaffinch was seen or heard each day, you could come up with the answers. In the process you will also have got to know the chaffinch a whole lot better and quite likely you will be motivated to study some aspect of its behaviour more closely.

The Indian myna is a conspicuous bird of town and country in the northern half of the North Island, above a line which runs from Wanganui in the west through Waiouru to Pahiatua in the east. Southerners consider themselves lucky that this aggressive introduction does not seem to be able to extend its range any further south. In recent years mynas have spread to the very northern tip of the North Island, but the southern boundary has been maintained except for occasional stragglers.

Mynas belong to Sturnidae, the starling family,

and you may see some similarities with the starling as they stride around a lawn. They are hole-nesters, too, and they tend to stay around human settlements, nesting in buildings. They roost communally in large trees, old phoenix palms being a popular choice. Mynas destroy nests and kill young birds of other species in spring. They move around an area in a gang, tearing apart nests and killing chicks. Of all their antics this behaviour is difficult to understand and is certainly one reason for their widespread unpopularity.

The white-eye (or silvereye or waxeye) is one of the most entertaining birds of the garden because of its tameness and its constant activity. They form flocks in winter and there is a movement down to lower altitude by birds which spend the summer in mountain forests.

White-eyes eat a wide variety of foods — fruit, insects, animal fats, etc. You will find that one of the first priorities of the winter flocks will be to clean up any apples or pears left on the trees, and they will also be accounting for aphids and scale insects all around the garden. Blight bird was a name given to them when they first arrived from Australia about 125 years ago. Many people find it hard to believe that this tiny bird found its way here over 2000 km of ocean. As if that wasn't enough, they have since spread to the Chathams and the subantarctic islands.

White-eye

They are easily attracted to food during winter and half an apple or a tin of old cooking fat tied up in a tree or on a fence will bring them to where you can watch them closely. All of them are not exactly alike as you may think initially — the chestnut flank is darker and richer on the male bird.

White-eye flocks give a great opportunity to study dominance and the constant struggle to preserve the pecking order within the flock. Watch how there is much threatening and chasing as near-to-equal individuals argue each encounter. When the bird at the top of the order arrives it will go straight to the food; low-order birds can be seen waiting until all the senior individuals have fed before they hurry in for anything that's left. Some white-eyes stay in the garden to nest and rear their young, but as soon as food becomes more plentiful in spring, pairs are formed, the flocks break up, and most of them move away from the towns.

Which other birds you have in your garden will depend on your locality and on what conditions you provide to attract them. A quarter-acre section in an established suburb which has plenty of trees and shrubs will support good numbers of the common species and there are likely to be interesting visitors like tuis, bellbirds and moreporks. Treeless new subdivisions are pretty much a desert for birds, with no more than the more adventurous sparrows and starlings — and of course neatly finished roofs won't even provide nest holes for them. One well-planted section in such an area will not be enough to attract the interesting species.

We need to realise that birds have to put up with a lot of disturbance in any garden. When this reaches a level which they cannot tolerate they will stay away permanently. It is unfortunate that any small garden which is well used by adults and children will have few birds. Dogs keep ground-feeding birds away, and of course cats not only disturb, but actively hunt and kill. Undisturbed areas of shrubs and trees are the most valuable environments for nesting. Regular mowing and weeding around a tidy garden often discourages birds at the delicate stage of nest site selection or commencement of building. When this happens there is little hope of the pair returning to nest there that season.

Winter can become an interesting time in the suburban garden through the visits of many birds not seen at other times. Finches and yellowhammers move in to the cities and towns when food becomes scarce in their usual habitats. Greenfinches appear in small parties which feed on the ground on seeds or chickweed. Males are smartly olive green with brilliant yellow flashes from wings and tail when they fly. Females are a sombre brownish green and may be mistaken for female sparrows if you do not note the heavy bill and stocky build. Goldfinches form flocks which can number hundreds of birds, but they usually move about the suburbs in small parties of three to ten, feeding on weed seeds, with a special liking for thistle seed. Their tinkling flight call is usually heard before you see the bright flashes from their golden wing patches. Chaffinches search the ground under shrubs and trees moving with a distinctive rapid shuffle that is neither hop nor walk. They also flutter around trunks and branches, displaying their white wing bars and white tail feathers while they catch moths. The handsome red-breasted male does not sing before late July but his strident "pink, pink" call is easily recognised. The female is delicately patterned in pale shades of grey and brown and also shows white in wings and tail in flight. Redpolls come into gardens from time to time in winter in those districts where they are common in the surrounding countryside, especially Christchurch and the towns of the South Island's east coast. They remain shy of buildings and are most often seen flying overhead quite high, invariably giving their distinctive flight call, "chi-chi-chi-chi". Seeded patches of weeds, especially fathen, will bring them back day after day until this food is exhausted.

The two buntings introduced to New Zealand, yellowhammer and cirl bunting, both range widely in winter but the rare cirl bunting is unlikely to be seen in town gardens. The other frequently comes on to bare ground and is still around in early spring to join sparrows stealing grass seed on newly sown lawns.

The hedge sparrow (which is no sparrow but brings its name down the centuries from the time when most small birds were "sparrows") may live in a well-planted garden all year round. Sadly there are now large areas where the strident song and cheerful "tseep" call of this shy little bird are no longer heard. Bare ground or short grass under shrubs and trees, or along hedges, are the places where it is most easily seen, searching diligently with jerky, shuffling motion. The greatest numbers of hedge sparrows are now found at the coast in sand dune lupins and scrub.

The close-mown lawns of parks and playing fields are popular resting places for gulls in almost all weathers, but especially when storms drive them away from the rocks and beaches. Black-backed gulls will be seen in all the colour phases which indicate the age of the bird: dark brown young of the year, through mottled brown and white until the adult plumage is achieved with smart white head and body, black back and upper wing surfaces. The bird is three years old by the time it sheds all traces of brown. It is a fact that the dark brown of the youngest birds creates an optical illusion that they are larger than the black and white ones, and young birds are often mistaken for a different species from their parents. The smaller red-billed gull is a regular lawnsitter too, using this safe place as a base for its scavenging around the streets and school playgrounds. After heavy rain, when sodden ground has driven worms to the surface, the flock spreads out to feast on the easy pickings. The black-billed gull is even more fond of worms and grubs but it seldom comes into town parks.

When a high spring tide backed by strong winds drives South Island pied oystercatchers off their usual roosts on the estuary shores, you may find them in tight flocks out on large areas of lawn. Their long red bills and black and white plumage make them conspicuous on the green turf, especially when they also cover the ground in search of worms. Having flown in to join in the party, white-faced herons and kingfishers can also be seen, the herons striding over the grass and the kingfishers using trees or goal posts as perches for frequent swoops down to the turf.

Chapter 6

Farmland

The open farmland which covers approximately 30%
of the area of the two main islands of New Zealand
does not carry a high number of birds. It is
interesting that nearly all of them are introduced
species. Is it that the new habitat of grassland heavily
grazed by animals is unattractive to native birds, or
have the introduced birds driven out the natives? You
will be able to make up your own mind about that
when you become familiar with the various New
Zealand habitats and the requirements of the native
species.

The short-cropped grass paddocks have ground-
feeding blackbirds, song thrushes, starlings and
magpies. All of these feed on worms and insects dug
from the soft ground.

The skylark is a bird of the grassland but it feeds
on seeds and above-ground insects, so it has some
preference for drier pastures. The native pipit (which
looks so much like the skylark) shares this habitat in
the rougher or tussocky places — so as to confuse
birdwatchers. The skylark and pipit are so alike that
identification of them could be taken as the
qualifying test of a field observer. You will have no
option but to use the methods which are described in

Chapter 2. Colour patterns give no obvious distinguishing marks, and going to a book for a coloured photograph or painting is not very likely to help either. But there will be no problem for you if you start by looking closely at the way the bird behaves, its "jizz". Firstly, the pipit has no sustained song, so the bird which pours forth a long and melodious song while hovering in the air is sure to be a skylark. On the ground skylarks may run a little as you approach, but normally they will fly off a hundred metres or so. Pipits behave quite differently. They have a distinctive habit of running ahead as you approach them on foot. They are often met on a track, where they run ahead in little bursts of 5 m or so, taking to the air only when you have gained on them and are within 25–30 m. Their flight will be for a very short distance and you will soon catch up again, and the pattern is repeated. You can drive a pipit quite a distance along a track before it chooses to circle round to land behind you. If you do not put pressure on it to run or fly, it will flick its tail up and down as it watches you. Pipits belong to the family Motacillidae which includes the European wagtails which are named for this tail-flicking habit.

Differences in the "jizz" of skylark and pipit can easily separate them if you are able to watch them closely. The skylark has a noticeably smaller head in proportion and the tail is a little shorter; it frequently erects its head feathers into a small crest, which the pipit cannot do. Pipits have a head more in proportion to the body size and a longer tail, which give a sleeker look; their light eyestripe is more prominent than the skylark's. So test your skill as an observer by distinguishing between these two really difficult ones.

A new arrival which is conspicuous on farmlands is the spur-winged plover. It has spread northwards slowly but steadily since it arrived at Invercargill (from Australia) about 1940. Look for it, or listen for its distinctive grating call in the open, especially near areas of wet, sour ground.

Around farm trees and along hedges white-eyes are likely to be met as they move through the branches, or form into energetic little flocks making their way between feeding places with a constant "peep, peep" contact call. Hedge sparrows feed on the ground near cover, chiefly where the ground is bare of grass and litter insects can be turned up. Thrushes and blackbirds, too, like to keep near cover. The side of a large grass field next to trees gets more attention than the centre where the birds would be very vulnerable to attacks from predators.

Fantails and grey warblers are probably the only endemic species normally found around farm hedges and trees. To them the insect fauna supported by hedges is a fair substitute for the forest margins which they lost when the land was cleared. Along roadsides and on areas of waste ground introduced finches and yellowhammers are attracted to the supply of weed and grass seeds. Yellowhammers are found in open country throughout New Zealand, but the closely grazed green grass pastures which make up a big proportion of our open country are of no use to them because they produce no seed. They thrive along roadsides and in riverbeds where growth and seeding continue in the natural cycle. Winter feedout of hay attracts very interesting mixed flocks of yellowhammers, chaffinches, goldfinches, sparrows, feral pigeons, and even cirl buntings in the regions where these occur. Grass seed shaken out of the hay lies along the feedout line after the hay has been eaten by stock, and birds soon learn to come to it each day. The weed we call fathen used to be common in crops and it attracted large flocks of birds if it was left to seed. However, modern selective sprays can eliminate most weeds and clean crops are of little interest to birds. The total number of finches and yellowhammers has most likely declined since they lost this valuable food supply.

Streams and ponds in farmland attract mallard and grey duck from time to time. There must be good cover such as raupo or rushes if the ducks are to stay throughout the year. The bogs and swamps which best suit ducks are unfortunately the very conditions which efficient farming sets out to eliminate, so they are more and more being driven to the remaining

lakes and larger rivers. Most pied stilts spend winter
on the coast, but from early spring gravelly riverbeds
and the boggy areas around ponds and farm dams
will resound with their yapping calls. Some of them
nest in riverbeds among stones, but more often small
colonies of a few pairs set their nests on clumps of
turf in wet places.

Pied stilt

Stilts go through an elaborate distraction display to
draw predators away from their nests and chicks. No
doubt this is an effective defence in most cases, but
for humans it acts in the opposite way by advertising
the nest. When the usual "yap, yap" of stilts becomes
more high-pitched and agitated, and the birds circle
closely around, you know there is a nest near by. By
careful manoeuvring you can lower the intensity of
the calling and diving as you get further from the
nest and increase it as you get closer. The parent bird
will then land a few metres away and go through the
peak performance. This calls for a realistic act of
dying slowly with plenty of flapping and crying.
There may be one or two flutters which take the bird

a little way off the ground, then it may lie flat and slowly flap its outstretched wings, crying out all the time. Maybe the original pied stilt was an Oscar-winning actor in the bird world soap opera. Very entertaining, but in real earnest of course, because the parent birds desperately need to get you away from the eggs or chicks which have only their cryptic colouration to protect them. Be *very* careful where you place each foot as you move through the nesting area. Not only are the eggs cryptically coloured, but the chicks are also very difficult to see when they "freeze" in response to their parents' calls. Don't stay in the vicinity too long, because on a cold day eggs or chicks could be chilled in a few minutes.

White-faced herons are also regular visitors to the wet places around farms. They come to stalk frogs, tadpoles or small fish in shallow water. This heron is not restricted to wet areas. Worms in a damp pasture or insects in dry grass are both acceptable. It is a common sight in a big variety of habitats. When you hear the sequences of guttural grunts which white-faced herons give as they glide into a roosting site, note the position and try to move to a spot where you can see them clearly. This way you can watch them through your binoculars when they are much more easily observed than when they are moving about in a swamp. They nest in tall trees, usually concealing the nest well up amongst the branches or next to the trunk of a pine.

Farm dams or ponds are also the most likely place to find the welcome swallows of this habitat, where they will be feeding on the insects which gather over the surface of the water. The vicinity of milking sheds is a popular place with swallows for the insects invariably found there.

Willow trees along the riverbanks in lowland farm country are as good a place as any in which to look for shining cuckoos in December and January. They are probably attracted to the willows to feed on the caterpillars of the willow-gall sawfly which are emerging from their hard brown leaf galls at this time of the year. The shining cuckoo is much more often heard than seen — its drawn-out call carries for hundreds of metres — but you have a much better chance of seeing them when they are in the willows than in native forest. Watch for a glossy shine on the back of any sparrow-sized bird which you see fluttering around the outer branches.

Paradise ducks (or paradise shelducks as they are more accurately called) are found on farmland over most of the country, as well as far into the foothills. The conspicuous white head of the female is the first thing to be spotted out in the open well away from cover. When they have seen you the distinctive duet alarm call will start: "quank" from the female, "honk" from the male. They are invariably in pairs as this is a bird which mates for life and the pair stays together throughout the year. They are such wary birds that they can never be approached closely.

There is a harrier high in the sky over farmland at almost every hour of the day. As well as this lazy circling they fly low to search the ground with care. No item of food misses the "eagle eye" but they are content to let the healthy and active escape while they feed on carrion, young or sick birds, lizards, and even frogs. This is one species which benefits from the hundreds of rabbits, birds and possums which are killed on the roads. In spring the courtship flight of a pair of harriers is a delight to watch as they circle round each other high up. Their piercing long drawn-out cry may first draw your attention to them. Harriers get a hard time when they wander too near to magpies' nesting trees. Three or four magpies will join an attack, circling and diving from all sides, sometimes until they drive it down to the ground. Usually the hawk rolls over in flight and defends itself with talons which are more than a match for the magpies.

Harriers' nests are placed in the centre of large rushes or reeds in remote gullies or in swamps, where the young can be safe from disturbance during the six weeks taken to grow their flight feathers. If you ever find a harrier's nest with young, you will see that they are of different sizes because like many birds of prey, the harrier starts to brood each egg as soon as it is laid. The result is that the eggs hatch successively instead of all on the same day. An interesting winter behaviour of these birds is to roost together on the ground or in reed beds. With careful observation of late evening flight lines you may trace birds to a roosting site containing as many as 50 birds.

Harrier

The age of a harrier can be judged by the darkness of its plumage: young birds are dark chocolate but as the years pass they become lighter until old birds are no more than tawny brown, even greyish in some lights. Knowing this, you can take an interest in which birds are in your district at any particular time. It is said that there is a larger proportion of dark young birds in more closely settled farmland and at the coast because the more valuable territories up-country are held by older birds which drive off the young ones. This is a common situation in the natural world where everything has to be earned. Harriers flying close to buildings, or showing no fear when coming to an animal killed on the road, are very often young birds driven to take risks through hunger brought about by their lack of experience in hunting.

Magpies are common over most developed farmland. They are conspicuous and unmistakable, but you must look closely if you are to distinguish the two species. Both white-backed and black-backed were introduced from Australia and they are similar except for the intense black of the mantle.

They are all very aggressive in defence of the locality of their nests, some individuals especially so. Magpies get some "bad publicity" in some part of the country every spring, when their attacks terrify humans as well as cats and dogs. Very often the birds are shot as a result. Fearless defence of nest and young may be admired, but we humans have a habit of treating every inch of the world's surface as our own territory. If you go near nesting magpies carry a twiggy branch above your head like an umbrella and you will never need to be afraid of getting struck by them.

No doubt birds have "followed the plough" since the first plough, many centuries ago, turned over the earth and exposed worms and grubs. A free lunch has always been welcome. Red-billed gulls are the most common followers of the plough in both North and South islands, but from Canterbury southwards the black-bill comes into its own as the true inland gull. Large flocks will often return each day to a paddock so long as it is being worked. They may be joined by black-fronted terns, especially within a radius of a few kilometres of their nests on the great riverbeds south of Banks Peninsula. A rich orange bill below a black cap is the distinctive feature of this graceful little tern. They spend the time floating lightly about 3 or 4 m above the ground, dipping down to pick up food but not landing to walk along the furrows as do the gulls. White-fronted terns may join the black-fronts and then you will notice that the bill colour and the lighter back and upper wings are the distinguishing points. Close observation is needed to note the black front/white front difference.

Throughout the night some bird activity continues. Pukekos and ducks take the opportunity to move out from swamps and streams to feed on pastures and crops. Moreporks are quite common in areas of the North Island where remnants of native bush are dotted through the grasslands. They greet the dark with a session of mournful calling then move off to hunt around the farm trees.

The little owl is limited to the South Island where it was first introduced early this century. It hunts by day as well as by night and is often seen on a fence post or a stump in broad daylight. It is particularly active in the early part of the night and its high-pitched "queea, queea" call is often heard around homestead trees or riverbed willows. Their nests are in holes of trees or clay banks, sometimes in old rabbit burrows. The first birds released in Otago came from Germany and they are still called German owls in some districts. That name was far too hastily chosen, because this species is *Athene noctua*, the owl of Athens and emblem of that ancient capital of the Greek Empire. However, this "Greek Owl" was not introduced to remind us of the cradle of Western civilisation but to reduce the numbers of sparrows and finches which were increasing rather too rapidly after their own introduction 30 or 40 years earlier. It is doubtful whether the owls achieved much in that respect because their main source of food has been shown to be large moths and insects, although they do take some small birds.

Chapter 7

Lakes, swamps and rivers

The birds of special interest in this habitat are on the ground or the water, so a quiet approach is important if you are not going to "put them up". It is pretty disappointing to find a good flock of ducks which flies off when you are still 200 m away. Keep in among trees or scrub as long as possible and take a long distance look at the area, planning your approach to the stretches of water which look most interesting. On lakes, these will be sheltered bays, shallow margins and reed-lined edges. In swamps, small areas of open water usually provide the best places for viewing. On rivers, slow-flowing stretches free from overhanging trees are likely to have the most birds.

Shallow lakes are more popular with birds that need to reach fish or vegetation growing on the bottom. In deep lakes, shallow margins or bays hold the biggest proportion of birds. Don't waste time on exposed banks where the shore falls away steeply into deep water because these places hold little attraction for birds.

Wind and weather are also important factors — wind especially. The sheltered side or sheltered bays are the birds' natural choice, enabling them to avoid

waves which in even a moderate wind give a swimming bird a very rough ride. In really windy conditions all the ducks stay on shore in a sheltered corner. This can be unsatisfactory for the birdwatcher who comes upon them unexpectedly at close range. They all take off in fright before there's a chance to identify them.

Your aim should be to see the bird before it sees you. Keep in cover not too close to where the birds have been spotted or where they are expected to be. Once swans, geese and ducks have been disturbed from their shoreline resting places they take a long time to return.

Swans feed on bottom weeds, reached with their long necks when the bird upends, so they are confined to shallow water. They come ashore to rest and preen where a gently sloping edge makes for easy landing, offers a good view of predators, and is preferably well sheltered. Muddy bays with a grassy margin but with short rushes 10 or 20 m back are a common choice because they fulfil those require- ments. You will find that popular loafing spots for swans and ducks get heavily fouled with their droppings — proof of their regular use.

For preference, swans, ducks and geese choose lakes large enough to allow them to swim well out of range of predators (including men with shotguns). Dogs anywhere near the shore will frighten birds out to the middle of the lake. On small areas of water they fly off whenever threatened, returning when all is clear.

The need to be able to swim to safety is important at the time of post-breeding moult. The birds seek out an area large enough to give them safe refuge during the time when the moult leaves them flightless, or nearly so. Lake Ellesmere is temporary home to several thousand Canada geese while they are in moult in January. These birds spend the rest of the year in the foothills of the Southern Alps around river flats and streams which suit the wary "honker" very well for feeding and nesting. However, there are no suitable wide areas of water there to use during the vulnerable flightless period.

Canada goose

A bird which is not confined to lakes but is nearly
always found somewhere around the margins is the
pukeko. It feeds on pasture grasses as well as on
aquatic plants, so it is often one of the first birds
you meet as you cross the paddocks. When a pukeko
is sighted out in the open, try to let it retreat slowly
and quietly to the shelter of the reedbeds. The noisy
squawks of alarmed pukekos will otherwise warn
every bird for hundreds of metres.

The soft edge mud, especially around reed beds, is
a place to look for the footprints of birds. Careful
study will reveal the "signatures" of nearly all of the
birds which are about. It would be too much to
expect you to identify different species of ducks from
footprints, but herons, swans, pukekos, crakes and
bitterns will all leave footprints which you can learn
to identify. You will then know what is worth
looking for on this visit or if you should come back
some other day.

Stalking birds around lakes often brings a
temptation to wade through the water as a short cut
or to get to some otherwise inaccessible spot. This is
a risky business and not recommended, especially if
you are alone. The depth of murky water is always
difficult to judge and there may be unexpected
channels or holes. Soft mud on the bottom is the real

danger, and this will probably start not at the edge where you step in but a metre or two further out. You could sink in up to your neck in water that is only waist deep if there is a similar depth of soft mud underneath. Close to beds of raupo (which are some of the most interesting places) there is usually a band of very soft and treacherous mud.

If you do wade in — and it can be good fun getting to the really secluded areas — don't wear gumboots or waders, which are a death trap if they become filled with water. Old sneakers are a much better protection for your feet. Another suggestion is to always wear a brightly coloured hat. Then when you sink out of sight the floating hat will let your friends know where to start digging.

Sewage treatment ponds are a type of artificial lake which has become known all around the world as a habitat for several species of birds. Those ponds which are last in the sequence of oxidation, and are therefore close to containing fresh water, attract ducks, swans and dabchicks. Waders come to suitable muddy or sandy edges.

Some enlightened authorities have gone to the trouble of leaving islands in the ponds, which become ideal nesting places for ducks. Ornamental plantings in places where there is very little human traffic attract more than the usual numbers of finches, white-eyes, etc. There are normally well-formed roads around the edges of all ponds, and these are useful for watching water birds from the cover of a car.

Before going to sewage ponds, phone the local authority, explain that you want to watch birds, and ask if you may have permission to enter areas not normally open to the public. You will find these people very helpful so long as they know who is where in the area. Remember that they are responsible for the installation and control of dozens of valves and pumps which keep the place operating as it should.

Pied stilts are often found around the swampy edges of lakes, although they are equally at home on estuaries, tidal mudflats and wet paddocks. They become accustomed to people in populated places, but in the countryside they tend to be wary and noisy with an insistent yapping alarm call.

Larger areas of raupo, say over 1000 m² (a quarter acre), support communities of birds, providing cover and a reliable food supply. Ducks feed about the edges and along the channels where water plants thrive in the shelter. Bitterns hunt frogs and small fish, and crakes quietly move back and forth through the dark tunnels of the fallen reeds.

The spotless crake is still one of our least known birds, but since it was discovered how readily it responds to a tape recording of its call many more have been located. They occur over all of the North Island, but rarely in the South. Their requirements seem to be met in large swamps, ponds and even small hillside gullies, so long as there is at least a small area which remains wet through all seasons with plenty of reeds, rushes or sedges for cover.

A simple description of crakes would be "miniature pukekos"; their long legs, long toes, dark plumage and short flicking tail all identify them as rails, of which the pukeko is our most common representative. The spotless crake and the marsh crake are small shy relatives which are seldom seen because they spend their lives well hidden amongst the reeds. The spotless crake's name isn't very useful as a description. (True it has no spots, and there is a spotted crake in Australia.) Its plumage is uniformly dark, and the overall length is 20 cm.

The rarer marsh crake is slightly smaller, blue-grey on head, breast and underparts, streaked brown and black on back and wings, with flanks finely barred black and white. They seem to prefer larger areas of protective cover, especially dense clumps of raupo on lake edges. Silent and secretive, these beautiful little birds may be quite widely distributed, but only two or three nests have ever been found in New Zealand.

The first sight of a bittern around the lake edge may be as it takes to the air a few metres ahead of you. This is because they are so cryptically coloured that they are often not seen until you are nearly on top of them. In these circumstances you may see their interesting behaviour of "freezing" with bill pointing skywards, making them very hard to distinguish from the reeds. A careful search of raupo beds with binoculars from a distance such as the other side of a lake may often pick out a bittern feeding at the edge or perched up in the raupo. In low flight a bittern is often mistaken for a harrier, until its head and long bill are seen.

Harriers are regular visitors to lakes, where they hunt for carrion at the water's edge or for unwary young birds. A harrier will swoop repeatedly at small ducklings out on the water, each time bringing the parent duck jumping out of the water in brave defence while her family dives under the surface. Large reed beds are often chosen by harriers as a site for their platform nests.

Three species of shags are commonly found in fresh water. The black shag, largest of them all, spends most of its time inland on lakes, rivers, ponds and even irrigation ditches. It fishes alone but nests in colonies like all cormorants, often choosing trees which grow on the cliffs of river gorges where the birds are free from persecution. Although fully protected, shags still get shot at by fishermen who believe that the birds are ruining their sport.

The little black shag is less common in the North Island and rare in the South Island except Tasman Bay. It seems to be as content to fish in lakes as in estuaries and harbours and in both situations it engages in pack hunting, which is rare in birds. A flock of shags, just a few or more than a hundred, will swim in formation to drive fish, some birds diving to feed on them while others swim on the surface.

The little shag has varying amounts of white on its undersurface and at one time two species were recognised as white-throated shag and little pied shag. This bird can be all black except for white on the face and chin, or the white may extend down the front of the neck to the breast. The little pied form has completely white undersides. Immatures are all black and you have to note their shorter bills and longer tails to distinguish them from little black shags.

Ducks are the most common birds of fresh water, but as there are several species which differ only slightly in size and shape, they present a challenge in identification. You will find that you have most success if you sort them out firstly by behaviour and "jizz". Fall back on plumage colours only when you need to, and when the bird is close enough and in a good enough light to let you see the colours clearly.

Dabbling ducks gather their food on the surface of the water, along muddy edges, or by upending in the shallows. This group includes the grey duck, mallard and New Zealand shoveler, three of our most common species. Unless disturbed, dabbling ducks are likely to be found near the edge of any area of water. They spend a lot of time around reed beds or loafing on the banks.

NZ scaup

Diving ducks find their food on the bottom, and their time is spent out on the deeper water, resting in small flocks far out from the shore. The New Zealand scaup (or black teal) is our only diving duck and it has the typical compact shape which distinguishes it from the longer-bodied dabblers. Scaup are usually in rafts of ten or more and when they are feeding there is a regular movement of little black bodies either popping up from below or disappearing on the next dive. This means that it can be quite a job getting an accurate count of a flock of scaup which is continuously growing and contracting. "Eight birds there — no, twelve I think — no, six . . ." In the clear waters of Lake Wakatipu by Queenstown wharf the whole sequence of their dives can be watched. They slip under the water without a splash (in contrast to dabchicks which make a little jump for their dive) and leave a swirl on the surface. Their webbed feed paddle strenuously to take them down to the bottom and continue paddling to keep themselves there while they search for plant growth. To resurface is only a matter of ceasing to paddle, raising the head, and the little diver shoots to the surface and bobs up like a cork. Their take-off from the water differs from other ducks'. The diving ducks patter along the surface whereas the dabbling ducks jump into the air.

Grey ducks can be found in almost any part of the country because they are happy to settle on almost any small area of water where they can be undisturbed. When they become accustomed to humans they become as confiding as any railway station sparrow, as you can prove any day along Christchurch's Avon River. Well-vegetated swamps are probably the grey duck's first choice, but it is also found on the slow-moving reaches and the quiet backwaters of large rivers, small streams, lakes, farm dams, ditches and ponds. They move widely about the countryside, usually at night, and whistling wingbeats and occasional gentle quacking can be heard as they fly overhead, always in a hurry to get to the next splashdown. In all of these habitats the grey has to compete with the introduced mallard in most parts of the country.

The mallard made a slow start after its introduction by acclimatisation societies as a game species, but it is now well established and its adaptability makes it a competitor of more than one native species.

There was much interbreeding with grey ducks as mallards spread across the country. Some years ago there was concern that there might be no true grey ducks left in a few years. However the position seems to have stabilised and pure grey ducks are holding their own in many districts, especially in Southland and Northland. When the two species and their hybrids are all together mallard drakes are always easily distinguished, but male and female greys are alike and rather similar to the female mallard. Hybrids add to the difficulty. Here are some points which should help you to sort out all but the most difficult — and some of them are difficult.

Mallards have orange-red legs whereas grey ducks' legs are olive-brown, and any orange in the legs is one simple indicator of some degree of mallard in the bird's pedigree. But ducks' legs are so often out of sight that you need to be able to distinguish plumage differences. There is always an overall greyness in the grey duck compared to the tawny brownness of the mallard female. The body feathers on the mallard are more strongly emarginated with buff than are the grey's with their thin white margin. The colour of the speculum is not a very reliable distinguishing feature because it may change in different lights and the speculum is often obscured when the wings are closely folded. The most useful feature for identifying the grey duck is the prominent stripe over the eye. A very pale buff stripe like an eyebrow runs from near the bill towards the back of the head. Although the mallard female has a similar stripe it is indistinct in comparison, and in hybrid birds it is never so clear or prominent as in the grey.

If you begin your duck-watching in popular places like park ponds or artificial lakes, be prepared to find ducks which can't be identified. Domestic varieties get into these areas and their hybrids come in all colours and sizes.

The grey teal is an Australian species which is now a common sighting on our larger stretches of water. It is thought that regular arrivals of small flocks come across the Tasman to add to those breeding here. The grey teal is a little smaller than the grey duck and can be identified by the noticeably paler chin and cheeks which give the impression of a different shaped head. In flight a white triangle shows prominently in the wing. Watch out for them on lakes and ponds throughout the country but especially near the coast.

The shoveler's large spoonbill distinguishes it from all other ducks and it often holds its head and neck in a hunched posture. In outline, far out on the water, the shoveler can be picked out from other ducks of the same size by these features. The male is very colourful in full breeding plumage, but when he goes into eclipse plumage it is not easy to tell him from the females.

Most ducks form flocks in winter. Shovelers form pairs and start their courtship displays while still in these flocks. Male and female swim side by side with regular head bobbing and a repeated "took, took" call. Around the reed beds during late winter or early spring this soft call may tell you that there are shovelers around before you have had a chance to see them.

An endemic species which is now our rarest duck is the brown teal. It prefers the densely vegetated and shady margins of large swamps, and it was once spread over most of the country. However this habitat has also been eliminated by the draining of swamps for conversion to farmland. Brown teal are now most likely to be found along the coastal area north and south of the Bay of Islands and on Great Barrier Island where they keep to slow-flowing creeks and partially modified swampland. A feature of this duck's behaviour is its habit of gathering into flocks at certain traditional sites during the winter.

Continued breeding in captivity has allowed the release of many brown teal in the Manawatu, in an effort to re-establish them in an area which was once one of their strongholds. Indications are that they are breeding in the wild and there are hopes that a self-sustaining population will soon be achieved.

Paradise shelducks are New Zealand's largest representative of the duck tribe but they are less a bird of lakes and rivers than they are of farmland and the foothills. In mid summer you may meet a flock of "parries" on a stretch of water large enough to keep them out of danger when they swim to the middle. These are moulting birds which are unable to fly when flight feathers have been shed. Right

through the year male and female keep the distinct-
ively coloured heads (female white, male black) and
these are so conspicuous that they provide sure
identification even without considering their large
size.

Swans look for the security of large areas of water
to raise their families. The choice is obviously
important, considering that it is up to six months
before the young are able to fly. Nests of black
swans are commonly placed on the open water side
of a reed bed, where a large mound of vegetation is
made and continually added to throughout the period
of incubation. The large colony of black swans on
Lake Ellesmere's Kaitorete Spit is on very open
ground which slopes gently to the water, but this is
not a natural choice. The acclimatisation society has
long encouraged the swans to nest there by active
discouragement elsewhere around the lake.

Mute swans build a similar nest at the water's edge,
sometimes a little way into a reed bed along a natural
channel which allows direct access from the water, so
that the heavy birds can avoid laborious walking to
and from the nest.

Canada geese which occasionally nest at a lake
choose a site concealed in rushes or tussocks, in a
swampy place or a little way back from the lake
edge. An interesting habit of the goose is to cover
her eggs with down whenever she leaves the nest,
which both camouflages them and keeps them warm.

Less common birds which are worth searching for
on any lake are grebes. They may appear very duck-
like when first seen swimming on the surface, but
they belong to a different order from the swans and
ducks, and accordingly have some very different
characteristics. Their bills are longish and pointed
and their feet are webbed with lobes along each toe.
Their tails are no more than a bump of feathers
above a rounded stern. They all give the impression
that they are poor fliers, skimming low over the
water with whirring wings. The downy young are
attractively striped and often ride on their parents'
backs. Grebes are divers, spending a great deal of
their time under water and often surfacing many

Marsh crake
(Don Hadden)

Western weka
(Rod Morris)

South Island pied oystercatcher
(Don Hadden)

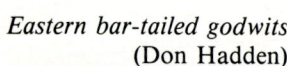

Eastern bar-tailed godwits
(Don Hadden)

Spur-winged plover
(Don Hadden)

Southern black-backed gull; immature at left
(Geoff Moon)

Caspian terns
(Rod Morris)

White-fronted terns
(Geoff Moon)

metres away from where they were last seen.

The handsome crested grebe is now restricted to the lakes of the foothills of the main mountain chain of the South Island, but individuals occasionally turn up near or at the coast in winter. The New Zealand dabchick is absent from the South Island but well distributed over the whole of the North Island, especially in the dune lakes of the western coast, but also in farm ponds, inland lakes and sewage treatment ponds. A relative newcomer should also be looked for. The Australian little grebe seems to be established in the Far North and it is found on lakes in all parts of the country from time to time.

All grebes engage in courtship displays and those of the crested grebe are one of the most flamboyant and highly ritualised displays in the world of birds. The pair nod and head shake in unison, and rush upright along the water in what has been called the "patter dance" — all an amazing display for anyone who is lucky enough to witness it.

Quiet, cautious stalking is very necessary for a successful survey of a small lake. A look around when you arrive is likely to find only half of what is there. Ducks emerge from the reeds or from hidden loafing spots on the shore, grebes and shags surface from long dives in progress when you first swept binoculars over that particular spot. But before you leave, it may be quite rewarding to make a quick noisy circuit of the area. Birds that you haven't seen may then fly up and you will at least get a brief look at them in the air.

The great braided riverbeds of the east coasts of both islands are a special habitat which supports large numbers of birds during the spring and summer. Many of these move down to the coast when the higher water levels of winter cover most of the gravel and sand and the harsher inland climate reduces the amount of food. At the mouth of a river there are likely to be small colonies of gulls and terns if there is somewhere secure and undisturbed for them to nest. There may be black-backed and black-billed gulls and white-fronted terns, probably with a few red-billed gulls. Banded dotterel territories may be spaced along firmly consolidated spits with the possibility of New Zealand dotterels north of Raglan and the Bay of Plenty.

It is commonly 1–2 km inland before the river is met at its full width. Then there are two benefits to the birds: the shallower water in the many braided streams makes prey more easy to capture than it is in one swift channel, and the dozens of small islands are potential nesting sites.

Pied stilts are on every riverbed, but they do not always demand the protection of a river island, and will often place a nest on the landward bank of a quiet stretch of the river. Indeed many of them nest away from riverbeds in wet places with a good food supply.

All other ground-nesting birds will avoid willow trees and other cover as widely as possible. The lupins which have become established on many of Canterbury's riverbeds have destroyed a large proportion of the nesting habitat of riverbed birds. Consolidated shingle islands with a few small ground cover plants and perhaps some driftwood is the natural habitat and the most preferred.

Colonies of black-billed gulls and black-fronted terns are easily located by the sight and sound of the birds. Black-bills may soon settle down to lay if returning to a nest site used before, but a new site may be occupied noisily for weeks before eggs are laid. There are often last-minute changes to a different site. They prefer an island with clean smallish stones and plenty of driftwood around which to place the nests.

Black-backed gull colonies may be spread over a long stretch of the riverbed, with one or two nests each 50 or 100 m apart. These birds also like to be in the middle of a wide riverbed well away from trees, but they are more tolerant of smaller vegetation. Both gulls see that the colony is surrounded by flowing water, and they seem to be able to judge the depth required to keep out ground predators. This is unlikely to be more than knee deep on all sides, but you will always have to bear in mind your own safety when you are crossing the river. Many people have come to grief in water not much over their knees, because in swift streams there is the added problem of unstable footing. As well as stumbling on large round boulders, it can be very dangerous when the current is rolling boulders along — one of these can easily knock you off your feet. Learn the techniques of safe river crossing before you go looking for riverbed birds.

Anywhere near the coast, colonies of terns or black-billed gulls will each have a small colony of red-billed gulls alongside it. These are scavengers for the scraps of food and dead chicks of the colony, and they are also active predators of any chick or egg left unguarded for a minute. Unawares, you can cause a lot of damage just by walking through a colony. When nesting birds are chased off, the red-bills seize the opportunity and small chicks are killed and eggs eaten.

Black-fronted terns nest on the riverbeds of Canterbury, Otago and Southland, sometimes in colonies of more than a hundred pairs. They choose islands in the middle of the river, and nests are widely spaced so the colony may cover a lot of ground. Right through the summer this beautiful little tern can be seen feeding in ones and twos up and down the river channels. It moves to the coast and to the north in winter.

After a winter sojourn on the mudflats of the Firth of Thames or Manukau Harbour, wrybills return to the riverbeds of Canterbury to breed. They are the most tame and confiding birds you will meet there. A pair found on an island of clean stones will probably have a nest, so sit down with the hope of locating it. A brooding wrybill will be willing to return to a nest when you are in full view as close as 3 or 4 m, and even without a nest they can be approached closely if you are patient. The eggs and running chicks are both cryptically coloured and very difficult to see, so it is necessary to take great care where you step. Running chicks will freeze motionless on the warning calls of their parents and become almost indistinguishable from the stones.

Banded dotterels behave in much the same way

although they are less confiding. The female can be watched back to the nest from a distance as the male performs his distraction display, often ending with wing fluttering as he lies on the ground with realistic cries of pain. (It is important not to spend too long in any nesting territory or you will risk the eggs or young being chilled.)

In suitable habitat banded dotterel nests may be spaced about every 50 m up the riverbed, and as you enter each territory the male, identified by the broader, brighter chestnut band, will come to meet you and fly or run around calling. If the neighbouring male has followed you it will quickly be chased off the territory.

The black-fronted dotterel, a newcomer from Australia, remains common on Hawke's Bay riverbeds where it first bred in the 1960s. It soon spread to the Wairarapa, and it is now prospecting the Canterbury riverbeds. Its preference is for the muddy edges of the backwaters.

A riverbed walk will usually find a few ducks, a black shag or two fishing in the deeper pools, and the weedy margins have interesting flocks of finches. White-faced herons are often about the backwaters hunting frogs and small fish, and they will rise with harsh "kaar, kaar" calls as they fly to perch high on trees. Their nests are likely to be in pines, macrocarpas or gums, not right by the water but perhaps a kilometre across the farmland.

Chapter 8

Forests

The approach to a forest often takes you through a
zone of rough scrub which acts as a natural wind-
break for the forest edge. It is also a nursery for
young trees growing as an extension to the matured
area. Do not ignore this scrubland which has its own
distinctive birdlife. Grey warblers can be seen
hovering around the tips of manuka or gorse.
Finches which are absent from the forest will be
common, especially if there are patches of seeding
weeds. Small flocks of goldfinches keep on the move,
and redpolls in ones and twos fly high before
swooping down to alight on the tip of a shrub where
you can see their bright red caps and the carmine red
breast of the mature males. Skylarks are often
present in quite large numbers, landing on bare
ground, but also exploring deep under the tussocks
of dried grass or weed.

California quail like this habitat, and in Northland
and the Bay of Plenty you may see the smaller brown
quail too. Pheasants join them to feed on weed seeds
amongst the scrub. Your quiet progress along a track
may be interrupted by the explosion of frantically
whirring wings as a cock pheasant does his vertical
take-off from the cover close beside you. Fernbirds

are sometimes there, so it is worthwhile listening for their distinctive calls as you move around places where manuka is dense and tangled with bracken.

White-eyes, familiar from suburban gardens, occupy the forest margins and places where wide tracks or other openings let in the full light of the sun. They feed among low-growing shrubs which need sunlight. It is here that their delicate little cup nest is hung in a fork near a branch end, usually less than 2 m from the ground. You see fewer white-eyes as you move deeper into the forest.

The fantail is there to challenge you as you enter the forest, dancing about and tossing its widespread tail just as the warrior prances with his taiaha during the ceremonial challenge to visitors to a marae. You may meet piwakawaka the fantail anywhere through the forest but he is most common around the margins.

Fantail

Two subspecies of fantail are recognised for South Island and North Island populations, but since they never occur together there is no great practical use in learning to recognise the difference in the tails' colour patterns. Something which is very striking is the appearance of totally black fantails. These are very rare in the North Island, but in the South Island about one in eight is black. This is not a different species but simply the other form of this dimorphic species.

New Zealand pigeons are large, obvious, beautiful and unmistakable when they are seen climbing around branch ends feeding on fruit. They are even easier to watch when they perch sleepily in the sun. They take frequent long rests, perhaps to help them digest after feeding. However, a pigeon is often heard before it is seen — the swish of wing beats as it swoops through the trees, often quite low, and sometimes along tracks taking advantage of the clearway.

NZ pigeon

The cooing call of the New Zealand pigeon is kept for the breeding season. It is seldom heard and the birds stop immediately they become aware of people, in contrast to many tropical pigeons and doves which coo almost incessantly. They are powerful fliers in spite of their heavy appearance. It is a delight to watch their antics — the climbs up to sharp stall turns, high speed swoops, and level full speed dashes. This performance could be described as "recreational flying" but is likely to be a mating display. A look-out point on a ridge may give you a chance to see this spectacular display over the treetops, especially in the early evening.

The whitehead is conspicuous from the beech forests above Wellington's eastern bays to the Bay of Plenty. It moves about in parties of up to 12 or 15 birds, always on the move, collecting insects as it climbs up the trunks, along branches, and right to the ends of twigs, often searching among the leaves. Females and juveniles may look very sparrow-like (though their behaviour is quite different) but the clear white head of the male makes him unmistakable. Whitehead song is so variable it is easy to confuse with other songs if you haven't sighted the bird first.

Parties of whiteheads moving through the bush keep up a small chorus of songs and chirps, so they are easily located. It is not difficult to catch up with them if you move quietly. At other times you will find that they move in on you and you are surrounded by whiteheads, feeding so actively that it's hard to get a good look at any one bird. A squeak bottle is useful to attract them and hold them at a time like that.

In the South Island the yellowhead (predictably named the bush canary by early settlers) behaves in much the same way. Unfortunately it is now quite rare, being restricted to a few of the largest tracts of virgin forest, with a preference for beech forests. Although the whitehead and yellowhead are congeneric (genus *Mohoua*), one is a hole-nester and the other builds a cup nest on a branch. It may be significant that the hole-nesting yellowhead has not survived as well since the arrival of rats and other predators.

Brown creepers are shy, inconspicuous little birds of the Stewart Island and South Island forests. Like the yellowhead they often move in parties. They have a delightful song which the male of a family group will proclaim from a branch while all the others busily continue their hunt for insects under leaves and loosened bark.

Maybe soon after entering the forest, or where tall timber has a good understorey of shrubs and saplings, the tomtit will appear suddenly beside you. Not so confiding as the robin but as curious, the tomtit will perch at your head height or lower and scrutinise you with its beady eye. The brownish females are not as brightly coloured as the males which are white-breasted in the North Island and yellow-breasted in the South. Much of their cheeky charm comes from having a head which is very large in proportion. A taxonomist with a sense of humour gave them the apt name of *macrocephala*, meaning big head. Well, bighead likes to know exactly what's going on in his territory, but as soon as he has inspected you, he will move off to continue feeding.

Within the forest the rifleman can be found going about its never-ending search of tree trunks and main branches for insects hiding in the bark. If your hearing is good you will locate the bird by its very high-pitched "zitt" call. It is given regularly, probably a contact call between a pair or family group. At 8 cm long the rifleman is our smallest bird. The males are green backed, the females and immatures have dark brown-streaked backs.

The bellbird's delightful song is easily heard either in patches of bush or large forest tracts. Bellbirds were eliminated from Auckland and Northland at the end of the last century, perhaps by disease rather than predators. Big populations on the northern offshore islands give hope of future re-colonisation.

The richest, purest song of the entire forest comes from the kokako, one of our most endangered species. The South Island subspecies (orange-wattled) may be extinct, but the blue-wattled North Island kokako hangs on in some undisturbed forests of the Bay of Plenty, Volcanic Plateau, the lower Waikato, Coromandel Peninsula and the Bay of Islands. The presence of kokakos could be taken as proof that the forest is in good heart because it requires a wide range of vegetation types. Weak of flight, it moves from ground level to the tops of the tallest canopy trees by "ladders" provided by various plant species. Where all of these are not present the kokako is seriously restricted in its feeding movements, as well as being deprived of a food source.

Some of the rich swelling notes of the kokako can be heard up to a kilometre away on a still day. Little wonder that early New Zealand naturalists wrote so much about its "organ-like tones" and others described it as the "true bellbird". These powerful notes make the bellbird chorus sound like the dings and dongs of handbells alongside a full peal from a cathedral tower.

In mature forest nectar-feeding tuis spend their time high in the canopy, often congregating in a flowering tree such as rata. Their bursts of song or the fluttering of wings during frequent disputes, will let you know there they are. You are likely to have unobstructed views when they visit garden trees during winter and early spring when nectar is in short supply in the forest.

Kakariki

Kakariki, our endemic parakeets, are heard more often than they are seen. Their cheerful chatter may be the only clue to their presence in mature native forest. However, a little careful stalking may allow you to see them clambering around in typical parrot fashion, their brilliant green plumage set off with a bright cap. In heavy forest it is often impossible to sight the head clearly enough to distinguish the red-crowned from the yellow-crowned species.

You may first note kaka when you hear their typical parrot screeches (kaa, kaa) as they fly over the treetops. Their musical fluting song is sometimes given in flight, but more often when the bird is perched. They feed high in the canopy taking fruit or nectar, or lower down tearing apart rotten timber for grubs. You should be able to locate them from their chatter and the sound of falling debris.

This is a bird which is dependent on mature forest which contains dead as well as living trees. There never was justification for the term "over-mature forest", and the kaka is a species which makes good use of dead timber before it falls to provide compost for the next generation of trees.

Seasonal fluctuations in the food supply are probably the reason behind the appearance of kaka far from forests. They are strong fliers. The gardens and shrubby second-growth areas around the slopes of Halfmoon Bay, Stewart Island, attract them quite regularly.

As soon as you have entered the territory of the New Zealand robin you will meet him face to face. There is nothing shy about the way the robin greets human visitors, and this fearlessness has made it favourite of all who go regularly into the bush. Unfortunately this lack of fear is probably a cause of its reduced numbers and complete absence from many areas. The robin spends much time feeding on the ground, where it is vulnerable to predators.

If you keep still a robin may stand on the toe of your boot or on your head. There are stories of frustrated photographers unable to get pictures of robins because they sat on top of camera and tripod!

Robins always manage to look rather scruffy,

because the underside feathers are not slicked down close to the body. The more positively coloured males are brighter than their sombre brown mates.

You can attract a robin by scraping back a small patch of leaf litter with your foot. Step away 3–4 m, keep still and the robin will readily accept your help in getting an easy meal.

Robin

If there are wekas in the forest it is likely they will find you before you find them. They are strongly territorial and soon investigate any human intruder. You will hear rustling in the ground cover and see the cautious movements of wily weka as it circles in. Wekas thieve anything shiny or colourful that looks faintly edible. The ones that live near picnic sites on well-used public tracks are especially bold. A forest ranger once tested a weka he met regularly at a certain point on the track. He stood quite still while the weka approached, stepped on the toe of his boot, then aimed a swift peck at his shin, and out gushed blood. That patient, dedicated man is now fully aware of what is likely to happen if an accident leaves him unconscious in the bush.

If you put food down for wekas more than one pair may be attracted. This is your chance to watch for encounters between the territory holders and the intruders. Expect crashes and squawks in the undergrowth, and high speed chases pursued far into the bush. The ones driven off usually manage to sneak back within a few minutes and then it's all on again.

Wekas are largely nocturnal, or to put it more accurately, they are active for most of the night, a species which seems to need little or no sleep. Their cries have kept many a camper awake for hours, but it is not an unpleasant sound. A pair will call with such quick co-ordination that it sounds like one bird. "Coo" from one bird to the right, "eet" from its mate on the left, sounds like one "cooeet" that comes from all around.

Weka

The two species of cuckoo which visit New Zealand from September to March are both forest dwellers. They are our only breeding migrants (other than sea birds). You are likely to first hear the shining cuckoo far from the bush, but the long-tailed cuckoo is confined to the larger areas of mature native forest.

Shining cuckoos feed on insects around leaves and branch ends. They are difficult to see in heavy bush even after you have identified their distinctive call. The host for this cuckoo's egg is invariably the grey warbler which hangs its little domed nest sometimes only a metre or two above the ground, usually in a shrub or manuka in the forest margin.

The handsome big long-tailed cuckoo is one of those birds which spend so much time sitting about, they never seem to eat. Most often you come upon one perched on a middle level branch and if you see it before it takes fright, you will be able to admire the broadly banded brown and fawn tail which gives it its name. Then it will be off through the trees at high speed, giving a loud "pet pet pet pet" call, apparently furious that it has been disturbed. It chooses whitehead or yellowhead as host for its young.

Long-tailed and shining cuckoos winter on a number of Pacific islands centred about the Solomons, approximately 3500 km from New Zealand. Both cuckoos travel over vast expanses of ocean to spend the breeding season here. Then a tremendous journey over the ocean faces young birds when towards the end of February instinct urges them to leave this country for the first time. There is no evidence that cuckoos gather into flocks. These young birds which have been raised by grey warblers and have never seen their parents, set off across the ocean with no guidance other than an inherited behaviour pattern. Evidence gained from a few banded birds shows that they return to the area of forest they occupied the previous year.

Some introduced birds have found a niche in our native forests. There is nowhere too dense, too wet or too remote for the chaffinch. This cheery little finch is probably the most widely-spread bird in the country, common in city, farmland, forest, mountain side and sea coast, showing a versatility others cannot match.

Blackbirds and, to a lesser extent, song thrushes are found right through the largest native forests. They become much more wary than the ones in suburban gardens. Food is plentiful — insects on the forest floor, and the fruits of several native shrubs. Kawakawa is popular with blackbirds. Obviously these introduced species compete for food sought by endemic species, such as the New Zealand robin which at the same time has to contend with introduced predators.

As darkness falls on the forest the native owl stirs from its roost in some deeply shaded spot, and announces itself with calls of "morepork, morepork". True to the legendary wisdom of the owls this one is able to call in three languages. Maoris heard him as ruru long before the first British settlers called him morepork, and across the Tasman the Australian Aboriginal knows him as boobook.

As well as this familiar call, the morepork uses a little hunting scream, quite frightening when heard close at hand. Although they have good night vision owls identify their prey by movement. The scream is given to startle prey into moving. Moreporks often hunt large moths and flying beetles which gather around bright lights. It is worthwhile watching for them around the lights of any camp or caravan park near a forest.

About 40 minutes after sunset the first kiwi calls ring through the forest. The call of a bird emerging from its burrow (repeated up to 20 times) is answered by its mate. The brown kiwi male's shrill "kee-wee" and the female's deeper, throaty "ah-eh" are sometimes synchronised to produce duetting between the two birds of a pair. The kiwi is a strongly territorial bird. Calling can continue all night in the breeding season as they defend territories in much the same way as passerines defend theirs with song. When kiwis are present you should have very little trouble hearing them call.

Seeing a kiwi is a much more difficult matter. It must be done at night because they are well hidden down burrows during the day. In the dark it is not easy to see a dark brown bird on the ground before your flashlight disturbs it. There are also shrubs, ferns, rocks and fallen logs to contend with. If you do stumble upon a kiwi it is likely the only view you will get is a disappearing rounded backside and hefty legs running. Like a little bent over man in brown shorts far too big for him. But hush, we are talking of our national emblem!

It is better to spend an unhurried half hour in a nocturnal house displaying kiwis in near-natural conditions. The birds in these displays have been gradually accustomed to a reversal of the day/night cycle. Visitors can watch their night time activity in a dark enclosure during the day. The birds move about freely, gently feeling with their bills or probing deeply into the leaf litter. At night artificial lights encourage the kiwi to retire into a burrow.

Unfortunately much native bush close to cities is second growth on hillsides burned or cleared within the last 50 years. This is of limited use to birds. Second growth gives cover and nesting sites for certain species, but is unable to provide the varied and balanced habitat which birds require throughout the year. It is made up of leafy shrubs and young trees with nectar-producing flowers and fruit, but several sources of food will be absent or very scarce. Missing items will include the insect fauna of deep ground litter and rotting logs, flowers and fruit of large canopy trees and many insects which depend on the rough bark of old trees for hiding and breeding. Second growth has grown up on ground where the original humus layer, built up over centuries perhaps, was destroyed by fire or in the drying out which followed clearing. It takes many years for rich ground litter to build up to the point where it provides a reliable food source for ground-feeding birds.

Even if they cannot make a permanent home there, many birds still make good use of second growth bush for the seasonal feasts provided by fruiting shrubs and trees. Tuis and bellbirds wander widely in search of flowering trees and New Zealand pigeons look out for ripe berries. Fantails, white-eyes and grey warblers are likely to come for flying and crawling insects, and they will probably nest there also. The number of bird species will depend on the location. Second growth beside a mature forest will be visited by more than those mentioned, whereas an isolated hectare or two amongst developed farmland may not even attract pigeons and tuis.

Forests of exotic pine trees, chiefly *Pinus radiata*, cover large areas of countryside in nearly every region. Unfortunately the shelter and safety provided by these forests is not matched with a good food supply, so they have a sparse bird population. The first requirement of a bird's habitat is a reliable year-round food supply. No New Zealand birds feed directly on pine tree leaves or fruit, but some insects are found on trunks and branches and in pine needle litter. Unfortunately the unnatural uniformity of trees, makes for a lack of insect variety. There are no understorey shrubs and saplings to host the leaf-eating caterpillars sought by many species of birds.

However, some native birds are found in older plantations of exotic pines where trees have been subject to the standard forestry practice of pruning. These plantations provide canopy protection and over the years the falling pine needles have built up some ground litter. Many understorey plants — rangiora, wineberry, five finger, tree ferns and ladder ferns — provide food for birds in one way or another. So white-eyes, tomtits, robins and grey warblers may occur in the plantations in a way that makes them dependent on the understorey but not on the pine trees themselves.

Other birds in and around pine forests will be those of the surrounding areas. In developed farmland where there are few trees, birds appreciate the cover which pines provide, if only for short visits. The outside branches of trees along the edge of a plantation spread much further than those within, and they are popular nesting sites for finches. It is worthwhile searching for them in September or

October at the peak of the nesting season.

In North Auckland there is an interesting exception to the rule that native birds avoid pine trees, and the bird concerned is none other than the brown kiwi. A study in Waitangi State Forest has shown that kiwis live in this exotic forest throughout the year. The birds find ground insects and worms in the pine needle humus. Moisture is retained where there is a good depth of needles but towards the end of summer when the humus dries out, the kiwis become more dependent on swampy areas or damp gullies with remnants of original native bush.

Chapter 9

The seashore

The distinctive habitat of the open shoreline makes birds easily visible at a distance as they feed on mudflats and around tidal pools. To get close enough to identify them is another matter. You may have little success until you are able to watch them on a roost.

We call many shore birds "waders" because they feed while wading. Strictly, waders are birds of the sub-order Charadrii — plovers, sandpipers and their close relatives. The common names of individual species are usefully descriptive in some cases, but often ridiculously long and even confusing. In New Zealand we use the name dotterel for many called plovers in other countries, and while we have several birds called sandpipers some in the sandpiper sub-family have other names. Remember that common names are only convenient labels; the bird's genus tells you its classification and relationships.

Waders must feed at low tide when mud is uncovered or water shallow enough to get at their prey, the worms and other invertebrates of the surface layer. Since feeding is dependent on the tide it may happen by day or night. When the tide is high the birds must roost in a safe place. An undisturbed

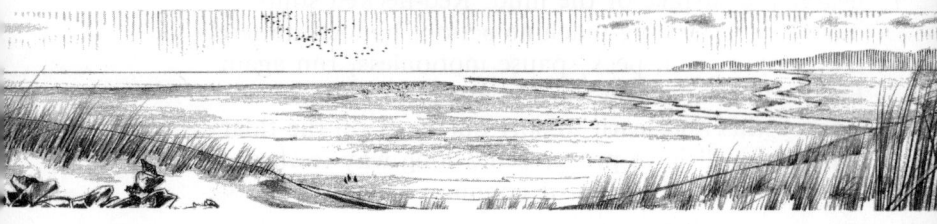

flock on a high tide roost will sleep soundly, each bird standing on one leg and facing upwind. In a strong breeze it can sway like a wind vane. The birdwatcher has plenty of time to study these birds, something rarely possible in a forest or swamp.

The first step towards finding the high-tide roost on any estuary is to watch waders flying in as high tide approaches or moving away after the tide turns. When you have an idea of the position you should be able to locate it by exploring the area at low tide, looking for a place which meets the requirements. Firstly it must be clear of cover and provide the birds with all-round visibility. Godwits, and to a lesser extent other waders, like the roost area to be free of all vegetation. Waders of small estuaries frequently roost on the open ocean beach which makes them very difficult to approach closely. Finally, you will know you are on the roost when you find the sand closely marked with footprints, heavily spotted with droppings and sprinkled with quite a few feathers. From there plan your observation point.

It is best to get settled into a place not so close as to make birds nervous. Try to have the light behind you. This is a great help when working out plumage details. There are many estuaries around the country where cars can be driven to within 100 m of roosting waders, where you can watch in comfort.

While the tide is low different species of waders feed together, but each has a method and style of searching for food. It is likely that each has a preference for particular species of invertebrates living in the mud. When you learn to recognise the methods and movements of the various birds, you will identify them more quickly than by looking at size, shape and colour. Godwits probe deeply with their long bills. Knots move more quickly, pecking nearer the surface of the mud. Red-necked stints have a rapid sewing-machine action; banded dotterels take a short run, peck, pause motionless, run again. Field guides give you the starting information. Absorb this and learn to sort out birds on the tidal flat. You will have progressed a long way towards the quick identification of common waders.

Godwits

As the rising tide chases them off the mudflats, waders come to the roost in small groups of 10 or 20 birds. Large flocks are formed only when a number have gathered on a shell bank and are driven off by the tide. It is amusing to see how they hang on determinedly to a place which is going to be covered by the incoming tide. The rising water forces them close together, then the water creeps up their legs until belly feathers get wet and they give in and fly off to another spot. As the height of the tide varies through the month so will the number of birds on the main roost. Only on very high spring tides do you get them all driven off minor roosts on to one which cannot be covered.

Knots especially are reluctant to move until they really have to. Like King Canute in the legend, they ignore the rising sea as if it might stop for them. This is why Linnaeus gave them the specific name *Calidris canutus*, and the English name knot is simply derived from the Scandinavian Cnut, in turn from Canute. (Nothing to do with a knot in a piece of string.) We should probably pronounce it k-not, but no-one does.

When rough weather sends spray splashing over high tide roosts all birds leave the estuary and fly a few hundred metres inland to an area of sand or stones, or a short-grassed paddock.

Your first visits to crowded wader roosts may leave you confused if you try to identify every bird. Start with no more than three species and get to know them well. Observe them resting, feeding, flying and so on, until you feel quite confident that you will know them anywhere. This may take more than one visit. Then add another one or two species, and gradually become familiar with all the ones usually present. When a rarity turns up you will spot it because it is different. Remember that identification starts from noticing what the bird *is not*, narrowing down the choices before you have to decide what it *is*.

It is very frustrating when a flock takes to the air as you are diligently counting or searching through it. The harrier is the only diurnal bird of prey at the coast, but the sight of it will put up a flock of a thousand waders. If you see a harrier in the vicinity you have some warning, but it isn't much help. There is sometimes no warning before a flock takes to the air. Birds in one part take off — perhaps one bird's nervousness starts it — and the rest follow. The movement often rolls along a large roosting flock from end to end. After a circle or two they usually return and the birdwatcher can resume. These sudden flights give you a chance to look over the flying birds, identifying odd species not seen on the ground. The different flight of a sandpiper, for instance, can alert you to look for it when the flock has landed.

As you get to know waders you will find it not too difficult to recognise many birds on the wing. It is always worth scanning edges of a flock with binoculars in the hope of seeing strays. As the flock comes to ground each bird seeks its own feeding niche. The strangers usually (but not always) rest on the edge of the flock as though needing to be with the crowd but realising they have joined the wrong club.

Knots fly in tight flocks and roost closely packed.

They are usually very difficult to count. The godwits fly into the roosts in strings and loosely formed Vs. They rest in a similarly scattered flock whenever there is room.

Many thousands of waders migrate to New Zealand after rearing their young in the Arctic — Siberia, Alaska, etc. They arrive about September and leave again in March, here for our summer, but in terms of their breeding cycle they are "wintering". We see them in winter or eclipse plumage which makes identification difficult. Species with distinctive colour markings in breeding plumage are often indistinguishable in drab eclipse plumage. In September and October some arrivals have not shed all their colour; in February and March many are getting brilliant breeding colours. Rich chestnut knots and godwits stand out in grey/fawn flocks as if they were different species. Rich pickings in our tidal mudflats fatten the migrants for their return to the Arctic where there is an "explosion" of insect life after the snows have melted. Their young, reared on a rich protein diet of insects will join their parents in the flight south before the brief Arctic summer ends.

Among these migrants there are often stray individuals or small groups from species which normally follow a different route. These rarities are keenly searched for, and over the years we have learned that many mistakes in navigation are made, though the straying birds represent only a tiny proportion of the vast numbers which move south each northern autumn.

Undoubtedly what gets people "hooked" on waderwatching is the ever-present likelihood of finding something rare. It is true there is little beyond identification in regard to the Arctic migrants which do not build nests, hold territories, raise chicks or engage in other activities which make birdwatching such a diverse and interesting occupation. But once you are able to identify the common waders there is always the chance of finding the only one of its kind ever seen on this estuary, or the first this season, or so far south, or perhaps the first one ever to be recorded in New Zealand. This possibility is a challenge. There is plenty of interest in searching big flocks in the hope of finding the rare one, or one you haven't seen before. Waders present some of the most demanding exercises you will meet in bird identification. To learn the finer points you need to go to the estuary with an expert, but never with two, or they will find a bird that gets them arguing feather by feather while you freeze to death in the cold.

Many Arctic waders congregate on the harbours of Auckland and Northland but Farewell Spit also carries very large flocks and smaller numbers are sprinkled throughout the country with many of our rarest visitors turning up as far south as Stewart Island. It is worth looking for waders on every estuary, coastal lagoon and shallow inlet.

The estuary in winter is more thinly populated with birds than in summer, but there are always some waders. Perhaps 10 per cent of Arctic migrants stay over our winter. It is thought these non-breeders are first-year birds which will return north with the others the following autumn and thereafter join the regular north-south migration.

However, winter is the time when internal migrants dominate the scene. South Island pied oystercatchers leave the riverbeds and farmlands east of the Southern Alps as soon as breeding is completed. Most of them go to the great harbours of Auckland and Northland but some find the sea coast of the South Island sufficiently mild.

Many pied stilts move in a similar pattern but are never absent from the coast. They nest around the estuary, competing with Arctic migrants for summer food.

The dainty black stilt, the rarest wader in the world, follows an internal migration route from its high country nesting area near the Southern Alps to winter on the west coast estuaries of the North Island: Foxton, Kawhia, Manukau, Kaipara. There are now so few black stilts that sightings at any of these places is quite an event.

There are oystercatchers around the world, all of them black or white and black, with a strong red bill. Mainland New Zealand ones are classified into two species, South Island pied oystercatcher (SIPO) and variable oystercatcher. (A third species is on the Chatham Islands.) SIPO has a white underside and breast, with the white coming up in front of the black wings in white "braces". The variable oystercatcher, includes birds which are pure black or with variable amounts of white on the breast and belly. Some are very like the SIPO, but never have the distinctive white braces in front of the shoulder. Pure black oystercatchers are more often found on open beaches or little rocky bays than on estuaries. All oystercatchers feed on worms, shrimps, etc., in mud or sand, and use their specially adapted bill for prising open bivalve shells, including oysters.

The pied stilt is another black and white wader. Whereas the oystercatcher appears solidly built both on the ground or in flight, the pied stilt is longer, has very thin black legs, slimmer body, and thin dark bill. Once seen together, they are unlikely to be confused. The stilt has an insistent call like a yapping dog. The oystercatcher's "whee-eep" is not heard quite so often. It also has a piping call surprisingly musical for a shore bird.

Oystercatcher

Another internal migrant is the wrybill, an endemic wader, unique in that its bill is bent sideways. Since its discovery 150 years ago there have been many theories on the value of a bill which bends quite sharply to the right about halfway along its length. Present day scientists can study it with the advantage of freeze-frame and slow-motion photography or video. As you will discover when watching wrybills feeding, the bill is used in a number of ways.

Don't try to identify the wrybill by its bent bill, which even at medium to close range is not conspicuous. Its pale grey back and upper wing are distinctive in all conditions.

Wrybills nest on stony riverbeds in Canterbury, scattered along suitable areas from mountain to sea. After breeding they move north, and Miranda on the Firth of Thames, Manukau Harbour and Kaipara Harbour carry almost the total population until about the end of July. The wrybill shares the rich mudflats with godwits, knots and sandpipers which have come twenty times as far from the opposite direction.

Wrybills on the riverbed and on the saltings behave rather differently. Breeding birds are spread out over measured territories and one meets each pair separately in the course of a walk up a riverbed. Wintering wrybills on the mudflats may spread out widely to feed but gather into tight little flocks on roosts. They wheel and turn together in the air with a sparkle of white from the underwing. Wrybill flocks have enraptured many visitors to the Firth of Thames, even if they have never met the quiet river bird that is so tame it will come as close as four or five metres.

Beaches and shell banks are the home of another endemic wader which is very reduced in numbers — the red-breasted or New Zealand dotterel. This has an interesting distribution, there being two distinct populations at either end of the country. One can be found in small numbers on beaches, sandspits and estuaries north of the Bay of Plenty, if they have not been disturbed by humans, their vehicles and dogs. On Stewart Island the other population is found on beaches and bare mountain tops. These birds sometimes cross the strait to Southland beaches but there is no evidence of movement between the two populations.

The banded dotterel is smaller, an estuary bird you are also likely to meet on sandy beaches, South Island riverbeds and dry stony paddocks, its chief breeding grounds. From banding studies it has been found that many migrate across the Tasman to winter on the coast from southern Queensland to Victoria. These non-breeders are subadults, having a trip to Aussie before settling down to family responsibilities.

Apart from waders, the estuaries and tidal flats carry small numbers of black-backed and red-billed gulls. White-fronted terns hunt for sprats in the shallows and Caspian terns come to search for fish in the channels. You may find them roosting among waders on shell banks. In the north, in summer they are joined by a few eastern little terns which are smaller and make comparatively rapid wing-beats.

Black shapes like driftwood on the mudbanks may be shags resting after a diving session. Three species of shags are common in this habitat. They have to be looked at closely to determine whether they are black shags, little blacks, or little shags in any variable form from white-throated to fully white underside from bill to tail.

Kingfishers are common on mudflats in winter, many having moved down from farmland or lakes to feed on the unending supply of mud crabs. Gannets wander in from coastal waters to catch unwary fish in the stream, and startle the area with their raucous "krark" cries.

The white-faced heron, a member of the estuary community in all seasons and at every point around the coast, is never difficult to spot when wading in the shallows or roosting on logs or shell banks. At low tide it follows waders to the tide line, and feeds in the water while the waders probe freshly uncovered mud.

In North Auckland harbours and tidal creeks the banded rail can be sighted by a patient watcher in

131

places where cover goes down to the water's edge. Under mangroves or among rushes this shy little bird seeks live or dead food left by the receding tide. This rail is nocturnal, so the most likely times to see it are the evening or early morning, or on grey days. Listen for its "swit, swit" call in the last hour of evening light.

In winter white herons are found on estuaries nearly as frequently as on freshwater wetlands. After spending the breeding season (August to January) at the nesting colony at Okarito, South Westland, they disperse in all directions, appearing in ones and twos throughout the country. It seems that individual birds usually return to the same place each year. Don't make a hasty decision on the identification of a pure white heron. There are five species if we include the royal spoonbill, now breeding in New Zealand. This can be picked out by its large black bill, flattened to a "spoon" at the tip. It flies with neck outstretched, unlike the herons which hold their heads back at the shoulders. We have no endemic herons. Although the white heron or great white egret (*Egretta alba*) has a special place in Maori mythology, it is found throughout the world. The little egret (*Egretta garzetta*) may often be seen on an estuary in winter because there is a regular migration of small numbers from Australia, though none has stayed to breed. It is noticeably smaller than the white heron. Widely-distributed flocks of cattle egrets (*Bubulcus ibis*) also come from Australia to stay from April to about November. These are birds of farmland rather than salt marshes. Lastly, there have been two records of the intermediate heron (*Egretta intermedia*) in New Zealand, another possible "white heron". When you see a white heron, look closely to be sure which one it is.

Open sandy beaches are too exposed to be attractive to many birds but there are nearly always a few gulls, especially at low tide. Black-backed gulls patrol the tide line and act as efficient scavengers of dead fish. Sometimes a black-back patiently tries to break open a bivalve shell. Time after time it will carry the shell to a height of 10 to 12 metres and drop it on hard sand until it cracks open.

Black-backed gulls fit well into the environment when in the naturally low numbers still found in remote areas of the coast or on offshore islands. However in closely settled areas, human garbage provides a huge increase in food supply and gull numbers are now a problem, especially as predators of other ground-nesting birds of the coastline.

Red-billed gulls are met along a beach singly or in small groups, often feeding on small invertebrates uncovered by the first wash of the tide. On summer days red-bills run this way and that chasing blowflies over the hot sand.

Terns use open beaches for resting after feeding in waters beyond the breakers. You will often add Caspian tern and white-fronted tern to your bird list after a walk along a few kilometres of beach. They are willing to choose fine sand as a base for their sparsely lined scrape. The very rare fairy tern nests on two or three Northland beaches, but usually seeks an estuary island or spit rather than the open beach.

Nesting colonies on sandy spits can be an exciting place to get among birds but must be treated with the utmost respect. Birds are very vulnerable to disturbance. Every year many succumb to vandals and, unfortunately, well-meaning visitors. It is best to watch from nearby vantage points without going into the nesting area, so as to avoid the risk of stepping on eggs which are difficult to see or on chicks hiding near the nest. If you stay in the colony for more than 15 or 20 minutes, parent birds will be kept off the nest long enough for eggs to chill and embryos die. The other danger is that human footprints may lead ground predators to the nests. The most satisfactory watching can be done from a position which does not disturb, such as the other side of a water channel recognised by birds as a safeguard. From there watch the life of the colony where there is plenty of action. Pick out one or two nests and follow the development of the chicks day by day in consecutive visits.

New Zealand pipits are often on the sands of open beaches. Skylarks may be there too, but are more often on grassy patches among the dunes. The dune area of lupins or scrub has an interesting assortment of passerines, especially in winter. Redpolls move about in small flocks feeding on weed seeds. Their almost constant "chi, chi, chi, chi" calls identify them more surely than any other feature. The sharp "tseep" of hedge sparrows indicate where they are although you may see few of them. Chaffinches are common in the dunes and are sometimes down at the tide line feeding on washed up seeds. It is interesting to note the sex distribution in chaffinch flocks. In winter males usually outnumber females, which may be entirely absent. Goldfinches gather in large flocks to feed on the seeds of *Salicornia*, or glasswort, one of the commonest salt marsh plants around New Zealand estuaries. If you arrive at an estuary at low tide when the waders are out on the mudflats, you should still be able to find enough birdwatching to make the trip worthwhile.

Chapter 10
Coastal seas

The seas around New Zealand are some of the richest
in the world for numbers of birds and variety of
species. This is to be expected with open seas on all
sides and our position north of the vast Antarctic
Ocean. The Snares, a small group of islands south-
west of Stewart Island, are home to more sea birds
than the entire British Isles.

The cold subantarctic seas are rich in food. Pelagic
birds, which spend their lives at sea, must come to
land once a year to lay their eggs and rear their
young. Therefore a few small islands where they
breed must support many millions of sea birds. One
species, the sooty shearwater, is estimated to number
three million birds.

The full range of sea birds are only seen by those
who regularly sail coastal waters, but weekend
boaties can build up a knowledge of many of them.
(For some opportunities provided by public sea
transport see page 144).

As you board the boat there are sure to be gulls
around. These scavengers of the coast have learned
that human activity means the chance of an easy
feed. Ornithologists call them gulls rather than
seagulls, because they are birds of the coast and

never venture out of sight of land. Red-billed gulls will probably be mixed in with large black-backs, but there are unlikely to be any black-billed gulls. The dark bills of immature red-bills make them look like black-bills, but the red-bill in flight has a white "window" in its black wing tip and this clears up any doubt.

A common sight around harbours is the black shape of shags drying their wings. Most water birds have waterproof plumage, the feathers having an extra coating of oil so that they shed water efficiently. But cormorants lack this and get very wet during their fishing sessions. When they finish feeding they hold their wings out to dry in the sun and wind as wet wings are of little use for flying. A wet shag when disturbed can only dive or flap across the water to escape. Shags are particularly fond of perching on fence posts which go into a lake or bay. These are low enough for a wet shag to fly on to and also provide safety from land predators.

Pied shag

Near the entrance of a harbour or inlet watch for roosting or nesting shags. This is a favourite place for pied shags (in trees) and spotted shags (on cliffs). Quiet manoeuvring of a boat can get you to colonies inaccessible from the land.

Shags have a long breeding season. Egg-laying is not co-ordinated as it is in tern colonies, for instance. Young about to fly might be flapping alongside a bird sitting on newly laid eggs. It is always a pleasant

surprise to hear the sounds from a shag colony —
young birds begging for food and adults greeting
each other in a constant chorus.

Spotted shags nest in large colonies on sea cliffs or
rock stacks. This is our most handsome shag,
ornamented with delicate white filoplumes (hairlike
feathers that lack vanes and occur between the
contour feathers) on the neck during a brief part of
its breeding cycle. It is strictly a marine shag. Long
strings of birds fly from the colony to feed in the
coastal waters.

Rock shelves and reefs around entrances are the
places to look for the reef heron, now uncommon
but present in less disturbed places. Its dark shape,
standing hunched and motionless above the tide or
stepping cautiously around rock pools, is easily
missed without a careful search with binoculars. The
rival white-faced heron is more likely to be seen on a
muddy inlet or sandbank in the harbour. It has
bicoloured wings, dark primaries and light wing
coverts and back, and in flight is easily distinguished
from the uniformly coloured reef heron.

Once the boat is in open water search for swimming penguins, especially in late afternoon or evening
when they are returning to nests or roosts among the
rocks. The little blue penguin is the most common
species on the main islands, and the only penguin
around the North Island. Like all penguins it swims
low in the water, the bill sometimes held above the
horizontal in a distinctive way. A boat will often get
quite close before it dives out of sight.

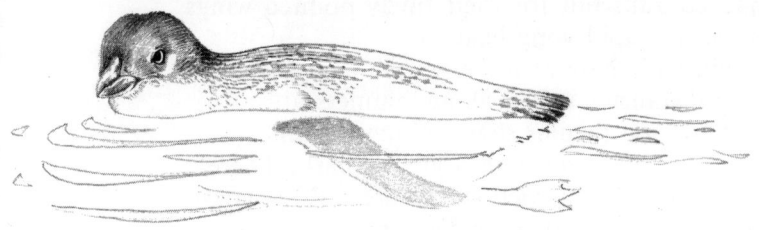

Little blue penguin

Terns may be seen in a harbour or up to a kilometre or so from the coast. The old name, sea swallow, conveys their graceful flight, their long pointed wings and deeply forked tails. All the terns are predominantly white with a black cap. It is size and shape, the placing of the black cap, and bill colour which are the distinguishing features.

The white-fronted tern is commonly known as the kahawai bird for its habit of feeding on shoals of small fish driven to the surface by hunting kahawai. The tern flies quickly five to eight metres above the sea, turning in a short circle when prey is sighted, then diving. After a pause the tern surfaces and flies away, swallowing its catch in the air.

Its name refers to the narrow white strip between the black cap and the bill. In black-fronted terns the cap comes down to the bill. This is too fine a point to help with field identification and you must rely on the "jizz" of the bird and some colour differences. The black-front has bright orange-red bill and feet, and its upper surface is greyish. The white-front's bill is black, its feet dark red. The black-front is an inland tern which breeds on the riverbeds of the eastern South Island. It usually meets up with the white-front in winter when it moves to estuaries and tidal lagoons in both North and South Islands.

In summer it is worth watching for migrant Arctic skuas among the white-fronted terns. These little pirates have a rough but effective method of getting their food. They wait for a tern to catch a fish, chase the tern until it drops the fish, then snatch it up in mid-air. Brown skuas may be mistaken for young black-backed gulls but for their finely pointed wings and distinctive rapid wing-beat.

The vivid whiteness of a gannet is distinguishable from long distances. Often alone, gannets are renowned for spectacular dives, plunging almost vertically into the water with a great splash. There are gannet colonies on rock stacks around the coast as far south as Foveaux Strait, but most are in the north, and northern waters are most likely to provide the spectacle of a gannet flock working a shoal of fish. A co-ordinated circuit is set up; each bird dives, surfaces, flies in a loop to gain height and joins again to take its turn for another dive. The effect must be decimation of the shoal of fish.

A kilometre or two from land, pelagic birds begin to appear, and the first to be seen may be prions, small blue-grey birds about 25 cm long which occur all round New Zealand. A broad "M" formed by dark markings on the back and wing coverts is the badge of the prions. They fly low over the water, usually in twos and threes, but sometimes up to twenty or more around a boat. They cross the bow or pass alongside, largely ignoring the boat while flying endless miles in search of food. When it is found they settle on the water for a minute or two.

Fairy prion

The most common species is the fairy prion. Considerable experience of small differences is necessary to distinguish the various species at sea. The broad-billed is an exception because its grotesquely large bill is easily seen.

Shearwaters are slightly, larger birds than prions and most are dark brown. They have long narrow wings and are faster fliers. The most numerous in southern waters is the sooty shearwater or muttonbird. Fluttering shearwaters, named for their rapid wing beats, are more common in the north. "Shearwater" is meant to convey the mode of flight — rising up over the water then shearing down on the wave tops. Several species are called "muttonbird" when the young are taken for food. The sooty shearwater provides the unfortunate young displayed as delicacies in fish shop windows. This species nests all around our coasts, but the greatest numbers are on the Muttonbird Islands, south-west of Stewart Island. They migrate each year to the subarctic seas of the North Pacific. The shearwaters seen most commonly from October to May, singly or in small parties, are likely to be breeding birds feeding many kilometres from their island nests.

Shearwaters feed in flocks on shoals of small fish driven to the surface by predators such as kingfish. The birds swim in tight groups. With little jumps they dive under to "fly" with half-open wings, chasing fish for several metres down. The dives can last 30 seconds or more. Flocks with thousands of birds can be met on the water near their main breeding islands in the far south and off North Auckland's east coast.

The large, dark brown flesh-footed shearwater is common in northern waters, especially the outer Hauraki Gulf and the Bay of Plenty. It is identified by its prominent light-coloured bill and pinkish legs and feet. It will follow a boat for hours, not closely, looking for anything thrown overboard. A bit of fish or bread often brings it close in.

Birds at sea can be classified into boat followers and boat avoiders. The followers regard a boat as a food source and keep near for hours (or days on the high seas). The boat avoiders give fewer chances to the birdwatcher, but keep a good lookout. They can be seen clearly as they pass by. Flesh-footed shearwaters and giant petrels are followers in northern inshore waters; cape pigeons and molly-mawks take their place in the south. From Dunedin southwards numbers of mollymawks and albatrosses increase and Foveaux Strait can produce an exciting variety in a single crossing. Despite seasonal changes, you can usually expect to see Buller's, white-capped and Salvin's mollymawks, and occasional wandering and royal albatrosses.

Plump little diving petrels emerge as a boat comes close, and take off with tiny wings beating at high speed. They are related to northern hemisphere auks, and are happier under water than over it. After a short flight they plunge into the water with little or no slowing down. It is said they sometimes fly through the crests of waves.

When a cape pigeon comes alongside it stays close, displaying smart black and white plumage as it flies alternating quick wing-beats with long glides. It is no pigeon, but a petrel with a name designed to confuse the uninitiated! Its other name, pintado petrel, is more appropriate. Pintado is Spanish for painted and the bird has a striking pattern different from other sea birds. Cape pigeons are bright little birds, addicted to boat following and almost always close to ships in southern waters. They are always ready to seize food thrown overboard, and many a seasick sailor has envied their confidence over the waves as he has hung green-faced over the rail.

Sighting of a storm petrel generates some interest in the most hardened seafarer. It is a matter of luck to find them inshore. On the right day you can see dozens, spread over a large area in ones and twos. As the name indicates you are most likely to see them near land when seas are stormy.

They were the first to be given the name of petrel because, like Saint Peter, they walk on water. They move over the surface with little skips and jumps, both feet together and wings lightly fluttering. No description can do this justice. It is one of those delightful surprises in nature which has to be seen.

Sea bird identification is difficult but from a good field guide you can learn what characteristics to look for. Underwing patterns are a more important feature than in most land birds. Birdwatchers, even the most experienced, smile when they speak of the "little brown jobs" which move through the bushes before they can be identified. If you are a beginner in birdwatching at sea, don't be ashamed to admit that most of the albatrosses and mollymawks are "big white jobs".

In Appendix 4 the Beach Patrol Scheme of the Ornithological Society is described. If you have the opportunity, examine storm-wrecked sea birds in the hand. This way of becoming familiar with small but important differences in plumage and structure is very helpful when identifying the bird at sea.

Sea bird watching with a telescope from clifftop or headland can be rewarding in suitable localities. Many sea birds may be seen inshore and a patient watcher will record a long list of species over a year. Obviously places with deeper water and inshore currents are likely to bring in more pelagic birds, especially when rough conditions offshore do not allow them to feed or to rest on the water.

Many places on the east coast of the South Island allow good views of sooty shearwaters migrating north in late April or early May. Hour after hour, birds fly past, skimming the wave tops. These are adults and that season's young on the first leg of one of the world's longest migrations. As far as we know, most sooties cover a great circle passing close to Japan and the Aleutian Islands, then fly down the coast of North America, across the equator and over the southern ocean to their breeding grounds off the south-west coast of Stewart Island, a journey of more than 30,000 km.

Other shearwaters, petrels, albatrosses and mollymawks often pass within spotting distance. When calmer conditions encourage those birds to stay out to sea, you can watch shags, gannets and terns going about daily routines, which are often governed by time and tide.

One of the most magnificent bird groups is the albatross and mollymawk family. These birds range over the seas circling the Antarctic continent and are common off both the east and west coasts of New Zealand. We are very fortunate to have a royal albatross breeding colony at Taiaroa Head at the entrance to Otago Harbour, because other colonies are on remote islands. Mollymawk is the old seafarer's name for the smaller species but they belong to the same genus as albatrosses. The distinction is not rigid — Buller's mollymawk and Buller's albatross seem to be equally acceptable.

Many albatrosses are devoted ship followers, but they may also be seen within sight of land around the southern coast. One can happily watch them for hours in flight: racing up to the ship, gliding silently past while scrutinising those aboard, then rolling off in a magnificent turn with the lower wing tip only a few centimetres above the waves. Every move is accomplished with rigid wings which seem incapable of bending. The colour of almost all albatrosses and mollymawks is simply white with black wing-tips and some grey or brown on the head. Careful attention to each feature is necessary to identify the species. Note the underwing pattern and bill colour before referring to a field guide.

Albatross

The wandering albatross leaves the nest site dark brown except for a white face and white underwing. It then passes through a mottled phase, sometimes called the leopard stage, when white gradually spreads and the back is brown-spotted. The mature bird is white with black wing-tips and some black on the upper wing. When food scraps are thrown overboard, watch the squabbling, splashing albatrosses. They may include wanderers in different age-plumages.

Albatrosses are surface feeders and go no deeper than plunging in head and neck. A large component of their natural food is squid caught on the surface at night. The birds' future must be threatened by commercial squid fishing which has developed rapidly. In 1985, 85,500 tonnes of squid were taken from New Zealand's Economic Zone.

The large, dark brown giant petrel or nelly is often mistaken for an albatross, but you will learn to recognise its slightly different proportions and less graceful flight. This bird is a scavenger and regular boat follower. Nellies usually join the inter-island ferries as they leave Wellington Harbour. They stay close alongside, ready to dive to every bucketful of slops which leaves the galley.

Unfortunately these days there are not many opportunities to get out to sea by public transport. The inter-island ferries provide the best of these. The withdrawal of the *Wairua* from the Bluff to Stewart Island run was a disappointment to many bird-watchers from New Zealand and overseas who used it to see albatrosses, mollymawks, petrels and shearwaters. In the Bay of Islands the celebrated "Cream Run" launch gets into waters which have pelagic birds in most weathers. Mail boats on Pelorus Sound meet small numbers of a variety of Cook Strait birds. The Hauraki Gulf is crossed by several boats from Auckland, listed in the Auckland district section.

As the boat returns to land, you have the opportunity to look for the same species of birds sighted on the way out, but time and wind and tide influence their movements. Your sightings of mobile species such as petrels and shearwaters may be quite different. Nightfall brings breeding sea birds ashore to their colonies. Summer breeders from October to February, winter-breeding species from May to August. When passing offshore islands you may see birds gathering in flocks a few hundred metres from the shore. This is especially likely for the outer Hauraki Gulf islands, the Mercuries, and Cook Strait islands. After dark, when they are no longer so vulnerable to predators, they fly in to nest burrows. There is a great deal of noise as each individual calls excitedly as it approaches its nest. It is a memorable experience to be near the coastline of a "bird island" on a moonless summer evening when thousands of birds arrive, each calling loudly, so the whole area vibrates with sound.

Chapter 11

Mountains

Birds are less common in the high country where plants grow more slowly and most forms of life are dormant during winter months, but there are some interesting species on the mountains which are seldom found elsewhere. New Zealand mountain sides have all undergone the shock treatment of browsing animals in the last hundred years, which must have greatly affected the plant food previously available to birds, but also brought many new weeds and seeding grasses. Two birds common on the open faces up to about 1500 m are introduced species which find weed seeds a good food source. These are the skylark and the redpoll. Pipits are there too, but they are dependent on invertebrates (as is the skylark, partly) and have been shown to avoid drier areas during the breeding season.

A drawn out cry of "kee-aaah" from the skies indicates you are a thousand metres above worry level. There is something carefree about the cry of that endearing old rogue, the kea. It is truly a mountain bird, found along the whole length of the alpine chain from Foveaux Strait to Cook Strait, but not at all in the North Island. The kea is very willing to supplement its diet of mountain berries, leaves and

insects, and regularly visits motorists' stopping places and mountain huts. The broad wings and hooked bill are unmistakable parrot features. Although most often seen in the open, the kea actually spends much of its time in the high altitude forest.

Flat-bottomed mountain valleys of the eastern side of the main alpine chain from Molesworth Station to Lake Te Anau have long been the main breeding grounds of the Canada goose. Any party tramping into the mountains can expect to disturb nesting "honkers" in early summer, from October to January. At lower levels the geese may be seen grazing on improved pastures or on turnip crops. Family groups or small flocks will be met on high country lakes and tarns. In any situation they are wary and difficult to approach.

Blue ducks are birds of the rapids of mountain streams within the forests of both islands. Finding them always involves a lot of walking along rivers, as they spend much of the day hidden under banks or vegetation. They are territorial all year round and with patience a known pair can always be located within its territory, which may be a stretch of river as long as one kilometre.

The chukor is found in open tussock country from about Roxburgh to Lake Coleridge, then again around the St Arnaud region at the headwaters of Marlborough's Wairau River. This handsome Asiatic partridge may be met singly or in small coveys. It is always wary and when disturbed is likely to fly across a valley, a short flight which takes it an hour's walk away. It is always worth keeping an eye out for it in tussock country from about 1000 to 1800 m especially in rough rocky gullies.

The rock wren is usually spotted as a tiny ball of life perched on a rock, actively bobbing and wing-flicking. It darts about catching insects on the rock vegetation, or collecting feathers to replace the lining of the nest set deep in the cavities between rocks. The rock wren lives in old and stable rock falls, clean or partly scrub covered, on the lower slopes of the mountains. It is well known only in Fiordland, Arthur's Pass and the Craigieburn Range, but probably occurs more widely in suitable habitat.

Unless a particular breeding territory is known (and it may be occupied for years) the falcon is not a bird to go looking for. Rather it is met, usually when a dramatic movement captures the attention. This may be the circling, climbing struggle as a falcon tries to out-manoeuvre a skylark or other small bird, or a high-speed chase of a pigeon in level flight. Falcons are common in much high country, but in this zone there are fewer harriers than in the lower hills.

Black-backed gulls range over the entire open country of both islands, and the mountain ridges are no exception. Breeding colonies are sometimes found on open tops with bare stony ground. Two such places have been the top of Mt Davey, at the southern end of the Paparoas, and on Mt Ruapehu near the Tama Lakes. However these colonies, like many smaller lowland ones, may be frequently moved about.

Hutton's shearwater is an unexpected mountain bird, but about 30 years ago its nest burrows were discovered at about 1500 m in the Seaward Kaikouras. At sea this bird is almost indistinguishable from the fluttering shearwater which nests on many islands in the Hauraki Gulf and elsewhere off the coast, but in nature there are always a few surprises. The last fingers of soil which stretch up to the rocky peaks of the Seaward Kaikouras are burrowed into by Hutton's shearwaters which come ashore to start cleaning out their burrows at the end of August, often before the snow has gone from the site.

Part III
Where to find birds

Where to find birds

The first guide to where to find birds in New Zealand was written by the late Ross McKenzie but it is now long out of print. The following district notes owe much to him, but there is an important change: Ross covered the country by moving in an imagined journey from Auckland to Stewart Island, treating all areas passed through, whether good or no good for birdwatching. Here, the aim has been to deal with only the best places for birds in each district. It is hoped that these notes will be useful to the tourist and holidaying birdwatcher so that time can be saved by going straight to the most productive areas and also having a guide to which birds to look for at each location. They can be only a general guide, since birds are often unco-operative things and will be absent from a once-reliable spot when they are most expected. But that is part of the enjoyment.

All birdwatchers have their own special places, known to provide plenty of interest at particular seasons, and you will still have to find these for yourself in your home district. By guiding you to the well-known places in other districts, these notes can form a framework for birdwatching trips. When you have become confident of identifying most birds that you see, you will get constant pleasant surprises from finding species where you haven't expected to see them.

You will note that bird names are often shortened for simplicity in locality sites: eastern bar-tailed godwits are called godwits, and so on. It would be pedantic to use the full name in cases where the only other species which it could be confused with are very rare stragglers. Care has been taken not to list species as expected when only a few individuals have been recorded at the locality over the years. With a bit of luck any regular observer should be able to add a species or two to any locality list every year.

Chapter 12

The North Island

Northland

Whangarei Harbour has extensive mudflats on its southern shore, with wader feeding grounds chiefly from Skull Creek to Takahiwai (with a major high-tide roost at Skull Creek) and at Oakleigh. Godwits and knots are common, with other Arctic migrants seen only rarely and small numbers of wrybill found in winter. New Zealand dotterels breed at various points around the harbour. The northern shoreline is mostly rocky and little blue penguins breed in many places. There are also variable oystercatchers there and a few reef herons. White-faced herons occur right around the harbour, and banded rails are in the mangroves. White-fronted terns and scattered pairs of Caspian terns nest around the outer harbour, and flocks of pelagic birds often wander in from Bream Bay, which is very rich in petrels and shearwaters. Fluttering shearwaters may often be seen in Urquharts Bay and Parua Bay.

Rangaunu Harbour is probably the most valuable bird harbour, but access is difficult; scrub and mangroves prevent viewing most areas from dry land, and a boat is the most effective means of travel. However, Kaimaumau Road takes you around the northern shore, and the south-eastern corner of the harbour can be looked over by following a disused road from the top of the hill just after the Lake Ohia school. The main wader feeding areas are on the northern side on a group of sand bars stretching towards the outlet, but most birds fly off to the ocean beaches to roost at high tide. Walker Island, near the neck, has large breeding colonies of Caspian terns, white-fronted terns and red-billed gulls, and some New Zealand dotterels breed there and on the dunes behind the ocean beach.

Wader numbers peak here in September/October and again in late January/February, indicating that this harbour is a stopping-off place for birds which spend most of the summer further south. At these times there are fairly large flocks of godwit and knot and several hundred turnstones. Throughout the year there is a big population of white-faced herons, pied stilts and red-billed gulls. Winter brings large numbers of South Island pied oystercatchers, but very few wrybills and banded dotterels.

The Bay of Islands has a number of boats catering for the many tourists who want to get out on to this beautiful bay. Most leave from Paihia, and some of them, especially the renowned "cream run" may take you out far enough to see Buller's shearwaters, fluttering shearwaters and fairy prions. Little blue penguins may be spotted on the surface anywhere in the bay, and gannets and white-fronted terns are always around. White-faced herons, variable oystercatchers and reef herons can be seen on the reefs and rocks.

Waitangi State Forest has the reputation of being one of the easiest places to see the brown kiwi. Kiwis have settled into the radiata pine forest, living on the invertebrates of the thick humus layer of pine needles in all but the driest seasons, when they tend to retreat to dense gullies which have been left in native shrubs. From Waitangi it is about 4 km (2 km from Waitangi Hotel) to the Forest Headquarters. Check in there for a gate key to give access to the forestry road (Wairoa Road) which should be followed on the north side of the forest to where it enters the forest at the junction with Bayleys (No. 21) Road. Walk along Bayleys Road on the right for the first good kiwi spot.

Wairoa Road may be followed right through to Kerikeri Inlet Road and Kerikeri township for a round trip of about 60 km back to Paihia.

Red-billed gull
(Don Hadden)

Black-billed gull
(Rod Morris)

Kea
(Don Hadden)

Morepork
(Rod Morris)

Kingfisher
(Geoff Moon)

Mallard drake
(Don Hadden)

South Island rifleman; female
(Rod Morris)

N.Z. pipit
(Don Hadden)

There are two other good places for kiwis which do not require going through the Forestry H.Q. Road. You may continue along Falls Road which skirts the southern edge of the forest and stop to listen for kiwis about 80–100 m past the Headquarters Road corner. A further kilometre along, this road skirts Mt Bledisloe where you should have no trouble hearing kiwis. This is outside the State Forest. Left at the next junction, Haruru Road goes south to Haruru Falls and a circuit can be completed back to Paihia. It is advisable to go to Forest H.Q. and tell them your intentions even if you are not planning to enter the forest — you will find them very helpful. Remember that kiwis should be listened and looked for in the 40 minutes following sundown. If you haven't found one by then, try the next night. The male normally calls as he leaves the burrow at sunset, and is answered by the female and other males in surrounding territories. Intermittent calling may continue through the night.

Where the road crosses a tidal inlet between Paihia and Haruru Falls there are banded rails, spotless crakes and fernbirds; search on the eastern (Paihia) side of the inlet up from the road.

Kokako can be seen in Puketi Forest where there are several known territories. Here, as in other forests, you will have more success if you use a taped call of a kokako. From Kerikeri drive to the Puketi Forest H.Q. (off Waiare Road) where there may be someone to give directions. For one good area, pass the H.Q. (turning left) and continue until you meet a locked gate. Park and walk on until the forest road branches. A few hundred metres along the left branch, and this junction, are likely places to see or hear kokako. Puketi also has tuis and pied tits, and in the scrubby margins there are fernbirds, pheasants, California quail and brown quail. Eastern rosellas are common throughout, and kaka and yellow-crowned parakeet are there in small numbers.

Omahuta State Forest is the western half of the same forest, entered by Omahuta Road just south of Mangamuka Bridge on Highway 1. Several walking tracks traverse the whole area. Forest remnants throughout North Auckland have kiwis which do some of their nocturnal feeding on farmlands. Pigeons, tuis and moreporks are common in all areas which retain patches of bush, and a conspicuous bird throughout is the eastern rosella. California quail, brown quail and pheasant are common in scrub and fern of dry country.

Ninety Mile Beach is usually seen from the comfort of the daily tourist bus to Cape Reinga, as few private motorists want to risk driving on the sands. The open beach is not entirely without birds, and occasional New Zealand dotterels, banded dotterels, New Zealand pipits and variable oystercatchers are seen, as well as black-backed gulls and red-billed gulls. At the low headland of Cape Maria van Diemen black-winged petrels (probably birds from the Kermadec Islands' population) have been attempting to get established for some years. This species would be a welcome mainland breeder, but it has suffered badly from wild cats, and petrel corpses continually litter the area. Birds can be seen in the air as they come in at night during their summer breeding season.

Rangaunu is a favoured wintering place for white herons and royal spoonbills. There is always the likelihood of seeing other "white herons" too, because little egret, cattle egret and yellow-billed spoonbill have all been recorded there. Take careful note of any large white bird. Big numbers of shags feed in the channels — black shags, little shags and a few little blacks. Duck of several species feed around the edges of mangroves where they are difficult to see and identify. The swampy margins contain the fernbird, bittern, banded rail and spotless crake.

The small lakes of the Aupori Peninsula north of Awanui vary in depth and condition. The bird life on them is rather unpredictable until you get to know them through frequent visits. Many of them have interesting birds, rarities are always possible, and you will seldom be disappointed. The Waipapakauri group is usually very productive. A map of this area is necessary to locate all the lakes and ponds; Ngatua, though easiest to find, is used for water skiing so has few birds. In the area there are black swan, paradise duck, grey duck, mallard, grey teal, shoveler, dabchick, Australian little grebe, black shag, little shag, pied shag, little black shag and spur-winged plover. Bitterns are quite common and spotless crakes have been recorded. The Australian little grebe seems to be more established here than any other place in New Zealand, and one flock of 20 birds has been recorded. The grey teal, renowned for its wandering habits, cannot always be expected.

Parengarenga Harbour's five-fingered spread has vast sand flats which support a great number and variety of waders. The most popular access point is Paua, where you can park near the wharf and walk around over the hard sand at almost any tide. This is a place to watch waders feeding in small flocks rather than crowded on to high tide roosts. In Parenga-renga's largely unaltered landscape there are several places where the birds roost. The flat land round Paua or the sands of South Head are two of them. The most fruitful time is in September when the flocks are arriving, or in February as they gather here after drifting up from southern estuaries. Turnstones are more common here than further south, and godwit, knot, banded dotterel and New Zealand dotterel are in good numbers.

The upper reaches of the Hokianga Harbour probably have the greatest number of banded rails anywhere in the country, but approach by boat is the only practical way for most areas. Mangrove edges and rushes invaded by high tide are always worth inspecting for banded rails in Northland; their footprints on the mud between tides may be the first clue to their presence.

Auckland

Every city likes to claim at least one ornithological attraction. Auckland is able to offer two. The Hauraki Gulf is rich in petrels and shearwaters, and the vast mudflats of Manukau Harbour and the Firth of Thames have large numbers, and probably the greatest variety, of shore birds in the country.

Harbour and gulf

Thirteen species of petrel and shearwater breed on islands of the Hauraki Gulf, and most can be seen on the waters of the inner gulf. Little blue penguins breed on all islands and are seldom missed on a day at sea.

The Waitemata Harbour has gannets, black-backed and red-billed gulls, Caspian and white-fronted terns, an occasional giant petrel in winter, and four species of shags — pied, black, little and little black. The spotted shag is a possibility also. Cross-harbour ferries seldom meet anything of interest but ferries to Rangitoto, Motuihe and Waiheke islands give you the chance to see gannets, little blue penguins and arctic skuas among the white-fronted terns in summer. Rangitoto Island hosts a large nesting colony of black-backed gulls.

The outer gulf beyond Rakino and Waiheke has many more pelagic birds. Depending on the season and weather, there may be giant petrel, flesh-footed shearwater, Buller's shearwater, fluttering shearwater, fairy prion, cape pigeon and white-faced storm petrel. Rough weather at sea brings birds into sheltered waters.

The ferry to Pakatoa Island travels further from the influence of the city, and if the boat goes round the outer side of Waiheke Island the chance of seeing Buller's and fluttering shearwaters is greatly increased. In summer there are a number of pleasure cruises in addition to the timetable ferries. They vary from year to year, so you should enquire from travel agents, the Auckland Public Relations Office or the Auckland ferry terminal.

Cruises to Great Barrier Island, normally lasting four days, are the most fruitful because the outer gulf is rich in bird life. Three rare endemic species are on Great Barrier Island. Black petrels and Cook's petrels fly over nearby waters, or gather on the sea near the island late in the evening during the breeding season. Brown teal can be found around Ohiwi and in small numbers in the harbours of the west coast.

The city

Tahuna Torea Nature Reserve on the Glendowie Spit is an excellent place for beginners to watch birds that will never be found in the garden. It is handy to the centre of the city, yet preserves much of the character of its original state. It has a good species list because at least four habitats are represented. The freshwater pond has mallards, grey ducks, black swans, pukekos, kingfishers and white-faced herons; welcome swallows are constantly feeding over the water. Native shrubs and trees are being encouraged along the western boundary and these contain white-eyes, grey warblers, chaffinches, goldfinches and other common species. The tip of the spit is a high-tide roost for the birds of the Tamaki estuary. South Island pied oystercatchers, godwits, knots, banded dotterels and occasionally other waders are there in summer, and pied stilts are always about. At low tide kingfishers are on the mudflats hunting crabs and white-faced herons tread the edges of the tide. Black shags and little shags are in the intermediate habitat of brackish ponds but often join the ducks to hunt fish in the freshwater pond. Pied shags from nearby colonies will be seen on the estuary. Gulls and terns are always about.

There are two points of entry to Tahuna Torea. One is a footpath half-way along Vista Crescent, off Roberta Avenue. The other is at the blind end of West Tamaki Road, where entry is by the viewing shelter that overlooks the freshwater ponds. A leaflet describing the reserve, its flora and fauna and how to get to it, is available from the Auckland Museum or the Auckland Public Relations Office in Queen Street.

Within the city two colonies of pied shags are easy to watch. One is at Panmure Basin, seen from the footbridge over the outlet channel. Here bird droppings are destroying the mature pine trees in which the birds have nested for many years, so the colony may not last long. The second, at Hobson Bay, is flourishing. The birds' white breasts are conspicuous against the foliage of large pohutukawa trees. Watch the shags from Waipipi Road or from the bridge at the eastern end of Orakei Road.

Western Springs has breeding black swans, coots, pukekos and ducks of several species and hybrids of many shapes and colours to test your identification skills. Little shags nest in a tree on the zoo side of the park.

Towards the western edge of the city, Pollen Island, a sand ridge protected by mangroves and mud in the Waitemata Harbour, hosts a small colony of fernbirds.

West and north-west of the city

The Waitakere Range, western boundary to Auckland City, has a picturesque covering of bush, much of it regenerated after sawmilling. There is not a high population of birds but you can find many bush species not easy to locate elsewhere. The Royal Forest and Bird Protection Society's Matuku Reserve contains 40 hectares of fine forest and swamp traversed by tracks. About halfway along Jonkers Road, 7 km from Waitakere (and about 33 km from Auckland Chief Post Office) watch for the Forest and Bird sign at the top of the narrow road down to the reserve. Drive 1 km to a parking area at the reserve gate. Birds to see include the tui, pigeon, fantail, grey warbler, and around the swamp and lagoon, mallard, shoveler, grey duck, bittern, fernbird, spotless crake, black shag, little shag, black swan, pukeko, kingfisher, welcome swallow and harrier. The eastern rosella is also in the forest, and around the margins the California quail, hedge sparrow, redpoll and yellowhammer. Kiwis were released in this reserve in the early 1980s but their present status is uncertain.

On the west coast, north of Auckland and handy to it, there is a gannetry, an exciting place to visit when birds are nesting between August and February. Leave Highway 16 at Waimauku (34 km from Auckland Chief Post Office) at the Muriwai signpost. It is 10 km to the beach, and just before the picnic area and main carpark take Waitea Road up the hill to the left; about 250 m on, turn right at the sign for Maori Bay to a large parking area (an old quarry). An unmarked track leads to the cliff top and around the cliff edge to the gannet colony. You will have sighted the gannets and have only a short distance to reach the fenced reserve. The colony was first on Oaia Island offshore, then it overflowed to the stack, now fully occupied. Further growth in the colony has brought birds to nest on the mainland, where after some initial failures through disturbance, they now breed in relative safety behind a high wire fence. Here they can be watched from a distance of 3 or 4 m.

Sharing the nearby stack is a small colony of white-fronted terns that extends to the mainland on cliff ledges out of sight below the gannets. The graceful terns in the air, and the nests and young on the rock stack are added attractions.

The long stretch of Muriwai beach is popular with beach patrollers who find large numbers of dead sea birds which have been blown in by westerly winds. Access is by a network of roads through Woodhill State Forest which covers the consolidated dunes behind the beach. A permit to enter may be gained from Woodhill Forest Headquarters down a well sign-posted road from Highway 16 about 6 km north of Waimauku. On South Kaipara Head, the long finger of land between the Kaipara Harbour and Muriwai Beach, there is a string of dune lakes commencing north of Parakai and stretching 15 km. Each lake varies in vegetation and water depth, and attracts slightly different bird life. Turning off Kaipara South Head Road into Wilson's Road leads you to Lake Kereta, which is perhaps the best. Dabchicks always breed on Kereta and bitterns are common. The Australian little grebe has turned up at Kereta No. 2 (close to the south) and it may become established. There are also grey ducks, paradise ducks, black swans, grey teal, shovelers, black shags, little shags, little black shags, Caspian terns, white-faced herons, kingfishers, pied stilts and pukekos at Kereta. There is a long-term lowering of water levels which has dried out areas of raupo swamp and some good ponds have been lost.

For several years this area has been visited each winter by a large flock of cattle egrets which may be seen (May to November) from the road as it crosses swampy farmland a few kilometres north of Parakai. At the top of the peninsula, the Kaipara South Head Road ends short of Papakanui Spit, a Wildlife Refuge where there is a colony of Caspian terns and where a few pairs of fairy terns continue to hang on. It can be reached by vehicle along Muriwai Beach.

Another great harbour, the Kaipara, is less than one hour's drive from Auckland. It ranks third behind Manukau and Farewell Spit for numbers of waders recorded in summer counts.

Wading birds at the more accessible southern end of Kaipara Harbour roost at Oyster Point and Jordans. Only small numbers are seen at Shelly Beach and the few other places where the harbour can be approached from South Kaipara Head. Jordan's Road leaves Highway 22 at the top of a hill and it should be followed down to the last house, where permission can be gained to cross to the mouth of a small tidal arm. If you turn off to the left at the foot of the hill, the road leads round to Oyster Point. These locations are the major accessible roosting places and you may see godwit, knot, turnstone and South Island pied oystercatcher in large numbers (according to the season). A small number of wrybill winter there with resident New Zealand dotterel and banded dotterel.

Day trips to Kawau Island (where you may see kookaburras introduced by Governor Grey a century ago) depart from Sandspit near Warkworth, and this trip meets up with a few fluttering shearwaters, Buller's shearwaters and little blue penguins. In the right weather conditions, difficult to judge in advance, fairy prions, flesh-footed shearwaters and white-faced storm petrels can also be seen. White-fronted and Caspian terns, gulls and little shags can be expected on inshore waters, and occasionally reef herons may be seen on rocky points or flying between islands.

Little Barrier Island is a closely protected sanctuary

for endangered species. There is no other part of the country where so many of our rare species may be seen. It is the sole stronghold of the stitchbird. From this thriving population stitchbirds have recently been introduced to one or two other islands. A very small number of kakapo have been released and these are surviving in the higher, more remote parts of the island. Recently introduced saddlebacks and kokako are breeding and becoming established. The small colony of Cook's petrels and the last remaining black petrels have a greatly improved chance of survival now that feral cats have been removed. The forests of Little Barrier have remained free of browsing animals, and they support a rich variety of species. As well as the rare and endangered species mentioned, there are kaka, red-crowned parakeet, yellow-crowned parakeet, tui, bellbird, robin, pied tit, whitehead, morepork, falcon, pigeon, brown kiwi, grey warbler, fantail, white-eye, pipit and several exotic species. A colony of pied shags is in trees overhanging a cliff near the homestead flat and little blue penguins nest around the coast. Both cuckoos are common in summer.

Permits to visit Little Barrier Island are obtained from the Hauraki Gulf Maritime Park Board, c/o Department of Conservation, Auckland. Bunkhouse accommodation is available to parties from recognised environmental organisations. Transport is usually arranged with charter boats working out of Leigh or Sandspit.

Tiritiri Matangi Island, off the tip of Whangaparaoa Peninsula, is being developed as an "open wildlife sanctuary". Anyone willing to treat the island with respect has free access to endangered plant and animal life. The North Island saddleback was one of the earliest introductions, and other birds will be added as the habitat is built up by extensive planting.

The East Coast Bays on Auckland's North Shore are so closely settled they have only the common birds of the suburbs. The long drive to the end of the Whangaparaoa Peninsula is worthwhile for those who like to engage in "sea-watching". An interesting assortment of the sea birds can be seen in comfort through binoculars without the risk of being seasick. These include Buller's shearwater, flesh-footed shearwater, fluttering shearwater, gannet and white-fronted tern. In late summer there will usually be Arctic skuas with the terns.

South of the city

South of Auckland city are the two great wader habitats, the Firth of Thames and Manukau Harbour. Right around the Firth of Thames there are wide mudflats, but the western shoreline from Miranda to Kaiaua (10 km) is the most easily approached, and this section carries the greatest numbers. From the city the direct approach is by Highway 1 to Pokeno, then turn left to Thames (Highway 2), turning off at Maungatawhiri where signposts indicate the road through Mangatangi to Miranda. At the Miranda Hall and carrier's yard keep straight on to the coast. The Miranda Naturalists' Trust property commences where this road (East Coast Road) turns north to run parallel to the beach. About 100 m from the corner you will see an entrance and sign.

The Miranda Naturalists' Trust was formed in 1975 by Auckland ornithologists to encourage the study of this area, in recognition of its great importance for migratory waders. The land between road and beach north of the river is leased and free access is provided for birdwatching. This is the Limeworks Site. A shelter is built among the foundations of the old works. Further out a wooden hide overlooks a mudflat used by waders roosting at high tide. This is available to visitors, and it contains a logbook to record birds seen. Further north (2 km) there is access to the beach for vehicles. Drive across the cattle stop and along the track to park at the water's edge for a superb view of waders roosting on the shell bank in tens of thousands, or feeding on the mud as the tide recedes. This place is Access Bay.

Unfortunately, the natural building of this shore is causing rapid silting up of the bay contained by shell banks, but when it finally dries out and the mangroves spread, there will be other shell banks for the birds to roost on, perhaps outside the present one or further north. At low tide, there are about 90 sq km of mudflat exposed. This rich food source is used by two important groups — Arctic migrants in the summer, and internal migrants in winter, after breeding in Canterbury and Otago.

High tide on this coast is the same time as for Auckland and is published in daily papers. The height is also important. Spring tides over 3 m cover all the mudflats and bring all birds on to the roosts; tides below about 2.7 m leave big feeding areas exposed and the birds also use many smaller roosting places. Main roosts are currently the shell bank at Access Bay, the mouth of the Taramaire stream and the shell bank spit at the limeworks. Big flocks gather sometimes behind the Miranda Hall on the muddy tidal reaches of the Pukorokoro creek bed, or north of Access Bay on the beach or shell bank, or on the paddock by the limeworks. Weather and height of tide influence the movement of flocks from day to day, but at Miranda you can always expect big flocks of waders.

At all times of the year you can expect to see godwit, knot, South Island pied oystercatcher, wrybill, white-fronted tern, black-billed gull, red-billed gull, black shag, white-faced heron, pied stilt and several other species. The numbers will vary according to season. From September huge flocks of godwit and knot dominate the roosts, but are joined and sometimes outnumbered after Christmas by thousands of South Island pied oystercatchers, moving north after breeding. Then the wrybill flocks arrive and February numbers may reach 20,000 birds of all species. After the departure of Northern Hemisphere waders in March, red-billed gulls and black-billed gulls arrive for the winter, more banded dotterels also, and pied stilts increase to several thousand.

Other summer migrants include curlew sandpipers, turnstones and red-necked stints in small numbers, and most seasons bring a few sharp-tailed sandpipers, Far-eastern curlews, little terns and Terek sandpipers. There have been sightings of a number of rare species over the many years the area has been watched.

Black-backed gulls nest on an open area of dry ground on the western side of the road, and rooks from the rookery near the top of Findlay Road flap across in twos and threes from time to time.

Many non-breeders of the summer migrant species stay over through the winter (and wintering birds stay through summer); thus there are a few hundred godwits, knots and odd Arctic waders through winter. In spring and early summer there are about a thousand South Island pied oystercatchers on the shell banks and at least one small flock of wrybills.

Those who know the wrybill as a confiding bird found in pairs on the larger Canterbury riverbeds will find that it is different in flocks at Miranda and more attractive. No-one fails to be moved by the beauty of tightly packed flocks of several hundred wrybills, clean grey, twisting and wheeling at high speed, then turning to sparkle with white as their underwings show against a winter sky. On the ground they roost in close flocks which can be approached, in contrast to the wary godwits.

Manukau Harbour

There are two popular areas for watching waders that feed on the Manukau mudflats — Karaka shell banks and the Mangere oxidation ponds. Karaka, on the southern shore, is reached by taking Kidd Road, which leaves the main road to Kingseat opposite Te Hihi School, then turn right into Clark Road, and left down a narrow road directly towards the harbour. For permission to cross this land ask at the house about 200 m on the left before the end of the road. A walk down the hill takes you to a semi-marine flat behind the beach, sometimes waterlogged and a popular roosting place for waders. The extensive shell banks further out will have been seen from the hill. There you may see godwit, knot, wrybill, South Island pied oystercatcher, white-fronted tern, pied stilt, white-faced heron, banded dotterel, small numbers of golden plover and red-necked stint and a few New Zealand dotterel. Black shags and little shags rest on the shell banks, and red-billed gulls are usually about. Karaka is a good place for rarer migrants and more attractive to whimbrel than the Firth of Thames.

The Manukau Sewage Purification Works of the Auckland Regional Authority is approached by Island Road, Mangere. At the office, ask for permission to go round the pools stating your purpose. The gates (open 8 a.m. to 5 p.m.) are locked at weekends but a key can usually be obtained from the office. The outer pools and the seaward dyke have waterfowl, waders and coastal birds in good variety, and there have been many records of rare vagrants. The artificial islands in No. 4 oxidation pond usually have good flocks of roosting waders. Without entering the works you can drive across Island Road to Puketutu Island, to see the spotted doves. These little doves may be seen or heard from time to time in many parts of Auckland, but there are few established breeding areas like this. Greenfinches, goldfinches, chaffinches and pheasants are all common there.

Around the oxidation ponds, there are often white-faced herons, black shags, little shags and pied stilts, occasionally a reef heron. Winter flocks of South Island pied oystercatchers on the lawns of Kiwi Esplanade at high tide can reach many thousands, and there is no better place to view them. There is free access through Ambury Farm Park where pukeko are also common. High tide on the Manukau is about three hours later than at Auckland.

Auckland
Recommended full day
Miranda on the Firth of Thames for shore birds, with a diversion to have a picnic lunch at Waharau Park about 10 km north on the coast road. Here you will find a good selection of bush birds. Then if the tides are suitable, cross to the Manukau Harbour (about one hour's driving, tide approximately three hours after Miranda).
Recommended half day
Tahuna Torea Reserve or Centennial Park bush walks, Waitakere.

Coromandel

The Coromandel Peninsula is a popular playground for Aucklanders who are attracted by unspoilt beaches on the east, picturesque bays and harbours on the west and rich forest cover over the rough inland range. The undisturbed beaches have breeding New Zealand dotterel and variable oystercatcher. The reef heron occurs in small numbers around the coast and banded rails are in the rush margins of many inlets. Fernbirds are in the rough cover of swampy places by many small estuaries. One very pleasant corner with all these habitats is Opoutere, which retains much natural charm, having less housing than most coastal resorts on the east. White-faced heron, kingfisher and pied stilt are there in large numbers, New Zealand dotterel can usually be found on the ocean beach and one or two pairs of variable oystercatchers breed there. Bellbirds and tuis are in the forest remnants, waterfowl frequent the estuary and a few godwits summer there also.

Among the remaining kauri and the hardwoods on the inland ridges a few pairs of kokako survive. Kaka and yellow-crowned parakeet occur in small numbers. Unfortunately whitehead is absent, and it follows that the long-tailed cuckoo is rarely seen. Pied tit is present and rifleman is recorded in the northern forests.

Waikato

The Whangamarino wetlands, a complex of 7100 hectares of swamp and bog, are the remainder of the original wetlands which once covered a very large area of the lower Waikato, and must have been very rich in ducks, bitterns, crakes and shags. Whangamarino now supports our largest known breeding population of bitterns but many of these birds move to river margins or lakesides in the region when water levels fall in summer and autumn. Many waterfowl (30,000–50,000) use these wetlands from late autumn to spring, and the rarest of our indigenous ducks, the brown teal, survives here in a population of less than 50 birds. The wetlands have large areas of willow, reeds and peaty meadow interspersed with islands of high ground. The main watercourses are the Whangamarino River and the Maramarua River, which join to enter the Waikato 3 km north of Meremere. The peaty meadows have large numbers of fernbirds; spotless crakes are most often around the margins of grazed pasture and bitterns are found throughout, except in areas of woody undergrowth. Grey teal are being encouraged to breed in the Maramarua River area.

Access can be gained from Meremere Road at the power station, linking on to Island Block Road, or from Te Kauwhata in the south, via Waerenga Road, Lake Road and around Lake Waikare. Bell Road (from the Pokeno-Thames highway) ends at a farm where permission is necessary to cross to the bittern and waterfowl habitat at the northern end of the wetland.

The bird list for Whangamarino includes bittern, spotless crake, white heron, white-faced heron, cattle egret, black shag, little shag, little black shag (occasional), pukeko, spur-winged plover, pied stilt, kingfisher, N.Z. pigeon, welcome swallow, pipit, shining cuckoo, and waterfowl: black swan, grey duck, mallard, shoveler, grey teal, brown teal.

Lake Whangape can be scanned from Glen Murray Road to locate the shags and ducks which are always somewhere on it, and the large numbers of black swans either on the water or up on the pastures. Where the road leaves the lake, turn down into Tikotiko Road to a small arm of the lake which is a good place for grey teal.

The Rangiriri district has attracted the largest flocks of cattle egrets in New Zealand, maintained in each successive winter, with some up and down variation since the dramatic build up in the late seventies. Cattle egrets arrive from Australia late in April and leave towards the end of October or early November. The lower Waikato is a likely area for them to establish their first breeding colony in New Zealand. This has been expected for some years now, but they may never stay and breed here.

Artificial Lake Karapiro beside State Highway 1 has scaup in its quieter corners and a few shags. Behind it to the west, the bush in Mt Maungatautari Scenic Reserve contains kaka, pigeon, whitehead, pied tit, bellbird, tui and long-tailed and shining cuckoos. It can be approached by crossing Karapiro Dam, then turning left, taking Luck-at-last Road or Hicks Road up to the mountain.

In the east, the bush on Mt Te Aroha is worth a visit for its interesting vegetation, and it has robin, pied tit, whitehead and the common bush birds. There is a steep track to the summit from the government gardens in the town. As the highway from Te Aroha to Matamata crosses the Kaimai Range, a turn off along Rapurapu Road takes you into good country for robins. They occur extensively along the western side of the Kaimai Range.

On the west coast, Kawhia Harbour and Aotea Harbour are places of considerable interest. These have always been popular wintering places for black stilts, and a few individuals of this rare wader may still be found on the mudflats of Kawhia or Aotea between March and August. From the vicinity of the village of Kawhia white-faced herons and kingfishers are always seen and godwits in the summer. At various points around the harbour both variable and South Island pied oystercatchers occur, also occasional knots. This coastline is the southern limit of the northern population of New Zealand dotterels. They occur again at Stewart Island, 1000 km to the south. A winding road follows the shore of the harbour to the remote southern peninsulas where limestone cliffs and rocky islets provide roosts for herons and waders. A large sand island in the middle is also a wader roost. Around this eastern shore there are several areas of rushes containing banded rails. Beyond, towards the coast, Lake Taharoa has waterfowl and some fernbird habitat and both banded and New Zealand dotterel are found on the slopes of the black sand dunes, near the point where sand is pumped to bulk transport ships offshore, for export to the steel mills of Japan.

Aotea Harbour is large and shallow and more

difficult than Kawhia to survey successfully without a boat. The limestone stacks across from the end of Pakoka Road are a home for reef herons. Gulls, shags and terns are around all parts of the harbour, also pied stilts and godwits. Banded rails are common around the margin wherever there is suitable habitat.

Raglan Harbour is rather poor in waders, having only the common estuary birds, but a relatively good population of reef herons. On the northern side of the harbour, castle-like formations afford them nesting places and security from the pressure of the white-faced heron. Ruakiwi, north of the harbour, is about the southern limit for white cockatoo ranging south and west from their base near Onewhero.

Pirongia Forest Park, inland from Kawhia, has held on to a rich bird life, in spite of its isolation from other large forests. It has kiwi, kaka, pigeon, red-crowned and yellow-crowned parakeet, falcon, pied tit, whitehead, bellbird, tui and a good population of kokako. Hauturu Road on the western side of the park is probably the best place to see or hear kokako, but an early morning climb on any of the park tracks will give you this opportunity. Eastern rosellas are common in the surrounding farmland and the edges of the bush.

Rotorua

Rotorua is the centre of a very beautiful region of lakes and forests and it has a great number of good birdwatching places. Water birds around the lakes are matched by the bush birds in some excellent areas of remaining native forest. Birdwatching can easily be combined with sightseeing around the geysers and thermal pools of Rotorua. Get a copy of the map NZMS 152 "Rotorua Lakes" and you will have a guide to the roads, tracks and places of special interest.

Close to the centre of the town is Sulphur Point, in a bay of Lake Rotorua which is strongly affected by thermal activity. The area is a Wildlife Refuge. A very pleasant walking path can be taken from the left of the Tudor Towers building through the Government Gardens to the lake edge and around by the golf course to Motutara Point. Another path starts behind the Travelodge car park and goes south around the lakeside to the Polynesian Pools. A long-established colony of black-billed gulls and red-billed gulls is on a low island at Sulphur Point, which has some thermal activity. This is one of the few places in the North Island where black-bills nest, and the unceasing action in the colony can be watched from about mid August to mid January. The high concentration of minerals in the water of some of the thermal areas does not deter the gulls. Birds' feet are not particularly sensitive to heat and cold, as you can guess from photographs of gulls standing on icebergs and geese on frozen ponds. A study some years ago showed that a large proportion of the gulls of Rotorua had the webs of their feet corroded by chemicals, and some had little or no webs left.

Little black shags have a colony near by and all around the Rotorua lakes there are good opportunities for comparing the three phases of the little shag and distinguishing it from the little black. Also in this bay are scaup, dabchick, mallard, grey duck and grey teal.

Mokoia Island in Lake Rotorua is visited by sightseeing launches from the town jetty. It is a Wildlife Refuge with a good number of bush birds including bellbird and tui. Wekas, introduced here many years ago, are the only ones in the North Island except for those at Gisborne and the Bay of Islands. Dabchick, scaup and little shag can be seen around the island.

There are many good areas of forest in the Rotorua region which should be explored for birds. Any of the Scenic Reserves marked on map NZMS 152 are worth a visit, and there is free entry to these. The indigenous Rotoehu State Forest contains some excellent habitat with a rich diversity of species. Control of this forest, which includes all the area north-east of Lake Rotoiti, is in the hands of the Officer-in-Charge, New Zealand Forest Service, Rotoehu Village, which is on the Te Puke side of the forest. Call there for information on the access tracks etc. Fire risk is the greatest concern for forest staff, so entry may be denied during summer. The plantations of exotics at Whakarewarewa, especially the giant redwoods, are well known for their populations of finches.

Spotless crakes are widespread through the district, and any area of raupo over half a hectare is likely to have a pair of them. Play a tape recording of their call at the edge of the swamp and you will soon get a response. If you get behind cover a little way back you may entice them out into the open.

Lake Rotomahana is a Wildlife Refuge and accordingly attracts a great number of birds in the shooting season, but there is a good population there at any time. It is not approached directly by any road but is reached by a walking track through the Waimangu thermal area. Nearby Lake Rerewhakaaitu has a good variety of bird life.

The Blue and Green Lakes have grey ducks, scaup and shags which can be seen from a very pleasant walking track through the Douglas firs about the car park which is on the ridge between the two lakes. Bush birds seen here include pied tit, robin, whitehead, bellbird, tui, fantail, grey warbler, shining cuckoo and long-tailed cuckoo. Lake Okareka has black swan, grey duck, mallard, grey teal, scaup, paradise duck and coot. The coots are much fewer than they were a few years ago. On the shallower edges there may be bittern as well as pied stilt and white-faced heron. Dabchicks occur also. Lake Rotoma, furthest east of the group, has dabchick, scaup and marsh crake, and these may be seen along the southwestern inlet which is bordered by a scenic reserve. Another scenic reserve is cut through by Highway 30 to the east, and this contains a good selection of birds including pigeon, pied tit, bellbird, whitehead, rifleman, tui and both cuckoos.

Around the southeastern corner of Lake Rotoehu (Te Pohue Bay) is a track which can be used for a quiet approach to the bitterns and spotless crakes in the grasses and rushes on the shallow edge.

The large expanse of Lake Rotoiti can only be

properly surveyed from a boat. The most easily approached area is the western end at the Ohau channel to Lake Rotorua and the arm which runs up to the Okere Falls. This is one place where you can see a fair sample of the lake's water birds, including dabchicks and coots, more common here than on any other lake in the district.

A large colony of little shags is located high in the gorge above Okere Falls, reached by a track on the eastern side of the river. These colonies move around and many of the birds here have probably come from the deserted site at Lake Rotoehu.

Rotorua
Recommended full day
Around the northern side of Lake Rotorua via Hamurana Springs and the Ohau channel to Okere Falls, returning via Lake Okareka and the Blue and Green lakes.
Recommended half day
Mokoia Island boat trip, or on foot to Sulphur Bay gull colonies.

Tongariro National Park

This whole area is very busy catering for skiers in winter and early spring but when they have gone and the last of the snow melts from the lower slopes it becomes a very rewarding area for summer bird-watching. The area is administered as a national park including wilderness areas at Hauhungatahi in the south-east and Te Tatau-Pounamu in the north, and there are indigenous and exotic state forests. For advice and any necessary permits call at one of the information centres, Whakapapa Village or Ohakune Junction, and get map NZMS 273, Tongariro National Park. About 2 km east of the turnoff to the Karioi Railway Station is the Forest Headquarters where permission may be gained to take the Rangataua indigenous forest or Karioi exotic forest roads.

On the eastern side of the mountains there have been very extensive construction works for aqueducts, tunnels and channels to direct water for hydroelectric schemes. The construction roads off the Desert Road offer access to the eastern slopes of Mt Ruapehu and Karioi State Forest. Much of the land on the eastern side of the Desert Road is Army Department training ground, where entry is either restricted to certain times or denied completely.

Paradise Valley Road 20 km north of Waiouru on the Desert Road runs east for about 5 km through army property to the edge of the beech forest. In the open country pipits and skylarks are common, and hedge sparrows also, at the lower levels. Banded dotterels are found on the dry eastern slopes down to the Desert Road. Finches are common above the bushline and there are colonies of black-backed gulls nesting high on Mt Ruapehu near the Tama Lakes.

The lakes of the north and west carry an interesting variety of birds. Lake Rotoaira has dabchick, bittern, black swan, scaup, shoveler, pukeko and a good number of spotless crakes. Fernbirds are also there. At Lake Otamangatau black swan, shoveler and a few pukeko can be seen, and around the margins there are pied stilts, banded dotterels, spur-winged plovers and abundant fernbirds. Welcome swallows are usual at all lakes. Lake Rotopounamu has shoveler, scaup and dabchick. In the south, Lake Rotokuru near Karioi, has dabchicks and coots. The many small hydro lakes in the east have only black swan, mallard and grey duck and pied stilt, but they will attract more birds as cover grows on their margins.

There is good access to Lake Rotoaira by the construction road alongside the Wairehu canal. This takes you across a large area of swamp to the edge of the lake. One of the very best combinations of bush birds and water birds can be enjoyed by leaving a car in the parking area at the Ponanga Saddle and taking the marked track through the forest and in a loop around Lake Rotopounamu. You will be back to the car in a little under two hours.

Guests at Chateau Tongariro or elsewhere at Whakapapa Village will find the best birdwatching along the Taranaki Falls loop track which crosses a good range of habitats and gives a chance to see the falcon, rifleman and pied tit among others. On the other side of the main highway, the hydro access road to Whakapapa Intake leads to a good area of bush with blue duck on the river.

The large indigenous forests have all the usual bush birds but the islands of beech forest to the east understandably do not have such a good range of species. Kaka are in the bush on Mt Pihanga and Mt Kakaramea in the north and Karioi State Forest in the south. Parakeets and kiwi are in both of these areas and also in the Erua State Forest in the west. Robins are in these, near Ohakune, and in the region of the Chateau. Falcons are on Mt Pihanga, and also in the native forests of the south and west.

Lake Taupo is deep and steep-sided so it has few birds except at the southern end. The northern and eastern shores are so popular with trout fishermen and boat owners that birds are much disturbed, though red-billed, black-billed and black-backed gulls are always about and willing to accept any scraps. Black, little black and little shags also occur right around the lake and they can be seen drying their wings on posts or dead branches in most sheltered bays. Australian coots breed in the reeds around the Motuoapa marina.

The southern shoreline is shallow, with large reed-beds which are a rich bird habitat. Near Tokaanu both spotless crake and marsh crake are in raupo, and fernbirds are common through the adjoining swampy areas. The little road to the Tokaanu jetty gives good access to the area if you are making a brief visit. This is one place where attempts to attract fernbirds with a squeaker can bring crakes, and vice versa. Both bittern and dabchick are numerous and there are shoveler, scaup, grey duck, mallard, black swan, pukeko and spur-winged plover. The two small shags are in big numbers along the southern end of the lake and at times they can be seen in the tail-race canal right up to the power house. The road to the west of the lake is well away from the shore and most access roads to the western bays are quite long and tortuous, although bush remnants there are worth exploring if you have the time.

Pureora Forest Park, west of Lake Taupo, has some of our finest remaining native forest, much of it preserved thanks to the long and bitter battle fought by conservationists in the 1970s. Approach is by Highway 30 from Te Kuiti on the west or Taupo from the east. On your first visit a call at the Headquarters Information Centre is advisable. The areas of greatest wildlife interest are the dense mixed podocarps and the podocarp/hardwood forest. Close to the Headquarters is the Pikiariki Ecological Area, and the southern half of the North Block contains the Waipapa Ecological Area, where the Outdoor Education Centre is located.

The chief attraction to birdwatchers are the kokako which are well distributed throughout the unlogged forest. You will be able to locate them by listening just after daybreak or in the evenings. But as well as these, Pureora has probably the richest fauna of any mainland forest, with falcon, kaka, both red-crowned and yellow-crowned parakeet, pigeon, whitehead, rifleman, robin, pied tit, grey warbler, fantail, bellbird, tui, long-tailed cuckoo, shining cuckoo and morepork. The blue duck is in the streams at higher altitudes.

On the eastern edge of the great area of exotic forest on the volcanic plateau, the hills and valleys of Whirinaki State Forest Park contain the remaining reserves of rich indigenous forest. Here are the country's finest stands of podocarps (rimu, miro, kahikatea, matai), great hardwoods (tawa, kamahi) and red and silver beech. Each forest type features some magnificent specimens, including 60 metre kahikateas. It is a delight to look for birds in conditions which must be near to their original forest habitat.

Go direct to the Forest Park Headquarters at Minginui for information and maps of the park and its tracks. Another approach is made about 5 km east along S.H. 38 from the Minginui turnoff, where a rough road takes you up the valley of the Okahu stream, by podocarp and hardwood zones and ending at a pleasant parking and picnic place close to the lowest beech forest. Kiwi, kaka and kakariki are in Whirinaki, also blue duck, robins, pied tit, whitehead and other bush birds. In summer it has a large population of long-tailed cuckoos.

Young plantations of exotic pine trees at Kaingaroa are almost empty of birds, but older stands can have an undergrowth of native shrubs and ferns, and these support quite a variety of bird life. The stable, undisturbed (temporarily) environment of the exotic forest is an encouragement to birds, and you will find them wherever there is some food supply, especially around streams or damp gullies left in native growth. Robins, pied tits and fantails are in the five finger, ferns etc., near the edges, and by firebreaks which let in the light. Annual grasses and weeds along the roadsides and firebreaks attract good numbers of finches; California quail and pheasants are in small numbers.

Entry to these forests, whether State or company-owned, is prohibited except by permit, because of the risk of fire. On most roads there are a few rest and picnic areas which allow access to the forest edges away from the roadside, and these present the best chances for a bird watcher to gain some impression of the birds of this artificial habitat.

Bay of Plenty

The northern end of Tauranga Harbour at Athenree is a very good area for shore birds but with the disadvantage that high tide roosts are on shell bank islands about 500 m off the Athenree beach. Large flocks of South Island pied oystercatchers and godwits can be seen there, and good numbers of turnstones. Caspian tern, New Zealand dotterel, variable oystercatcher and white-fronted tern nest there, and New Zealand dotterel and banded dotterel also nest on Bowentown beach. Bowentown Head has nesting little blue penguins and reef herons. The area has banded rail, fernbird, bittern and spur-winged plover, and cattle egrets can be expected each winter.

In Tauranga, Sulphur Point is an important wader roost with godwits, sometimes a few knots and other migrants including whimbrel and little tern. It is also the only place in the Bay of Plenty where wrybills are likely to be seen (late summer to August) and is a breeding ground for New Zealand dotterel, banded dotterel and variable oystercatcher. Regular visitors are reef heron, white-faced heron, pied shag, little shag, Caspian tern and white-fronted tern.

Maketu Estuary, east of Te Puke, is an excellent area for waders and waterfowl. The estuary is easily reached from Maketu village, and a walk at low tide gives good views of many species of waders including godwit, knot, variable oystercatcher, New Zealand dotterel, banded dotterel, and maybe golden plover, turnstone, red-necked stint, sharp-tailed sandpiper, whimbrel and curlew. Pied stilts are common and there are occasional occurrences of little tern, wrybill and pectoral sandpiper. The Kaituna Cut lagoons (reached by taking Kaituna Road then Ford Road to the end) have grey teal, Canada goose, paradise duck, mallard, grey duck, white-faced heron and spur-wing plover. Black-fronted dotterels join them in winter. Banded rails are relatively common: one of the best places to see them is on the left side of the straight stretch of road just before Maketu village. Pied shags and black shags nest in nearby pine trees. As with many Bay of Plenty estuaries, sea birds can be seen offshore, especially fluttering shearwaters and Arctic skuas in late summer.

Little Waihi (Bledisloe Park) estuary has most of the waders which are listed for nearby Maketu. New Zealand dotterel and variable oystercatcher nest on Pukehina Beach near the mouth of the estuary and along all of this coast there are small numbers of black-billed gulls between the end of April and early August. Little egrets are often in cover around the edges, particularly at the upper reaches. There are bittern, fernbird and banded rail.

The Matata lagoons at Tarawera River mouth can almost be guaranteed to have a white heron in winter, and waterfowl are plentiful: paradise duck, shoveler, grey teal, grey duck and mallard in thouisand. Little shag, black shag and little black shag are all common on the lagoons and pied shags roost on the beach. In the cover round the edges of the lagoons there are bittern, fernbird, marsh crake, spotless crake and brown quail. During late summer Arctic skuas are often seen among the feeding flocks of white-fronted terns and there are occasional Pomarine skuas also. Reef herons occur right along this coast in small numbers and grey-faced petrels still breed on the mainland cliffs in several places.

The Awaiti Wetland Reserve is approached by turning right into Grey Road after crossing the Tarawera River by the main road bridge. Paradise duck, shoveler, dabchick, bittern, spotless crake and marsh crake are here, and also a mixed colony of black shags and little shags. Cattle egrets and black-fronted terns can be seen in nearby paddocks in winter. Thornton Lagoon at the mouth of the Rangitaiki River is noted for scaup and good numbers of bitterns, and it is one place where you are sure to see dabchicks. Ohope Spit by Whakatane is an important breeding ground for New Zealand dotterel and it is also the main high tide roost for waders which feed on the mudflats of Ohiwa Harbour. Flocks of New Zealand dotterel and banded dotterel can be seen there in late summer and autumn.

The Motu River has many pairs of blue duck, also found on the upper reaches of other rivers. Local guidance will be necessary on your first visit to this heavily bushed area. Bush birds include kiwi, kokako, kaka, yellow-crowned parakeet, tui, bellbird, whitehead and falcon.

A good place to see a variety of bush birds is Otanewainuku, on No. 2 Road from Te Puke. Walking tracks start 200 m along Mountain Road (to the right off No. 2 Road) and in this forest there are kiwi, kokako, pigeon, whitehead, tui, bellbird, robin, pied tit, morepork, long-tailed cuckoo, shining cuckoo and occasional kaka.

Gisborne — East Cape

The East Cape district was a stronghold of the paradise shelduck before its rapid spread over the country in the last two decades. The recently grassed hillsides and artificial dams of the large farming developments remain a very suitable habitat for these handsome birds. In the high country to the west, the bush streams of the Raukumara and Ruahine ranges carry good numbers of blue duck. Finding them in the steep gullies usually requires a good deal of walking, but that is part of the pleasure, and you will also have the chance to see many bush birds. As well as the commoner species, there are tui, pied tit, bellbird and whitehead. Robins, kaka and both yellow-crowned and red-crowned parakeets are also in the higher country, and falcons occur throughout.

From Gisborne north to Tokomaru Bay the North Island weka is common. When between 1916–30 wekas disappeared suddenly from the rest of the North Island (some avian disease is suspected as the cause), a pocketful of survivors hung on at Gisborne. There they increased rapidly in the 1960s and 70s, but in 1984–5 they began to leave areas where they had been common for a long time, so there is some concern that this population may also be in danger. There has not been much success in getting North Island wekas established in other districts. The eastern Bay of Islands around Rawhiti is the only other mainland locality where this subspecies continues to thrive.

About 16 km south of Gisborne on State Highway 2 and on the northern side of Young Nicks Head, the Muriwai Lagoon can be overlooked from a high point near the roadside or approached from Karua Road on the north or by the Muriwai settlement on the south. Small numbers of interesting waders have been recorded here and there are banded dotterels, gulls and terns. At Nuhaka, a side road leading to Oraka Beach skirts the side of Maungawhio Lagoon. Ducks and waders can be watched here, occasional herons and terns, and spotless crakes. Any small shore bird habitat along a coast such as this which does not have large estuaries is always worth checking for waders. Some rare and interesting birds have been found on them, probably having a short stopover during movement up or down the coast.

Beside the highway closer to Wairoa, the big shallow Lake Whakaki holds large numbers of waterfowl and also shags and dabchicks. Around the shoreline there are bitterns, and banded and black-fronted dotterels. The whole area is very interesting. Smaller lakes closer to Wairoa are back from the road in private property. These are Paeroa, Wairau and Big and Little Ohuia. Then comes the long tidal Ngamotu Lagoon parallel to the beach and joining the mouth of the Wairoa River. On the western (town) side of the river, Lake Whakamahi has a good selection of ducks, black, pied, little and little black shags, white-fronted terns, white-faced herons and black-backed, black-billed and red-billed gulls.

Lake Waikaremoana, at the south-eastern edge of Urewera National Park, is surrounded by magnificent forest, rich in bird life. There are few better places in the country to study bush birds, and as well as the main lake and its little brother Waikareiti, there are a number of smaller lakes and tarns with water birds. The whole area is well tracked and as an introduction the broad track to Waikareiti can be taken through some good beech forest, though its popularity means that birds are considerably disturbed in the holiday season. The Aniwaniwa Valley road and track lead off from near the park headquarters to follow a cleared valley with heavy bush easily accessible on either side. Blue ducks are on streams throughout the forest. Rangers at Park Headquarters will be able to tell you where they know these territory-holding birds to be, some near the lake but more in the rough streams far back in the forest. Black shags and little shags are around the lake shore, and black swan, paradise, mallard and grey duck, scaup, shoveler and dabchick are at various places around the lakes. The bush has robin, pied tit, pigeon, morepork, falcon, tui, bellbird, long-tailed and shining cuckoos, kaka, yellow-crowned parakeet and rifleman. Outside the forest there are pheasant, California quail and brown quail.

Hawke's Bay

The large gannet colony at Cape Kidnappers is one
of the great ornithological attractions of New
Zealand and every summer thousands of tourists visit
Hawke's Bay between August and February to see the
gannets.

It is possible to walk along the beach (11 km) on
the northern side of the peninsula at low tide, but the
majority of visitors take one of the tourist company
vehicles which drive along the ridge or along the
beach. Bookings can be made at travel agents.
(Private cars are forbidden.) It is a great opportunity
to experience the thrill of standing on the edge of a
great throng of nesting birds, watching all the life of
the colony carrying on undisturbed.

The slow movement of these handsome large birds
enables you to identify each separate display, some
modified into amusing rituals: the greeting of
returning mates, threat and defence in boundary
squabbles, food-begging by chicks of various ages,
and other fascinating behaviour.

Finches, especially goldfinches, are a feature of the
orchard country around Taradale and Hastings.
Rooks persist in small numbers.

Three large rivers cross the plains to enter Hawke
Bay. Their shingle riverbeds rival those of Canterbury
for the number and variety of breeding birds. The
most convenient method to survey them is to enter
the riverbed at one point and arrange to be picked up
(or have a car left) at another place downstream.
Don't underestimate the distance which must be
covered in a day. Surveying a riverbed involves
crossing and recrossing streams, and the distance is
much longer than a straight line along the riverbed.

For the Tutaekuri River go through Taradale
towards Redcliffs Bridge. Roads go upstream on both
sides from here. For the north-east side turn right
before the bridge into Springfield Road and go
towards Puketapu. There are a few access points to
the river, and it can be reached elsewhere through
private property. For the south-west side cross the
Redcliffs Bridge, incline right, then take Omarunui

Road where some approaches to the river are possible. Cross the bridge towards Puketapu, turn left on to Dartmoor Road and go on to Mangaone, with access to the riverbed at several places. Nesting birds are black-fronted and banded dotterel, pied stilt and black-backed gull. At the common mouth of the Tutaekuri and Ngaruroro rivers black-billed gulls nest at times, along with white-fronted terns. In autumn and winter black-fronted tern and black-fronted dotterel like this area.

The Ngaruroro River is of little interest below Fernhill, where there is access for some way upstream past the hotel on the south side and across the bridge and upstream on the north side, and about a kilometre downstream. These are good places to find black-fronted dotterel.

From the lower bridge over the Tukituki River roads go upstream on both sides with some public access to the riverbed. Ask permission to cross private property. For the east side leave the lower bridge by Tukituki Road, but few branch roads or tracks go to the river.

Two roads give good access on the west side: River Road from the junction of Te Mata and Mangateretere roads, or Matangi Road which swings off to the right of Waimarama bridge approach. This takes you to Horseshoe Bend. It runs parallel to the river and is high enough to give an excellent view.

The best way to approach the upper part of the river is to leave Havelock North by Middle Road through to Waitukai Road and on via Patangata to Waipawa. This route is roughly parallel to Highway 2 as far as Waipawa.

Horseshoe Lake is reached from Waipawa by following the Tukituki River to Patangata. There turn right across the river and right again into Mangarara Road to the lake. Seek permission at the homestead. Birds to be expected are dabchick, black and little shag, white-faced heron, bittern, black swan, paradise duck, mallard, grey duck, grey teal, shoveler, scaup, pukeko, coot, black-fronted dotterel, pied stilt and welcome swallow.

For Ahuriri Lagoon, cross from Napier to Westshore and turn on to a causeway across a shallow lagoon. Here, or at the main lagoon beyond you may see black swan, Canada goose, paradise duck, shoveler, grey duck, grey teal, pukeko, black-fronted dotterel, banded dotterel, wrybill, turnstone, pied stilt, godwit and knot. In summer there are usually some less common migrant waders, including sharp-tailed, pectoral and curlew sandpiper and red-necked stint. White heron, little egret, royal spoonbill and gull-billed tern have all been recorded here. Lake Poukawa, opposite Te Hauke on Highway 2, can be surveyed from the highway or approached with permission. The peat marshes and lake attract a great variety of water birds, including mute swan, black swan, mallard, grey duck, paradise duck, grey teal, shoveler, black shag, little shag, pukeko, spur-winged plover, black-billed gull, pied stilt, black-fronted and banded dotterel. There is a rookery on nearby Colin White Road. Cattle egrets visit in winter, and in autumn there are large flocks of goldfinches, chaffinches, greenfinches and yellowhammers.

Southern Hawke's Bay is an area of farmland with only common birds but there are interesting wetlands to the east. Lake Hatuma, close to Waipukurau, has shags, ducks, spur-winged plovers, banded dotterels and pied stilts, and other waders visit occasionally. Cattle egrets are there from May to August. Lake Purimu, 25 km further on towards Porangahau, has more waterfowl, little black shags and dabchicks. Wanstead swamp is also worth visiting and Hiranui Road provides convenient observation points.

Porangahau Lagoon at the river mouth is reached through private property, after securing permission. It is a good walk to the lagoon, but worth it. There are black and little shag, white-faced heron, bittern, black swan, paradise, shoveler, mallard and grey duck, pukeko, South Island pied oystercatcher and variable oystercatcher, banded dotterel, pied stilt, black-backed, red-billed and black-billed gull, white-fronted, black-fronted and Caspian tern, and a few waders. Gull and tern nesting colonies are located in varying places on the north or south spits.

Hawke's Bay north of about Takapau is the

principal area in the North Island for black-backed magpies. They are more common here than whitebacks.

South of Dannevirke the Manawatu River has large shingle beds used by banded and black-fronted dotterel, pied stilt and other river birds. There is access by road at several places, one by Oringi Road about 11 km south of Dannevirke. Ask at Gaisfords Station for permission to turn down to the river and drive along the flats to explore the shingle beds.

Lake Tutira, on the road to Wairoa, is a sanctuary for waterfowl made famous by the pen and camera of H. Guthrie-Smith, a pioneering runholder and a great amateur ornithologist. It carries a good number of black swan, mallard, grey teal, scaup, paradise duck, pukeko and coot, and a few dabchicks. Little Lake Orakei on the west side of the road over the hill should be checked out as well. Rooks at Tutira nest in the tall gums skirting the highway south of the lake.

Taranaki

Consider this district as starting from the mouth of the Awakino River in the north, where a small estuary beside the golf course has a few waders. It is also worth looking for reef herons there. Along the coast road to the south the mouths of several small rivers are places of much ornithological interest, but provide little wader habitat. The wild forests of inland Taranaki are the most interesting part of the province, but few people can undertake the sort of expedition needed to explore the remote valleys and ridges of the Matemateonga Range. Narrow coastal strips and intensively farmed lowland have the common birds, but where the highway cuts through heavy bush there are opportunities to see many species. At Mt Messenger tui, bellbird, pied tit, whitehead, parakeet, shining and long-tailed cuckoo, kaka and robin can be seen. The falcon is also present here. On the inland road at Tahora, kokako might be added to this list, and robins are quite plentiful.

On the coast, the mouth of the Waiongana River is a good place for birds but access is across private property. Waders, terns and herons are there. The mouth of the Waitara River has these birds too, and has turned up a few of the rarer waders over the years. Like other west coast estuaries, they are likely to receive new arrivals from Australia, and that irregular visitor, the little egret, is an example. A small flock of cattle egrets visits each winter. Nearer New Plymouth, Bell Block oxidation ponds and nearby lagoon have dabchick, pied stilt, and a few bittern, a bird that is difficult to find in Taranaki.

On the edge of the city, Barrett Lagoon wildlife refuge has a good selection of water birds, including Canada geese, and bush birds. Close to Port Taranaki, the Sugarloaf islets are protected as wildlife refuges, but they are natural sanctuaries in any case, with breeding populations of diving petrels, white-faced storm petrels, black-backed and red-billed gulls, white-fronted terns, little blue penguins and a few reef herons.

The lower slopes of Mt Egmont are heavily forested, but although the common bush birds are there you cannot expect to see falcon, kaka, parakeet, or robin.

Wanganui

The mouth of the Waitotara can be approached by road from the north, with a 2 km walk required at the end. There is a good selection of waterfowl, and wader records include godwit, knot, variable oystercatcher, wrybill, golden plover, turnstone, sharp-tailed and curlew sandpiper. Small temporary lagoons on the south side of the river often have waders during rough weather. The Waitotara River should be followed right back to the Matemateonga Range if you want to get a good variety of bush birds in this district. There the kiwi is common along with pied tit, robin, whitehead, pigeon, bellbird, tui and shining and long-tailed cuckoo. Falcons are also there, and blue duck further back.

Spotless crakes have been recorded in a number of

swamps in the low country in from Wanganui. Taped calls should be tried at any swamp which has permanent water, no matter how small. Many crakes have been overlooked in such places before there were tapes to attract them. The California quail is present in suitable habitat throughout the area.

The Royal Forest and Bird Protection Society's property at Bushy Park, 6 km north of Kai Iwi, has accommodation in a nature reserve with many bush birds. Two other places worth visiting for their bush birds are south of the city — McPherson's Bush in the Turakina Valley and Price's Rahui Bush, both Forest and Bird Society reserves. In the hills near Hunterville there is a long-standing colony of white cockatoos, and at Marton the oxidation ponds should be checked in winter for gatherings of New Zealand dabchick.

Virginia Lake lies within the city's northern boundary. The surroundings are attractively laid out and the birds to be seen are little black and little shag, mute swan, black swan, mallard, grey, shoveler and paradise duck and Australian coot. This was one of the first places in the country for the Australian coot to become established and it is still a good place to watch them diving for lake weed and mixing with the ducks for handouts.

The mouth of the Wanganui River at Castlecliff is worth visiting if you have a telescope. Sooty and fluttering shearwaters, gannets and giant petrels are among the species which may be sighted offshore. Shags and gulls are always about the lower reaches of the river.

Manawatu

The estuary of the Manawatu River at Foxton Beach is an excellent place where almost anything may turn up. Access is easy on the north side, where you can search for waders, terns and gulls from the ocean beach up to the narrowing of the estuary above the boat club. Some hundreds of black-billed gulls spend the winter on this coast, and red-billed gulls are there too. A very good assortment of waders has been recorded though none of them in large numbers. After breeding in the south, a small flock of royal spoonbills spends the autumn and winter on this estuary, and black stilts were winter visitors when they were in bigger numbers. Odd ones still turn up.

A track along a stopbank allows you to search upstream and across the mid-stream islands to the southern shore. Black and little shags, black swans, mallard and grey ducks are usually in this area. Access from the southern side is possible along the beach from Waitarere, or much more conveniently through the forest roads. Apply for a permit from the Waitarere Forest Headquarters, near Waitarere township.

The beaches north and south of Foxton and up to Himatangi have been New Zealand's most profitable stretch of coast for beach patrolling since the Ornithological Society first began to keep regular records some 40 years ago. The shape of the island forms a scoop into which the prevailing westerly winds drive pelagic birds. Corpses of storm victims or other dead birds can be collected easily from wide clean beaches. Regular patrolling of these beaches gleans a sample of the bird life of the southern Tasman Sea and the interesting variations which take place from year to year and season to season.

Lake Horowhenua near Levin supports an interesting selection of birds. You can drive to the water's edge in the domain, where there are mallard, shoveler, grey duck, black swan, red-billed and black-billed gull, pied stilt and little shag. Some rare species of tern have been recorded in this attractive habitat over recent years by one or two keen-eyed observers. The less disturbed parts of the lake and the reed beds at the southern end have dabchick. White heron and little egret have also been recorded.

Close to the coast between Turakina and Bulls, there is a group of small dune lakes, mostly in private property so permission to enter is required. Like those further south between the mouths of the Rangitikei and Manawatu rivers, these dune lakes are delightful places and have a large range of species. Duck, shag, pukeko and white-faced heron can be expected at all of them, and will be nesting at many. The little grebes are of special interest. New Zealand dabchick is on those lakes where the water level remains stable. Look for the Australian little grebe, and the hoary-headed grebe is a possibility. The small flocks of grey teal from across the Tasman usually turn up initially on western lakes. Bitterns are found where there are large reed beds. Marsh and spotless crakes are present. Pied stilts are often around shallow edges, and welcome swallows feed on insects over the surface of the water. The black-fronted dotterel is moving into this area.

Pupuke Lagoon is a Wildlife Management Reserve where scientists from the New Zealand Wildlife Service have for some years been conducting research into birds and mammals of the wetland habitat. Understandably, public entry is prohibited.

Rangitikei River estuary has road access from north and south. Although most birds gather on an extensive island in the river mouth, there is the chance to see black and little shag, white-faced heron, mallard, shoveler, grey duck, grey teal, variable oystercatcher (and occasional S.I. pied), banded dotterel, godwit, knot, golden plover, wrybill, pied stilt, white-fronted tern and all three gulls. Rarer migrant waders have also been recorded here.

The extensive area of closely settled land to the north and west of Palmerston North has the usual birds of the open. The welcome swallow is widely distributed and there are a few rooks five miles north of Feilding.

Near Ashhurst the Pohangina River comes down through the hilly country from the north-east and joins the Manawatu River near the western end of the Manawatu Gorge. It has shingle beds and backwaters suitable for dotterel, pied stilt and some paradise and other duck.

About 15 km up the river is Totara Reserve, a quite extensive area of fine native forest running up a broad easy valley. Breeding birds are pigeon, bellbird, tui and smaller bush species. Travelling 15–25 km further on, roads from Umutoi and further north lead off to the bush of the Ruahine Range, or to other good stands of native forest, where rifleman, pied tit and whitehead are found.

The Manawatu River from the Manawatu Gorge down to Opiki has extensive shingle beds where many banded dotterel and pied stilt breed, and black-fronted dotterel should be looked for. The best area is between Longburn and Opiki. From Route 56 turn down Jackey-town Road or Hamilton's Line Road and drive to the river.

From Shannon a narrow winding road (subject to slips in bad weather) climbs to the three Mangahao dams in the Tararua Range. It passes through bush and ends at the top dam, whence several walking tracks go on through the Tararua Range. Along the road may be seen pigeon, shining cuckoo, rifleman, pied tit, bellbird, tui and other more common birds. On the walking tracks, not far from the road, kaka, parakeets, long-tailed cuckoo and whitehead may be added. On the dams there are usually black shag, mallard, grey duck and shoveler. Kahuterawa Road is also a good approach to the forest and in any part of this higher country the falcon can be seen.

Wairarapa

Much of the Wairarapa's farmlands have only the common birds but there are points of interest throughout. There is rich bird life in the forests of the eastern mountains and the swamps of the wetlands in the south. As a break from field work, it is well worth visiting the Mt Bruce National Wildlife Centre, 28 km north of Masterton and 13 km south of Eketahuna. This establishment is run by the New Zealand Wildlife Service for the study and captive breeding of endangered species. It provides an opportunity to see birds such as the takahe (*Notornis*) and saddleback which the average New Zealander is not likely to see in the wild. The centre is open to visitors from 10 to 4 daily, and there are picnic facilities, toilets, etc. If given 48 hours' notice, a wildlife officer will be available to accompany groups of visitors. The New Zealand Wildlife Service has earned an international reputation for the success of its work with endangered species and a visit to Mt Bruce will give you an insight into their work.

The Tararua Ranges have an extensive system of tracks which are well used by trampers at all seasons of the year. There are several access points but a recommended one giving access to mixed forest is the Mt Holdsworth Reserve, where you can find kaka, pigeon, red-crowned and yellow-crowned parakeets, whitehead, tui, long-tailed and shining cuckoos, bellbird, rifleman, and pied tit. Eastern rosellas are common along the forest edges.

In winter the Masterton sewage ponds at Home-bush get an influx of dabchicks from the surrounding district and the same occurs at Carterton ponds.

South of Masterton the rivers begin to acquire wide shingle beds which suit riverbed breeding species, and banded dotterel, black-fronted dotterel and pied stilt appear. Black-fronted dotterel prefer the edges of backwaters or quiet stretches with muddy edges and the Hauhungaroa River supports more of these. The Ruamahanga River between Masterton and Martinborough has good dotterel habitat, especially where there are stretches of braided channels below the junctions of the contributing rivers, Waingawa and Waiohine. The Tauherenikau River runs through boulders and coarse gravel unattractive to birds until below Featherston, about 2 km before it enters the lake. Black-billed gulls should also be looked for on the Mangatainoka and above the gorge of the Manawatu River.

Among the bare and otherwise uninteresting western hills, Korarau Dam has mallard and grey duck, black swan, black shag, pukeko and dabchick. You will be able to note the lower proportion of grey duck in this district. At one time it was feared that the native grey would be crowded out by the intro-duced mallard or their hybrids.

Lake Wairarapa is still an extensive area of wetland although much has been drained for farming. Rather different habitats are found around the various parts of its long shoreline, and with Lake Onoke and Onoke Spit you have a very rich area for birdwatching. Lake Reserve, at the north end near Featherston, is a picnic and boating place, but you have only to take a track to the left of the boatsheds to get to swampy places which contain marsh crake and spotless crake, bittern and ducks. The road round the eastern side to Lake Ferry gives the best approach to the Boggy Pond area but the Western Lake Road must be taken if you intend to go on to Onoke Spit at the coast. The Boggy Pond area has the best marsh and swamp areas for waterfowl, and it is a first class place out of the duck-shooting season. Further south on this eastern side is less interesting except for the long-standing colony of rooks on the south side of Turanganui River, near Pirinoa.

A list of species recorded at Lake Wairarapa includes Canada goose, black swan, paradise, mallard, shoveler and grey duck, grey teal, coot, pukeko, pied stilt, spur-winged plover, oystercatcher, white-winged black tern, Caspian and white-fronted tern, white-faced, white and Nankeen night heron, cattle egret, bittern, dabchick, marsh and spotless crake, banded and black-fronted dotterel. Waders in small numbers can be added. It appears that as well as carrying a very good range of wetland species, the lake shores attract stragglers and rarities, many of these probably drifting in after moving up the east coast of the South Island.

The long shingle spit at the coast has extensive mudflats on the inner side, where a few godwits, knots and other waders occur. Banded dotterel are common on the drier portions of this area and they nest along the spit. Nesting colonies of black-backed and red-billed gulls are placed in varying positions on the spit each summer, and there is usually a small colony of Caspian terns also. Lake Onoke is worth scanning for terns at all seasons. Black-fronted terns can be expected in winter, and black-billed gulls also on migration from their South Island breeding grounds.

Wellington

Wellington city is a place better suited to floating a share issue than watching birds, but the beautiful harbour has many birds of interest. Surprisingly, there are still many reef herons around the harbour, not only in the undisturbed areas on the eastern shores, but also at Days Bay, Petone Beach, Ngauranga and even about the wharves from time to time.

A few years ago wandering albatrosses were regular visitors, providing a great opportunity for those who never get out on the deep blue sea. The food attraction was the waste from freezing works at Ngauranga, now long closed. There is a story that a scientist embarked on a study of the occurrence of albatrosses in the harbour, with the aim of determining when they were there and what conditions brought them in. Weather out at sea was suspected: was it a long blow from the south-west that made them seek sheltered waters, or perhaps a sudden change to easterlies? After gathering a lot of data he was able to state that they came in on Thursdays. It seems that Thursday was the day when most offal went out from the works and the albatrosses were there to meet it. Wellington Harbour now has much cleaner waters and unfortunately the great white shape of an albatross sitting high in the water is seldom seen. But in summer it's worth looking out for a royal albatross that has been a regular summer visitor to the grassy slopes above the Seddon Memorial at Mt Crawford.

Flocks of shearwaters come in frequently. Even in these good viewing conditions, deciding whether they are Hutton's or fluttering shearwaters is the cause of many an argument, but that does not detract from the pleasure of seeing them. They come close inshore, sometimes feeding a few metres from wharves where they can be watched diving and "flying underwater" chasing fish. They probably follow shoals of fish into the harbour. A flock may be seen about different parts of the harbour for a day or two, feeding on the same shoal until it escapes to open water.

On a rock stack close to the road at Scorching Bay a nesting colony of white-fronted terns continues to thrive. This must be the only place in the country where this species can be seen on the nest from the window of a corporation bus.

A small group of crimson rosellas has inhabited the western suburbs of the city for some years, adding their brilliant colour to the gardens of Kelburn, Highbury and Karori, when feeding on fruiting shrubs, and often visiting the higher parts of the botanic gardens. They have gained some protection by nesting in the waterworks reserve where the public may not enter. They originated from cage escapes, and if caught would still be valuable cage birds. The eastern rosella has crossed over the Rimutaka Range from the west Wairarapa population to become established in the upper Hutt Valley, but it is not yet in Wellington City.

Somes Island sits in the middle of the harbour as a convenient sanctuary for nesting birds. It is used as an animal quarantine station of the Ministry of Agriculture and Fisheries and permission to land is rarely given to the public. It provides a safe nesting place for hundreds of black-backed gulls, and also little blue penguins and a few variable oystercatchers. A small colony of spotted shags nest on a stack attached to nearby Leper Island. Ward Island (free access) has nesting little blue penguins which also nest under rocks in quite a few quiet corners of the harbour.

Houses in Days Bay, York Bay and Eastbourne have beech forest and second growth bush coming down the hills to their back doors, and there are whitehead, pigeon, rifleman, bellbird, pied tit, tui and long-tailed and shining cuckoo. The falcon appears at times. Several tracks climb up into the forest. At Days Bay take Ferry Road, Kotari Road and Korimako Road, then a walking track for about half an hour for a good bush walk. The Butterfly Creek track leads off Muritai Road at Karaka Street, Eastbourne. Falcons are regularly seen in the Orongorongo valley.

The road from Upper Hutt to Waikanae over the

Akatarawas passes through some good bush which has pigeon, pied tit, rifleman, whitehead, bellbird, tui, long-tailed and shining cuckoo and falcon. There are not too many parking places through the bush, but as the road crosses the saddle at the top, there is ample parking. From here an access road runs north and along this you have the best chance of seeing red-crowned or yellow-crowned parakeets, kaka and other bush birds.

The two arms of Porirua Harbour once had extensive mudflats to attract waders, but urban development has changed that. It is now cut across by the railway and main highway and closely settled around much of the shoreline. Porirua city has replaced the marshland at the southern end. In spite of all this, white-faced herons, pied stilts and the occasional reef heron still frequent the outer arm, and around Paremata there are white-fronted terns, black-backed and red-billed gulls and some black-billed gulls in winter. The inner arm, Pauatahanui Inlet, is in the process of recovery. The upper end of it is a wildlife refuge under the management of the Royal Forest and Bird Protection Society. Progressively the area is being improved as bird habitat, and hides and tracks are provided for birdwatchers. From the main highway, it is best approached around the north side past some small beaches and the mouths of one or two streams, where there are mallard, white-faced heron, pied stilt, maybe black swan and paradise duck. Harriers from the surrounding hills are frequent visitors, hunting for carrion. The historic cottage at the top of the inlet is occupied by the Forest and Bird custodian (look for the signpost) who may be able to give up to date information on less common birds such as godwits, black-fronted dotterels or South Island pied oystercatchers. Black and little shags and kingfishers are always present.

Kapiti Island squats brooding off the west coast in full view of travellers on the highway which winds along the coastal strip by Paraparaumu. It is rich in the violent history of Te Rauparaha and early European settlement, but since it was declared a fauna and flora reserve in 1897, it has been developed into a most valuable sanctuary for native birds, in spite of rats and possums. It has a few sooty shearwaters nesting at the top of the western cliffs, and there are waterfowl in Okupe Lagoon at the northern end. Black-backed and red-billed gulls nest near the shoreline around the northern tip and many little blue penguins nest under the tangled scrub of the flats. A few pairs of brown teal (introduced in 1968) still hang on in the swamp on Rangitira Flat, but they are seldom seen. Paradise shelducks rear their young near the mouth of Waiorua, the northernmost stream. There are a few pukeko and pied stilts around the lagoon and harriers regularly visit from the mainland.

But it is the bush birds which are the delight of Kapiti: North Island robin, whitehead, pied tit, fantail, rifleman, grey warbler, bellbird, tui and white-eye are all common. There are good numbers of kaka, some of them half tame, eyeing visitors in the hope of a handout. Red-crowned and yellow-crowned parakeets are found throughout, and so is the morepork. Weka are everywhere — hybrids of the North Island and Stewart Island subspecies, descended from liberated birds. Both shining and long-tailed cuckoos are there in summer; the large whitehead population on the island acts as nest host to big numbers of long-tails. Recent introductions are two endangered species, stitchbird and North Island saddleback. There are a few brown kiwis and a good population of little spotted kiwis. Most of the introduced birds of the mainland occur there also and a nearby islet carries a large starling roost.

A day visit to Kapiti is an excellent opportunity to see a good range of bush birds in an environment where the birds and the bush receive first consideration.

A permit is necessary to land on the reserve but this is easily obtained. Call on, write to, or telephone the Department of Conservation, Wellington District Office, for an application form. You will be asked the date of your visit, the names and addresses of those in the party, the reason for visiting and the transport you intend to use. A permit is then issued if the date is free. Only one party is permitted each day. There is no charge for the permit. Its purpose is to record and control the number of visitors in the interests of protecting the reserve. The ranger meets all parties and can give advice on which tracks to use to see different birds. Private boats may be used but visitors may not stay overnight. Two boat charter firms are Kapiti Tours and Dave Bennett, Paraparaumu — refer to the telephone directory yellow pages. Use of charter boats for two or three people is expensive and it is practical to share the cost among ten or fifteen. Environmental groups regularly make the trip.

Cook Strait

The inter-island ferries provide New Zealand's best opportunity for seeing pelagic birds by public transport. A good number of species can often be seen during the two hours the ship is in Cook Strait. Weather conditions and the season influence which species are present and it is difficult to predict what will be seen on any day.

As the ship moves out of Wellington Harbour, the following red-billed and black-backed gulls are joined by giant petrels, and these stay behind long after the gulls have dropped back to land. Then it is time to search for cape pigeons, diving petrels, and dark brown shearwaters — sooties, Hutton's and flutterers — which can only be distinguished if they come in reasonably close, and large black petrels which could be either the black petrel from the north or the Westland black. Prions in groups of three to ten birds are nearly always encountered, the most likely species being the fairy prion which breeds in thousands on islands in Cook Strait. Solitary albatrosses and mollymawks can be seen and occasional gannets. Storm petrels are rare. In calmer weather, and more especially on the Marlborough side as the ship approaches Tory Channel, there is the chance that you will see a mixed flock of birds working on a shoal of fish. Shearwaters, prions, petrels and red-billed gulls put on an exciting show as they flutter and splash about over the surface, each species using its own technique to secure a meal.

Wellington

Recommended full day
Waikanae estuary and Waimeha lagoon, returning via the Akatarawa road to Upper Hutt; or Lake Wairarapa.

Recommended half day
Eastbourne, the eastern bays and Butterfly Creek track.

Chapter 14

The South Island

Nelson

The natural boulder bank which runs north from
Nelson city has nesting white-fronted terns, black-
backed and red-billed gulls and some banded
dotterels. Some waders occur around Nelson Haven
and spotted shags can be seen on Fifeshire Rock out
from Rocks Road. The Waimea and Mapua inlets
have mudflats and sandbars where many waders and
shore birds can be found. These include white heron,
little egret, royal spoonbill, white-faced heron, South
Island pied oystercatcher, godwit, knot, turnstone,
golden plover, pied stilt, the three gulls, black swan,
Canada goose, mallard, shoveler, grey duck. The
numbers are never large but it is an interesting
estuary with a reputation for rare stragglers. One
high-tide roost is along a stopbank to the west of the
inshore end of the bridge to Rabbit Island, and the
bridge provides a good viewing point. All corners of
the estuary are worth searching.

In Golden Bay, bush birds can be found up the
Cobb River valley. This area is the northernmost
limit of the kea. The forests of Abel Tasman
National Park may be entered from the road in to
Totaranui, or from Marahau near Motueka. Kaka,
pigeon, weka, yellow-crowned parakeet, bellbird, tui,
robin, yellow-breasted tit, brown creeper and
rifleman occur there.

The main attraction for ornithologists in Golden
Bay is Farewell Spit, a very important wader habitat.
The wide tidal mudflats sheltered by the hook of

Farewell Spit support many different species. The national wader count of November 1984 recorded nearly 42,000 waders there, a higher number than at any other location. This included nearly 20,000 knots, almost as many godwits and 1000 turnstones. It has a reputation for sightings of very rare stragglers, though it is remote and visited less frequently than Auckland and Northland harbours. There is some evidence that birds on an internal south/north migration use the spit as a jumping-off place to cross to the North Island. They would certainly have the advantage of prevailing westerly winds. Several species of duck and a large population of black swan share the tidal flats with the waders. In the vegetation among the sand dunes there are wekas, California quail, hedge sparrows, skylarks, pipits, goldfinches, redpolls and chaffinches.

The Spit is a fauna and flora reserve, so public access is restricted to a point 2.5 km along the inside beach or 4 km along the outer beach measured from the vehicle track connecting the two beaches. Advance application may gain permission to go further. Permits are given to fishermen to fish from the outer beach, and Collingwood Motors run tourist trips along the beach to the lighthouse. This is an interesting trip but too fast for the birdwatcher who wants to stop and study. The nearest camping ground is by the beach at Pakawau; camping is not permitted on the Spit or on Puponga Farm Park.

Great sand dunes make up the Spit, unstable ones along the outer edges, inner ones stabilised with vegetation comprised of lupins, akeake and other shrubs as well as marram grass, with some areas of pasture grasses on the flats. Spring tides invade the dunes on the ocean coast to create extensive temporary lagoons. Waders come to these when high tides drive them off the inner mudflats. Many rarer migrant waders have been found in these areas, especially whimbrels which occur at Farewell Spit more than any other place. The large high tide wader roosts are usually on the ocean beach.

The pine plantation near the lighthouse is a refuge for many passerines which feed in the dune country, and the morepork is there too. Beyond the lighthouse (3 km or more) the Shelly Banks are high enough to provide nesting places for colonies of Caspian terns and red-billed gulls, and there is a small colony of gannets.

An expedition to Farewell Spit should also take in Westhaven Inlet for bittern and fernbird, as well as more waders, and the small lakes of the region for duck, pukeko, banded rail and spotless crake.

West Coast

Along the length of the West Coast there are rich native forests with bird life which has been only briefly studied. Unfortunately, this indicates unwillingness on the part of birdwatchers to get into wet and difficult conditions. The birds of the western Paparoa Range, between Westport and Greymouth, are probably typical of many areas: near the coast there are yellow-breasted tit, bellbird, tui, pigeon, white-eye, grey warbler. Further back, are kaka, yellow-crowned parakeet, robin, brown creeper and rifleman, and blue duck are in the mountain streams.

Many areas such as the forested terraces above the Totara River, would reward some closer study. Out of the breeding season white herons from the Okarito colony can be found on estuaries, lakes and swamps throughout the region. Wekas are plentiful north of Harihari, and falcons occur through most of the forests. Roa, the great spotted kiwi, is common in the Paparoas and is also in the forest of the Karamea Bluff hill. It would be necessary to stay in the bush edge for an hour after sunset to have the chance of seeing or hearing it.

There are many estuaries worth visiting, though the number of birds is small by east coast standards. Orowaiti Lagoon at Westport is a wader haunt, both close to town and further upstream. Pied stilt, variable oystercatcher and South Island pied oystercatcher, pukeko and spur-winged plover can be expected, along with ducks and shags. In the north, the estuaries of Karamea and the Little Wanganui River have a few waders, white-faced heron, and

*Yellow-breasted
(South Island) tit*
(Don Hadden)

South Island pied fantail
(Rod Morris)

South Island fernbird
(Rod Morris)

White-eye
(David Stonex)

Yellowhammer
(Geoff Moon)

Goldfinch
(Geoff Moon)

Yellowhead
(Don Hadden)

Bellbird; male
(Geoff Moon)

Tui
(Geoff Moon)

banded dotterel. On the south side of the Buller River mouth at Cape Foulwind, the Okari and Totara rivers join to form a common estuary which has shags, white-faced herons, ducks, oystercatchers, banded dotterels, pied stilts, gulls and terns. Caspian terns are not plentiful on the West Coast but white-fronted terns are numerous.

At Perpendicular Point, south of Meybille Bay, you can look down from the parking place to see spotted shags on the cliffs below. A weka will probably appear hoping to share a sandwich.

Near Barrytown the Westland black petrel breeds in winter under the heavy forest which covers the rough coastal faces of the Paparoa Range. Looking for the birds in the forest would be futile and dangerous as the area is very steep and intersected with limestone bluffs and cliffs. It is a fauna reserve for which an entry permit is required. The petrels can be seen from the roadside as they fly into their nests during the breeding season from April to December. Scotchman's Creek, about 4.5 km south of Punakaiki, is one place where in midwinter they come in over the coast at about 5.30 p.m. and leave in the mornings at around 7.30 a.m. The numbers that come ashore on any one night vary greatly according to the weather. This is one of the largest petrels, with a powerful bill, probably the reason for its having survived against introduced predators.

Around Greymouth there are pools at the river mouth, on the south side and on the Cobden side, which attract herons and other shore birds. Inland, fernbirds can be found in the pakihi areas among the second growth bush. Lake Brunner, also Kangaroo Lake and Lake Poerua beyond, have crested grebe, black swan, scaup, paradise, mallard, shoveler and grey duck, pukeko, spur-winged plover, Canada goose, and South Island pied oystercatcher.

Hokitika River has some nesting black-backed gull, also black and little shag, white-faced heron, black-billed gull, white-fronted tern and banded dotterel. Lake Kaniere is set back towards the mountains and the approach road passes through some choice native forest in which to look for birds. The lake has crested grebe, and both marsh crake and spotless crake have been found there. Bush birds include kaka, robin, yellow-breasted tit, brown creeper, yellow-crowned parakeet, shining and long-tailed cuckoo, weka and falcon.

South of Hokitika, entry to the bush at any convenient place will give you the chance to see yellow-breasted tit, brown creeper, bellbird, tui and pigeon. Robin, kaka and parakeet are not common, and the weka is rare (but common again in Fiordland). Fernbirds are present in scrub and pakihi country right down the coastal strip.

The road drops suddenly on to Lake Ianthe. This is a good place to see crested grebe, scaup and grey duck. A recommended place to find robins is on Mt Hercules, 6 km south of Harihari. When Okarito appears on the map, it is a reminder that you are close to New Zealand's only nesting colony of white herons. Permission to visit the heronry must be obtained from the Department of Conservation, Hokitika, and arrangements made to have a ranger accompany each party. Travel is by horse or tractor up the spit, then by boat up the Waitangiroto River to the colony. White herons may be seen in swamps, rivers or estuaries around this area at any time.

Tracks around the reserves at Franz Josef and Fox Glacier will give the chance to see many of the bush birds already mentioned. Keas are frequent visitors but these wide-ranging birds are not always where you expect them. Further south, Lake Mapourika, Lake Paringa and Lake Moeraki all have crested grebes; falcons are common throughout and keas often come down from the mountain sides. The Fiordland crested penguin is in small colonies along the coast from about Bruce Bay southwards, and Jackson Bay has a well-known colony.

Marlborough

East of Blenheim, the Wairau River enters Cook Strait with a large area of lagoons attractive to shore birds. Most notable of these are the royal spoonbills

which have nested there since deserting their former
site alongside the white herons at Okarito, South
Westland. Fortunately the place is remote enough to
be undisturbed. These handsome big birds can be
seen about the estuary all through summer.
Spoonbills fly with their necks extended, and are
easily distinguished from white herons which hold
their heads back against their shoulders. White
herons and little egrets also occur on the Wairau
lagoons. Black, pied and little shags all nest in the
lagoon area, and also present are white-faced heron,
black swan, mallard, shoveler, grey duck, grey teal,
pukeko, South Island pied oystercatcher, variable
oystercatcher, godwit, knot, pied stilt, black-fronted,
Caspian and white-fronted tern. The long Wairau Bar
has nesting banded dotterel, Caspian terns and gulls.
Access to the river mouth is along Wairau Bar Road.
To reach the lagoon area and the bar, which are on
the south side, take Highway 1 as far as Riverina and
turn off on Redwood Pass Road.

Upstream, the Wairau is a typical shingly river and
Highway 63 runs along it for about 80 km though
seldom close enough to observe the birds. On the
north side from Tuamarina access is better for a
short distance. In spring and early summer the
riverbed has nesting banded dotterels, pied stilts,
South Island pied oystercatchers, black-backed and
black-billed gulls and black-fronted terns.

Queen Charlotte Sound is travelled from end to
end by the inter-island ferries, and it is also busy
with pleasure boats and tourist launches from Picton,
so there are fewer birds than in the quieter Pelorus
Sound. However, the little blue penguin is found
throughout, gannets are occasional visitors, and
fluttering shearwaters come in from time to time
from the strait. Pied and little shags and occasional
variable oystercatchers can be spotted on the rocks or
beaches.

In Pelorus Sound, there are spotted shag colonies
on the outer islands and also straggling along the low
cliffs of the eastern side of the sound. Pied shags
also nest in a few localities around Forsyth Bay and
the outer sound. The rare endemic king shag nests on

Duffers Reef and Sentinel Rock (beyond the Chetwode Islands) and there are a few on Stewart Island close to D'Urville Island. This is the shiest of the shags and will leave its nesting or roosting rocks long before a boat is close. They should not be approached in the breeding season because of the risk of nest desertion, but one or two may be seen fishing in Pelorus Sound and can be recognised by the white shoulder patch. The mudflats around Havelock are occasionally visited by waders. There are a few pied stilts and white-faced herons. From Havelock, mail boats go down the sound to the outer bays and these provide very pleasant birdwatching. Picnic and charter cruises are also available. Enquire at Glenmore Cruises Ltd in Havelock.

At Pelorus Bridge the main road touches the edge of a large native forest containing the finest podocarps in this part of the country. It contains good numbers of pigeon (especially in riverside willow trees in springtime) and tui and bellbird which can be seen feeding on the "honeydew" on the trunks of beech trees. Sometimes there are yellow-breasted tits, brown creepers and wekas.

From the outskirts of Blenheim, south to the Ure River and up to 16 km inland the cirl bunting is more numerous than anywhere else in New Zealand. This is our rarest introduced bird. It is a challenge to identify it when yellowhammers are also present in the same habitat of rough grass and roadside ditches.

Lake Elterwater, beside the highway, is worth visiting. Except in drought years, when it may dry up, it has a good collection of waterfowl — black swan, mallard, grey duck, shoveler, grey teal, Canada goose and paradise duck all occur there. This has been a favourite haunt of the Australian little grebe for many years, and the hoary-headed grebe has also been found there. South of some roadside willows a little raised ground beside the road gives a good vantage point for looking over the lake without disturbing the birds.

The Kaikoura district has many interesting bird places. The road along the northern side of the peninsula is a popular approach to the seal colony. It also takes you within sight of the very large red-billed gull colony on the rock platform beyond the point, occupied by breeding birds from July to the end of January. On the way along, it is worthwhile searching little beaches and rocks for herons and oystercatchers, and the rock platforms and pools where Siberian tattlers have been found. There is a good selection of bush birds in the forest remnants about Kaikoura. In a reserve on the banks of the Kowhai River intensive studies have been carried out on South Island robin, yellow-breasted tit, grey warbler and other native passerines. Bellbirds are common. The New Zealand falcon is common throughout the Kaikoura Mountains and the Hundalee Hills as far south as the Conway River.

At Rosy Morn Bay red-billed gulls nest on a rock stack close to the road. Oaro and other bays along this rocky coast provide excellent opportunities to see Hutton's shearwaters, which gather offshore in large flocks during the summer and are often seen feeding close inshore, perhaps right into the kelp among the rocks. This bird has its nest burrows in the steep tussock slopes of the Seaward Kaikouras at about 1600 m above sea level.

Approximately 4.5 km north of Cheviot on the main road, watch the western side of the road for the entrance to St Annes lagoon and domain, marked by concrete gateposts and double iron gates but still not easy to see. It is a delightful place for a stop and there is always plenty of bird life. Mallard, grey duck, shoveler, grey teal, scaup and paradise duck are on the lake, along with Australian coot, little grebe, black and little shag and pukeko. Hundreds of paradise ducks gather there to moult in late summer. Redpolls and finches are common in the exotic trees and you should watch for black-backed magpies here where they first became established in New Zealand.

Christchurch

There is no native forest near Christchurch, but the area has many good places to see shore birds and waterfowl. Introduced passerines are in particularly good numbers, and the little owl is well distributed in mature pines and willows around the outskirts of the city. The large Avon–Heathcote estuary can be watched from many vantage points on the Sumner side, at Bromley or the Brighton spit. It has South Island pied oystercatchers, banded dotterels and godwits in summer (sometimes joined by other migrants), and resident white-faced herons, little shags, pied stilts, Caspian and white-fronted terns, and the three gulls.

At the end of Rockinghorse Road, which runs the length of the New Brighton spit, walk through Stilt Lane to see the main high tide wader roost for the estuary. (A careful approach is necessary.) Alternatively, the birds will roost on the ocean beach opposite. Bromley oxidation ponds were designed with plantings and islands for birds and are worth visiting. Permission and key for entry may be sought from the Engineer's Office, Christchurch Drainage Board. Black swan, Canada goose, mallard, shoveler, grey duck and grey teal can be seen there, with particularly high numbers in the duck-shooting season — a time for the city reaches of the Avon River to be crowded with mallards and greys. The pukeko is very common and the royal spoonbill is a regular visitor.

There are many spotted shag colonies around the coastal cliffs of Banks Peninsula. One at Sumner can be easily viewed. Take Scarborough Road, which zigzags up the hill from the Sumner waterfront, and turn left at the top to park by the pine trees. Opposite, a grass path leads to the top of a high cliff to give a view of a small part of the large colony where thousands of shags build nests on the narrow cliff edges. Individual birds may be seen with the ornate plumage crests and plumes they assume briefly at some time during the extended breeding season of the colony.

The richest bird habitat near Christchurch is Lake Ellesmere, which has some marvellous places for birdwatching. It would take a long time to get to know the long shoreline well, but its diversity enables you to select the birds to see by the area you visit.

The season and the weather must be taken into account. Wind across the large expanse of water can raise the water level a long way up gently sloping edges on the downwind shore. Bear this in mind to avoid being caught with water deeper than it was when you crossed it. The area near the lake is a maze of roads in flat country and it is easy to get lost. Always take a map and save yourself hours, and litres of petrol.

Black swan are always in view on the lake, not in the huge numbers they were in the 1960s, but in little groups around the reed beds, feeding in the shallows or resting far out in the middle; on hot days they blend with the mirages over the lake. When disturbed near the shore they swim off with dignity to take up positions where they can watch everything with safety. One has the feeling that this is exactly one metre beyond shotgun range.

Apart from the sanctuary area of Harts Creek Reserve, there is a great deal of waterfowl shooting around the lake during the winter duck-shooting season and when special seasons are declared for swans or geese, so it is advisable to check these out with the acclimatisation society if you are planning to birdwatch.

Kaituna Lagoon, at the north end, has a good assortment of ducks, some black swan and pukeko among rushes and weed islands in a fairly open area. The Akaroa highway comes close to the lake edge here and you can survey the lagoon from the roadside. After the road leaves the lakeside a little further on, turn off to the right into Bayleys Road to drive along Kaitorete Spit. The 22 km long spit is dry and stony, with breeding banded dotterels, skylarks and pipits. Open mudflats on the lakeside are often used by waders, but access to the lake shore is limited here.

The southern end of the lake includes the outlet at Taumutu, Lakeside Domain and Harts Creek Refuge. The outlet area usually has a few terns and shags (including spotted) and Lakeside Domain has pukeko, mallard, grey duck, shoveler, grey teal, black swan, Canada goose and pied stilt. The first welcome swallows to breed in the South Island built their nest in a boat here, and it is still a good place to see them. New Zealand's largest feral population of mute swans breeds in the dense raupo of Harts Creek. They can always be seen around this area, with downy cygnets following their parents in November. Harts Creek is the only part of the lake with any quantity of raupo, and this, together with areas of willow and rushes, makes it an excellent place for breeding waterfowl. Marsh crakes are there too.

Ellesmere has a reputation for rare and interesting waders, and these are most often found on the wide mudflats of the central section of the western shore. Best access is from Embankment Road. Take Springs Road from Highway 1 beside Wigram Airbase, following it right through past Lincoln College, across McDonald Road into English Road, left along Davidsons Road and right into Embankment Road which goes straight to the lake. The gate at the end of the road (free public access) takes you on to 5–6 km of mudflats where waders may be found at the lake edge or at pools higher on the shore. They will be in small numbers and it is hard to predict species, but waders recorded here include golden plover, wrybill, turnstone, pectoral sandpiper, curlew sandpiper, sharp-tailed sandpiper, greenshank, red-necked stint, godwit and knot.

A nearby place worth visiting is Selwyn Huts, at the end of Days Road which leaves the Ellesmere Junction Road between Lincoln College and Springston. Ducks, shags and occasionally bitterns can be seen along the banked channel of the Selwyn River, and shining cuckoos are in the willow trees in summer.

South of Lake Ellesmere, Coopers Lagoon has some waterfowl and small numbers of waders. At the northern end, 8 km beyond Kaituna along the Akaroa highway, Lake Forsyth fills a valley which was obviously an arm of the sea in ages past. It carries large numbers of waterfowl and is the moulting place for thousands of Canada geese which congregate here (and on Lake Ellesmere) in January after the completion of breeding.

Between Kaituna and Lake Forsyth, side roads into Kaituna Valley and Prices Valley lead to patches of bush, but for the best selection of bush birds in this region go a further 9 km for the turn-off to Okuti Valley. Patches of bush here have brown creeper, bellbird, tui, pigeon, yellow-breasted tit, grey warbler and fantail.

North of the city, the Spencerville–Brooklands lagoon has waders and some waterfowl and it is a great place for finches. For convenient birdwatching, the Forest and Bird Society has a walkway and hides on the Spencerville side. A few cirl buntings have been recorded in that area. The lowest reaches of the Waimakariri River now have few birds. The Ashley riverbed does not provide good habitat until above Rangiora, upstream from about where the Okuku joins. There are nesting colonies of black-billed gulls and black-fronted terns and scattered pairs of banded dotterel and wrybill where the riverbed is clear of vegetation. The mouth of the Ashley River at Waikuku in summer usually has knots, red-necked stints, turnstones, whimbrels, South Island pied oystercatchers, pied stilts, and white-fronted, black-fronted and Caspian terns. White-faced herons are on the riverbeds and wet places throughout the district.

Christchurch
Recommended full day
Lake Ellesmere, either central area at Embankment Road and Selwyn Huts or the northern shore at Kaituna and on to Okuti Valley for bush birds.
Recommended half day
Avon–Heathcote Estuary and the spotted shag colony at Sumner.

South Canterbury and North Otago

Lake Wainono on the coast east of Waimate is a rich island of bird habitat in a sea of intensively farmed flat or rolling country. Always present on or around the lake are black swan, Canada goose, paradise duck, grey teal, grey duck, mallard, shoveler, black shag, little shag, white-faced heron, bittern, pukeko, marsh crake, black-backed and black-billed gull, white-fronted tern and a few Caspian tern, harrier, rock pigeon, little owl, welcome swallow, South Island pied oystercatcher, pied stilt, banded dotterel, spur-winged plover and many small passerines. White herons are there in most months of the year and royal spoonbills have been recorded most often in December and January. Black-fronted terns are common except in spring, when they are nesting on local riverbeds.

Access around the southern edge off Highway 1 is by Foley Road across the railway, left into Hannatons Road, then the first road on the right, across a bridge and right through a gate to follow a track out to the shingle bank. From the bank you are able to survey the whole lake. Before leaving it is worth checking the ponds and flats 1 km south for waders. The western edge is reached by a narrow road opposite the restaurant at the Waimate junction. Along this western shore you may see royal spoonbills in summer and white herons in winter. Resident bitterns and marsh crakes are in the rushes and dense vegetation and along the banks of the two inlet streams.

Being the most important extensive wetland in the 250 km coast between Lake Ellesmere and Karitane estuary, Wainono attracts a number of migrant waders, and there have been many records of rare vagrants. Sharp-tailed sandpipers stay all summer, but godwits, turnstones and knots leave by mid December. Wrybills visit the area between August and January, with peak numbers in September and October. This lake is seriously disturbed by duck-shooting during May and June.

The mouths of nearly all South Canterbury rivers have tidal lagoons with resident shags, gulls and terns. Red-billed gulls and white-fronted terns nest at many of them. Hinds, Rangitata and Orari river mouths are accessible and are moderately populated with estuary birds. The Opihi riverbed has black-fronted dotterel on the lower 10 km and its estuary is particularly good. Caspian, black-fronted, and white-fronted terns are there, and the white-winged black tern is frequently there or at Spider Lagoon a few kilometres north. This is probably the most likely area in New Zealand in which to find white-winged black terns, an interesting visitor which is taking a long time to decide whether to settle here.

Browns Beach and Spider Lagoon are reached by turning off Highway 1 at the Winchester School, into Rise Road, which goes straight to the beach. Just 150 m north you will find black-fronted dotterel, banded dotterel, pied stilt and waterfowl.

Washdyke Lagoon, on the nothern outskirts of Timaru, is suffering from growing urbanisation along its shore, but ducks, oystercatchers, stilts and shags are there, and also white-fronted, black-fronted and a few Caspian terns. White herons can be expected in winter. Brackish ponds to the north have produced some rarities, and the *Salicornia* flats at the southern end should be searched for waders, including wrybills from August and October. The northern approach is from Washdyke, turning off on the north side of Washdyke Creek bridge, through the industrial area and across to the northern end of the lagoon. For the southern end turn into Bridge Road at the top of the hill towards the freezing works, from where you can overlook the lagoon.

The wide beds of the great rivers, Rakaia, Rangitata and Waitaki, are of more interest in the upper and middle sections than near the coast. As bird habitat they have been badly affected by vegetation covering the shingle islands and a restricted water flow after damming or diversion of the headwaters. There is a connection between the two, because the plants which colonised the mid-stream islands used to be swept away by floods. Depending on the recent behaviour of the river, and how clean the riverbed is, it may be worthwhile searching for colonies of black-billed gulls or black-fronted terns between October and January, especially near the main road bridge over the Waitaki. Banded and black-fronted dotterels can be found on the shingle banks and the edges of quietly flowing side streams.

The breakwater at Oamaru Harbour is a resting place for spotted shags, black-backed gulls, red-billed gulls and white-fronted terns. Yellow-eyed penguins may be seen there and mollymawks follow fishing boats close to the harbour entrance. Stewart Island shags occur here too, their most northerly point. From the rocks around to Cape Wanbrow, sooty shearwaters may be seen close inshore, especially on summer evenings. The cliff top, reached by Bushy Beach Road, is a good place for sea-watching for other pelagic species. Further south along this picturesque coastline, Shag Point (true to its name) always has some Stewart Island shags on the rocks. There are sometimes seals as well. During the two or three weeks from mid October sooty shearwaters pass close inshore on their homeward migration. In a wide and continuous stream, hundreds of thousands of birds hurry past on their way to the "muttonbird islands" to the south-west of Stewart Island. The return journey can be seen early in May.

Central Otago and inland Canterbury

Central Otago and inland Canterbury comprise an area characterised by large open space, hot and dry in summer, cold and largely deserted by birds in winter. The great treeless mountain sides and ridges have an enduring beauty. Harriers circle lazily over them, and skylarks abound in the tussocks, but there are few other species in this dry habitat. Close to rivers, lakes or farm dams you will find more birds. Pied stilts nest around any wet place, South Island pied oystercatchers are well distributed, nesting sometimes well away from water but never where it is really dry. The white-faced heron is always on the hunt for frogs, and spur-winged plovers are widespread.

At Queenstown there are always scaup by the wharf close to the town centre. It is fascinating to watch them diving in the clear water there, paddling constantly to keep themselves down at the bottom. They don't know about skindivers' weighted belts, and when paddling stops and heads are pointed upwards, they shoot to the surface like corks. There are usually a few other waterfowl and some red-billed and black-billed gulls around Queenstown Bay, but most of the lake is too deep and steep-sided for birds.

At the head of Lake Wakatipu the wide shingle beds and wet areas have nesting black-billed gull, black-fronted tern, South Island pied oystercatcher, pied stilt and banded dotterel. Canada goose, paradise duck and spur-winged plover are common. Up the valleys of the Rees and the Dart you meet the edge of beech forests rich in birdlife. You can see robin, yellow-breasted tit, pigeon, bellbird, tui, kaka, yellow-crowned parakeet, rifleman, yellowhead, brown creeper, shining cuckoo and long-tailed cuckoo. The yellowhead which is now in reduced numbers and gone from the northern part of the island, has its stronghold in these forests, particularly in the Caples Valley on the western side of the lake.

In summer, roads to skifields provide very convenient access to birds of the high country. Redpolls are common on the slopes, and skylarks and pipits will test your identification skills. The road to the Rastus Burn skifield may give you the chance to see chukor.

Chukor were introduced as a game bird to take advantage of this habitat and although they are widespread they are never in large numbers nor easily seen. Look for them in rough, rocky gullies (altitude 1000–1800 m). They are seen occasionally at the roadside and the Crown Range road would be a likely place.

Lake Hayes is about 15 km from Queenstown on Highway 6 towards Arrowtown. It is a most picturesque little lake, shallow enough to provide lots of food, and therefore well stocked with birdlife. The coots which breed there were one of the first groups to establish themselves in New Zealand. The lake has black swan, Canada goose, grey duck, mallard, shoveler, grey teal, paradise duck and pied stilt. Pukeko are common and marsh crake and bittern are also in the extensive raupo reed beds. Spur-winged plovers are on the surrounding fields, and finches are common in the trees.

California quail are common in the gorges of the dry country and black shags forage for fish up all the watercourses. Small numbers of wrybills are on a number of high country riverbeds in summer, including the Matukituki, Makarora, Hunter and Dart. In the lower hills feral rock pigeons are met on the riverbeds and other weedy ground. They nest on cliffs in undisturbed places.

At Alexandra the confluence of the Manuherikia and Clutha rivers is a good birding spot at any time of the year. Nearby Lanes Dam has little shag, black shag, mallard, pukeko and a resident population of coots. Taieri Lake below Ranfurly sometimes has very large numbers of birds, and several rarities have turned up there. Many of these lakes are worth an extended visit and a careful search, and experience gained that way will teach you the most rewarding places to return to.

At Wanaka the waterfront usually has some ducks, but Ewings Bay and the mouth of the Matukituki River at West Wanaka are much more rewarding, with a selection of species which includes white-faced heron, black swan, Canada goose, mallard, grey duck, grey teal, paradise duck, scaup, shoveler, pied stilt, South Island pied oystercatcher, banded dotterel, spur-winged plover, pukeko. Take the opportunity to walk part of the riverbed and you can see pied stilt, South Island pied oystercatcher, banded dotterel, wrybill, black-billed gull and black-fronted tern all nesting between September and November.

Once you have passed through Omarama going north you are in the crisp clean air of the Mackenzie country. Here the wide riverbeds and quiet backwater streams are the home of the black stilt, one of our most endangered species and, sadly, the rarest wader in the world. Numbers are so low it is exciting to see any but there are still places where there is a good chance of seeing them in the summer. First choice would probably be the homestead tarn of Benmore Station, at the corner where the road from Omarama forks to Lake Ohau (left) and Twizel (ahead). The tarn is not visible from the road; ask at the homestead for permission and directions. White-backed magpies are very common through this area.

Lake Tekapo has some places of special interest. First, near the outlet of the lake, Mt John is known for the observatory on its summit, and the road up to the observatory provides an opportunity to get up among the tussocks. This is one of the best places to see chukor, which come around the observatory for handouts.

The delta of the Cass River, midway along the western shore of Lake Tekapo, is a likely place to see black stilts, often around the margins of ponds or stable streams. They share this habitat with South Island pied oystercatchers and wrybills which breed in the Cass River valley. You can also see spur-winged plover, pied stilt, banded dotterel, black-fronted tern, black-backed gull and black-billed gull. The white-winged black tern occurs regularly between October and February.

Nearby Lake Alexandrina is probably the richest bird lake in this district. Crested grebes are there in greater numbers than at any other lake. In the raupo across the northern end the marsh crake is common, which cannot be said of any other place in New Zealand. This is a popular fishing lake, with fishermen's cottages, but the birds are not seriously disturbed. Waterfowl include black swan, paradise duck, mallard, grey duck, grey teal, shoveler, scaup. These are also on nearby Lake McGregor, which also has coots. It is only a 3 km walk over the hill to the north to the Cass River delta, though you can drive around. Chukor should be watched and listened for on the hillsides.

Visitors to the Hermitage, Mt Cook, should look out for birds on the edges of Lake Pukaki or on tarns near the road. The mouths of small streams entering the lake usually attract birds. Call at Mt Cook National Park Headquarters for a Bird Checklist and some seasonal advice. In the area you may see black swan, Canada goose, paradise duck, mallard, grey duck, scaup, shoveler, wrybill, pied stilt, white-faced heron, spur-winged plover, South Island pied oystercatcher, black-fronted tern, black-billed gull and black-backed gull. Chukor are on the mountain sides and you may be lucky enough to see a falcon which is present throughout this area. The delta and wide shingle flats of the Godley River which flows into the head of the lake, have nesting banded dotterel and wrybill. Black stilts also occur at the delta.

Keas are around the lower slopes of the mountains and they come down to the Hermitage and to Ball Hut. Small patches of native forest in this district are worth investigating for yellow-breasted tit, rifleman, brown creeper, bellbird, grey warbler and fantail. Away from the mountains you should listen at night for both morepork and little owl as the ranges of these two owls seem to overlap here.

Motorists crossing the island pass through some interesting habitat by either northern route, but this is big country and you must not expect to see much during a brief stop. Plan your trip to give at least an hour to wander about and see and hear all the things that are missed from a speeding car. On the Arthur's Pass route, Klondyke Corner near Bealey gives easy access to beech forest. A short diversion at the Hawdon River takes you into an excellent place for bush birds. Right by the highway, Lakes Pearson and Grassmere are the easiest places of all to see crested grebes. On the Otira side of the Arthur's Pass summit, an off-road viewing area looks down the Otira Gorge. Stop here to take in the view and you will probably see keas come down for handouts.

From the Lewis Pass road the bed of the Waiau River is really too wide and vast to be tackled in anything less than a well-planned expedition. At the Hope River, a side road (running south-west) goes to a parking place which can be the starting point for a good walk. Birds in the forest here include kaka and yellow-crowned parakeet. Over the Lewis Pass you meet the rich, wet forests of the West Coast.

Queenstown
Recommended full day
Head of the lake and Routeburn valley.
Recommended half day
Lake Hayes.

Dunedin

Otago Peninsula has the most interesting birds of the Dunedin area, but there are also several other places of interest. Within the city, Woodhaugh Gardens and the botanic gardens have tuis, bellbirds and N.Z. pigeons. Riflemen are in the town belt and in many patches of bush around the city. Eastern rosellas are in the Leith Valley, Whare Flat pine forests and the slopes of the Dunedin side of Flagstaff Hill. A white heron has wintered on Lindsay Creek, Normanby, for several years. The twin Tomahawk lagoons at Ocean Grove have several species of waterfowl including mute swan and pukeko. Ross Creek Reserve is an attractive bush area with brown creeper, yellow-breasted tit and rifleman. It can be approached from the Balmacewen golf course or by coming down the Pineapple Walkway from Flagstaff. Tomtits are plentiful at Whare Flat, and the Douglas Fir plantations along the Three Mile Hill road have good numbers of South Island robins, which the other conifers do not.

On the peninsula, the drive along the harbour side will usually show variable oystercatchers as well as little shags resting on the ramps and jetties of boatsheds, and occasional kingfishers on the power lines. Dicksons Knob, up from Portobello, has rifleman and brown creeper, and there are yellow-breasted tits in the bushed valley between there and Harbour Cone. The inlets on the ocean side have small but varied wader populations in summer. Eastern curlew have been recorded there, as well as black-fronted dotterel, banded dotterel, godwit, pied stilt, and both variable and South Island pied oystercatcher. The likelihood of seeing either fur seals or Hooker's sea lions adds interest to the ocean beaches of the peninsula.

The Taiaroa Head colony of the royal albatross is certainly the most famous ornithological site near Dunedin, and rightly so. The area occupied by the colony is securely fenced and entry is possible only with an accredited guide. Bookings must be made in advance and it is no use turning up at the gate.

Attempting to view from outside the fence is either unsatisfactory or impossible. You can probably see more with a telescope from the mole at Aramoana on the other side of the harbour entrance. All arrangements are made through the Government Tourist Bureau, Princes Street, Dunedin. Enquire there (phone Dunedin 740-344) before planning your trip. Opening times depend on the season and the activities of the birds, but normally the sanctuary opens for visitors in the last week of November, on Mondays, Wednesdays, Thursdays and Saturdays, extending to Fridays from January. Own transport is necessary except in December, January and February when a coach leaves from the G.T.B. in Princes Street at 1.30 p.m. (Reservations are necessary.) From 1 February the timetable reverts to four days a week, and from about mid March there are visits on Mondays, Wednesdays and Saturdays only. Non-breeding birds leave the colony at the end of March. There is less activity, but access continues through the winter, depending on the birds. The sanctuary will be closed, for instance, when young albatrosses are wandering around the colony and cannot always be seen. Visits by the parent birds are less frequent during this period.

Stewart Island shags and large numbers of spotted shags are on the cliffs below the albatrosses at Taiaroa Head.

Yellow-eyed penguins may also be seen at a commercially developed viewing area called "Penguin Place". This is handy to Taiaroa Head and coaches visiting the albatross colony call there as well. Afternoon visits can be made by private transport or arrangements made for other times. A "Penguin Place" sign on the roadside before Taiaroa Head (and after passing Harington Point) directs you to McGrouther's farm. The yellow-eyed penguin exists in such small numbers it is regarded as the world's rarest penguin. This organised viewing will give you a good look at the birds without risk of disturbing them at their nest sites.

South Island fernbirds are on Mt Cargill, along the walking track by the summit and along the southern and south-eastern ridges just below the summit. The walk up to the summit from Bethunes Gully usually produces a variety of interesting species. Another good place for fernbirds is between Lakes Waipori and Waihola. Around the picnic place overlooking Lake Holm on the Clarendon–Berwick road (1 km south of N.Z. Forest Service headquarters), fernbirds are in the wetlands and also across on the lake side of the road.

Lake Waihola and, behind it, the large wetland of the Berwick Swamp (Sinclair's swamp) are valuable habitats for waterfowl. Shoveler, grey teal, mallard, grey duck, black swan, paradise duck are there, and also white-faced heron, bittern, pukeko and king-fisher.

Dunedin
Recommended full day
Otago Peninsula — the royal albatross colony, yellow-eyed penguins and small forest patches for bush birds.
Recommended half day
Ross Creek Reserve.

Southland

The neat green grass paddocks of eastern Southland's efficient sheep and cattle farms have only the common species of birds, but coastal wetlands and inland riverbeds provide some very rewarding birdwatching. From the mouth of the Oreti River a long estuary reaches to Invercargill, where urban-isation has made it rather unattractive to birds other than black-backed gulls, but the lower reaches open out to broad mudflats where waders feed. There are high tide roosts on the eastern side, chiefly between Clifton and Woodlands, approached (through private property) from the Bluff Road. Caspian terns and white-fronted terns nest there. Omaui, at the outlet to Foveaux Strait, gives better access to places to see godwit, knot, turnstone, South Island pied oystercatcher, Caspian tern, black-fronted tern, white-fronted tern, pied stilt, black-backed gull, red-billed gull, black shag, little shag and possibly Stewart Island shag.

Before Omaui the road passes through Greenhills Bush, and you should stop there to look for pigeon, yellow-breasted tit, bellbird, tui, brown creeper, rifleman, fantail and grey warbler.

Through Bluff township to the southernmost end of Highway 1 at Stirling Point, you come to a good place for sea-watching. Albatrosses and petrels may be seen in the strait or following fishing boats into the harbour mouth.

Awarua Bay, the eastern extension of Bluff Harbour, has turned up many interesting waders over the years, though the numbers are never large. The western and southern sides of this large area of swamp and sedge are reached from Tiwai Road. Turn left before the crossing to the aluminium smelter. There you may find godwit, turnstone, variable oystercatcher, South Island pied oystercatcher, golden plover, banded dotterel, New Zealand dotterel, pied stilt, and white-faced heron. Waterfowl can include black swan, shoveler, grey teal and paradise duck. Black shags and little shags are common. Fernbirds are right through this area, and redpolls and finches are common in drier places. Waituna Lagoon is adjacent to the eastern side of Awarua Bay and can be approached by road from the north. The same species can be expected there.

Up-country, the cold days of winter bring flocks of introduced finches and yellowhammers around the farms and along hay feed-out lines, and into town parks and gardens. In spring and summer nesting birds come to the riverbeds, the waders early, gulls and terns later. Take every opportunity to scan any open shingle riverbed from bridge or road to locate colonies of black-billed gulls and black-fronted terns. Some colonies are very large and return to a stable site year after year, but there are many which must find a new site each season when winter floods have altered the contours of the shingle beds. Nests of South Island pied oystercatcher, pied stilt and banded dotterel will be located from the river bank or on a walk along the shingle. The little owl is a common bird of Southland farmland, heard at night and often seen on tree stumps or fence posts during the day.

The spur-winged plover first settled in New Zealand near Invercargill, taking nearly 50 years to spread over the rest of the country. Its rattling call and distinctive flight make it a conspicuous bird anywhere. There is now no open country in Southland without spur-wings.

West from Invercargill, Riverton Estuary has white-faced heron, paradise duck, South Island pied oystercatcher, pied stilt, and small numbers of migrant waders. Both white herons and royal spoonbills occur there in winter. Riverton Rocks provide another good vantage point for sighting mollymawks and petrels offshore. It is about 15 km further to Lake George, which always has an interesting variety of birds. Some exciting rare migrants have been found there. The very good wetland known as the Henderson Extension has paradise duck, mallard, grey duck, grey teal, shoveler, pukeko and marsh crake.

As far west as the road will take you, Lake Hauroko nestles into the eastern edge of Fiordland. It is approached through some fine forests, and the shore of the lake at the road end has many kaka and falcons. A delightful walk (1 km) along a track to the lookout point will give you the chance to see robin, yellowhead, yellow-breasted tit, yellow-crowned parakeet, bellbird, tui, brown creeper and rifleman. The morepork is here too and you may find crested grebe on the lake.

Fiordland

At Te Anau, scaup can be seen on the lake at many places, especially near the National Park Headquarters and often in a large flock after the breeding season. A small number of crested grebes occur around the lake edge. The Te Anau Bird Reserve of the New Zealand Wildlife Service is open daily from dawn to dusk. Takahe (*Notornis*) are kept there, also a selection of native parrots and waterfowl. At the Lake Te Anau outlet – the start of the Waiau River

— a walk across the dam structure into the beech forest should allow you to see yellow-breasted tit, brown creeper, rifleman and yellow-crowned parakeet. Falcons may be seen anywhere around Te Anau, especially young birds in autumn. A little to the south, at Horseshoe Bend on the Waiau River (nearly opposite a road sign for Wapiti Park), a track along the edge of the extensive terrace overlooks a swampy area near the river which has good numbers of fernbirds.

The tourist trips from Lake Manapouri to Doubtful Sound usually meet keas when the bus stops on the top of Wilmot Pass, and they are often around the Deep Cove hostel. On the boat trip down the sound into Hall Arm you should see the Fiordland crested penguin — there is a colony at Elizabeth Island.

North from Te Anau, as the road to Milford climbs steadily up the beautiful Eglinton Valley it passes through the beech forests of the lowest slopes and across grassy river flats. These forests offer excellent birdwatching. The area about the 45 km peg is probably the best, with robin, yellowhead, yellow-breasted tit, brown creeper, yellow-crowned parakeet and long-tailed cuckoo being some of the most interesting species.

At Cascade Creek, the excellent Lake Gunn track makes it easy for anyone to make the ten minute walk through magnificent red beech trees to the lake. This is probably the best place to see yellowheads, and there are also kaka, robin, yellow-breasted tit and rifleman. At Mirror Lakes there is a lookout platform from which you can see scaup, and this is another good place for long-tailed cuckoos and other bush birds.

At the eastern end of the Homer Tunnel, rock wrens can be found in and around the rock falls on the lower slopes, some quite close by. Keas are never far away, and they are likely to come down to see any visitors to their domain. Remember that they like shiny things (as well as butter and cheese) so while you are hunting rock wrens, keas may be dismantling your car. Count the wheels before you drive off. On the descent from the tunnel on the western side you pass across an area of alpine vegetation which is again the realm of kea and rock wren. Parking places are limited, but it is well worthwhile to stop for a minute and get out to watch the kea wheeling across the mountain sides while you breathe in the cleanest air in the world. It seems an unlikely place for parrots.

Milford Sound usually has a few red-billed gulls and black-backed gulls around the head of the sound. Wekas are present, and may be heard at night if not seen during daylight. The shallow tidal area near the Milford hotel has variable oystercatcher and paradise duck and white herons sometimes visit. Black shags and little shags come ashore here after feeding in the sound. A boat trip to the mouth of the sound may give you a chance to see a Fiordland crested penguin.

Stewart Island

Stewart Island has a good selection of birds and most of them are quite accessible. Many visitors to the island take a plane from Invercargill airport, but so long as there is a ferry service the birdwatcher should make every effort to cross Foveaux Strait by sea. By air you miss what is probably one of the best 30 km trips for albatross viewing in the world. Weather and the season influence both the number of birds and the species. Make sure you brush up on your knowledge of the finer points of identification of the albatrosses before you sail, because they can be very difficult. It can be worthwhile to take a few stale loaves of bread to attract the big birds. A conspicuous white loaf thrown overboard will float long enough to bring nearby birds in close. In Foveaux Strait you may see Buller's mollymawk, royal albatross, wandering albatross, shy mollymawk, Salvin's mollymawk, sooty shearwater, diving petrel, giant petrel, Cook's petrel and prion. If you are not able to identify all the prions, you should at least distinguish the broad-billed prion by its heavy bill. You may meet a penguin or two, and these could be

Fiordland crested, yellow-eyed or little blue penguin. The southern skua breeds around Stewart Island and may be seen in coastal waters between September and May; at other times it is far out at sea.

On the island, pigeons are common in Oban in December, and kaka are in the garden trees in November, a treat the early settlers had in many parts of New Zealand but now seen nowhere else. The northern part of the island is well covered by walking tracks. In spite of the effects of past sawmilling and recent deer and possums, the forest has survived and regenerated to support kaka, tui, bellbird, pigeon, weka, red-crowned and yellow-crowned parakeet, shining cuckoo, long-tailed cuckoo, morepork, rifleman, brown creeper and yellow-breasted tit. The Stewart Island robin is now in reduced numbers and not easily found. Kiwis are in the bush further back, and flights by light aircraft are offered to remote Mason Bay where kiwis can be seen more easily than anywhere else in the wild.

Boat day-trips are available out of Halfmoon Bay and into Paterson Inlet. A visit to Ulva Island is usual, and there you have the chance to meet most of the bush birds. The beaches at The Neck sometimes have a small flock of godwits and New Zealand dotterels. These dotterels will be from the southern population which nests on the bare ground on the tops of Stewart Island high country, chiefly on the western side. Variable oystercatchers can also be expected here.

Further up the inlet Stewart Island shags roost on headlands and islets. This is a dimorphic species, and it is interesting to see the mixture of the bronze and pied forms. They nest outside the inlet, on Whero Rock. Pied shags nest at the Waipipi inlet, and on the rock known as Dirty Island there is also a colony of blue shags, that beautiful subspecies of the spotted shag of the north.

From Oban, a walk to the lighthouse at Ackers Point on a long summer evening can be rewarded by seeing sooty shearwaters coming into burrows and wekas may be met along the way. Nearly every small beach has its resident pair of variable oystercatchers.

Appendices

Appendix 1

New Zealand birds

A list (in taxonomic order) of the birds occurring on or around the main islands of New Zealand, but excluding rare migrants and stragglers. Introduced species are marked with an asterisk (*).

Kiwis (family Apterygidae)
North Island brown kiwi	*Apteryx australis mantelli*
South Island brown kiwi	*Apteryx australis australis*
Stewart Island brown kiwi	*Apteryx australis lawryi*
Little spotted kiwi	*Apteryx oweni*
Great spotted kiwi (roa)	*Apteryx haastii*

Penguins (family Spheniscidae)
Yellow-eyed penguin	*Megadyptes antipodes*
Northern blue penguin	*Eudyptula minor* subsp.
Cook Strait blue penguin	*Eudyptula minor variabilis*
Southern blue penguin	*Eudyptula minor minor*
White-flippered penguin	*Eudyptula minor albosignata*
Fiordland crested penguin	*Eudyptes pachyrhynchus*

Grebes (family Podicipedidae)
Southern crested grebe	*Podiceps cristatus australis*
N.Z. dabchick	*Podiceps rufopectus*
Hoary-headed grebe	*Podiceps poliocephalus*
Australian little grebe	*Tachybaptus novaehollandiae*

Albatrosses (family Diomedeidae)
Wandering albatross	*Diomedea exulans exulans*
Northern royal albatross	*Diomedea epomophora sanfordi*
N.Z. blackbrowed mollymawk	*Diomedea melanophrys impavida*
Grey-headed mollymawk	*Diomedea chrysostoma*
Yellow-nosed mollymawk	*Diomedea chlororhynchos*
Buller's mollymawk	*Diomedea bulleri*
Shy mollymawk	*Diomedea cauta cauta*
Salvin's mollymawk	*Diomedea cauta salvini*

Petrels and **Shearwaters** (family Procellariidae)

Giant petrel (nelly)	*Macronectes giganteus giganteus*
Cape pigeon	*caption capense capense*
Grey-faced petrel	*Pterodroma macroptera gouldi*
Mottled petrel	*Pterodroma inexpectata*
Pycroft's petrel	*Pterodroma pycrofti*
Cook's petrel	*Pterodroma cooki*
Black-winged petrel	*Pterodroma nigripennis*
Broad-billed prion	*Pachyptila vittata*
Fairy prion	*Pachyptila turtur*
Black petrel	*Procellaria parkinsoni*
Westland black petrel	*Procellaria westlandica*
Flesh-footed shearwater	*Puffinus carneipes hullinus*
Buller's shearwater	*Puffinus bulleri*
Sooty shearwater	*Puffinus griseus*
Fluttering shearwater	*Puffinus gavia*
Hutton's shearwater	*Puffinus huttoni*
North Island little (allied) shearwater	*Puffinus assimilis haurakienis*

Storm petrels (family Hydrobatidae)

White-faced stormpetrel	*Pelagodroma marina maoriana*

Diving petrels (family Pelecanoididae)

Northern diving petrel	*Pelecanoides urinatrix urinatrix*

Gannets (family Sulidae)

Australasian gannet	*Sula bassana serrator*

Shags or **cormorants** (family Phalacrocoracidae)

Black shag	*Phalacrocorax carbo novaehollandiae*
Pied shag	*Phalacrocorax varius*
Little black shag	*Phalacrocorax sulcirostris*
Little shag	*Phalacrocorax melanoleucos brevirostris*
King shag	*Leucocarbo carunculatus*
Stewart Island Shag	*Leucacarbo carunculatus chalconotus*
Spotted shag	*Stictocarbo punctatus punctatus*
Blue shag	*Stictocarbo punctatus steadi*

Herons, egrets and **bitterns** (family Ardeidae)

White-faced heron	*Ardea novaehollandiae*
White heron	*Egretta alba modesta*
Little egret	*Egretta garzetta immaculata*
Reef heron	*Egretta sacra sacra*
Cattle egret	*Bubulcus ibis coromandus*
Australasian bittern	*Botaurus stellaris poiciloptilus*

Spoonbills (family Threskiornithidae)

Royal spoonbill	*Platalea leucorodia regia*

Swans, geese and **ducks** (family Anatidae)

*Mute swan	*Cygnus olor*
*Black swan	*Cygnus atratus*
*Canada goose	*Branta canadensis maxima*

Paradise shelduck	*Tadorna variegata*
*Mallard	*Anas platyrhynchos platyrhynchos*
Grey duck	*Anas superciliosa superciliosa*
Grey teal	*Anas gibberifrons gracilis*
Brown teal	*Anas aucklandica chlorotis*
N.Z. shoveler	*Anas rhynchotis variegata*
Blue duck	*Hymenolaimus malacorhynchos*
N.Z. scaup	*Aythya novaeseelandiae*

Eagles, goshawks, etc. (family Accipitridae)

Australasian harrier	*Circus approximans gouldi*
N.Z. falcon	*Falco novaeseelandiae*

Pheasants and **quail** (family Phasianidae)

*Chukor	*Alectoris chukar*
*Brown quail	*Synoicus ypsilophorus*
*California quail	*Lophortyx californica brunnescens*
*Pheasant	*Phasianus colchicus*
*Peafowl	*Pavo cristatus*

Rails (family Rallidae)

Banded rail	*Rallus phillippensis assimilis*
North Island weka	*Gallirallus australis greyi*
Western weka	*Gallirallus australis australis*
Stewart Island weka	*Gallirallus australis scotti*
Marsh crake	*Porzana pusilla affinis*
Spotless crake	*Porzana tabuensis plumbea*
Pukeko	*Porphyrio porphyrio melanotus*
Notornis (takahe)	*Notornis mantelli*
Australian coot	*Fulica atra australis*

Oystercatchers (family Haematopodidae)

South Island pied oystercatcher	*Haematopus ostralegus finschi*
Variable oystercatcher	*Haematopus unicolour*

Plovers (family Charadriidae)

Spur-winged plover	*Vanellus miles novaehollandiae*
Pacific golden plover	*Pluvialis fulva*
N.Z. dotterel	*Charadrius obscurus*
Banded dotterel	*Charadrius bicinctus*
Black-fronted dotterel	*Charadrius melanops*
Wrybill	*Anarhynchus frontalis*

Curlews, snipes, etc. (family Scolopacidae)

Far-eastern curlew	*Numenius madagascariensis*
Asiatic whimbrel	*Numenius phaeopus variegatus*
Eastern bar-tailed godwit	*Limosa lapponica baueri*
Siberian tattler	*Tringa brevipes*
Terek sandpiper	*Xenus cinereus*
Turnstone	*Arenaria interpres*
Knot	*Calidris canutus canutus*
Sharp-tailed sandpiper	*Calidris acuminata*
Curlew sandpiper	*Calidris ferruginea*
Pectoral sandpiper	*Calidris melanotos*
Red-necked stint	*Calidris ruficollis*

Stilts (family Recurvirostridae)
    Pied stilt   *Himantopus himantopus*
                                     leucocephalus
    Black stilt   *Himantopus novaezealandiae*
Skuas (family Stercorariidae)
    Southern skua   *Stercorarius skua lonnbergi*
    Arctic skua   *Stercorarius parasiticus*
    Pomarine skua   *Stercorarius pomarinus*
Gulls (family Laridae)
    Southern black-backed gull   *Larus dominicanus*
    Red-billed gull   *Larus novaehollandiae*
                                     scopulinus
    Black-billed gull   *Larus bulleri*
Terns (family Sternidae)
    White-winged black tern   *Chlidonias leucopterus*
    Caspian tern   *Hydroprogne caspia*
    Black-fronted tern   *Sterna albostriata*
    White-fronted tern   *Sterna striata*
    Fairy tern   *Sterna nereis*
    Eastern little tern   *Sterna albifrons sinensis*
Pigeons and **doves** (family Columbidae)
    N.Z. pigeon   *Hemiphaga novaeseelandiae*
    *Rock pigeon   *Columba livia*
    *Malay spotted dove   *Streptopelia chinensis*
Cockatoos (family Cacatuidae)
    Kakapo   *Strigops habroptilus*
    *White cockatoo   *Cacatua galerita*
Kakas and **keas** (family Nestoridae)
    North Island kaka   *Nestor meridionalis*
                                     septentrionalis
    South Island kaka   *Nestor meridionalis*
                                     meridionalis
    Kea   *Nestor notabilis*
Rosellas and **parakeets** (family Platycercidae)
    *Crimson rosella   *Platycercus elegans*
    *Eastern rosella   *Platycercus eximius*
    Red-crowned parakeet   *Cyanoramphus novaezelandiae*
                                     novaezelandiae
    Yellow-crowned parakeet   *Cyanoramphus auriceps*
Cuckoos (family Cuculidae)
    Shining cuckoo   *Chrysococcyx lucidus*
    Long-tailed cuckoo   *Eudynamis taitensis*
Owls (family Strigidae)
    Morepork   *Ninox novaeseelandiae*
    *Little owl   *Athene noctua*
Kingfishers (family Alcedinidae)
    N.Z. kingfisher   *Halcyon sancta vagans*
    *Kookaburra   *Dacelo novaeguineae*

New Zealand wrens (family Xenicidae)
    North Island rifleman   *Acanthisitta chloris granti*
    South Island rifleman   *Acanthisitta chloris chloris*
    Rock wren   *Xenicus gilviventris*
Larks (family Alaudidae)
    *Skylark   *Alauda arvensis*
Swallows and **martins** (family Hirundinidae)
    Welcome swallow   *Hirundo tahitica neoxena*
Wagtails and **pipits** (family Motacillidae)
    N.Z. pipit   *Anthus novaeseelandiae*
Accentors (family Prunellidae)
    *Hedge sparrow   *Prunella modularis*
Warblers, flycatchers, thrushes, etc. (family Muscicapidae)
    North Island fernbird   *Bowdleria punctata vealeae*
    South Island fernbird   *Bowdleria punctata punctata*
    Brown creeper   *Finschia novaeseelandiae*
    Whitehead   *Mohoua albicilla*
    Yellowhead   *Mohoua ochrocephala*
    Grey warbler   *Gerygone igata*
    North Island fantail   *Rhipidura fuliginosa placabilis*
    South Island fantail   *Rhipidura fuliginosa fuliginosa*
    Pied tit   *Petroica macrocephala toitoi*
    Yellow-breasted tit   *Petroica macrocephala macrocephala*
    North Island robin   *Petroica australis longipes*
    South Island robin   *Petroica australis australis*
    Stewart Island robin   *Petroica australis rakiura*
    *Song thrush   *Turdus philomelos*
    *Blackbird   *Turdus merula*
White-eyes (family Zosteropidea)
    White-eye   *Zosterops lateralis lateralis*
Honeyeaters (family Melaphagidae)
    Stitchbird   *Notiomystis cincta*
    Bellbird   *Anthornis melanura*
    Tui   *Prosthemadera novaeseelandiae*
Buntings (family Emberizidae)
    *Yellowhammer   *Emberiza citrinella*
    *Cirl bunting   *Emberiza cirlus*
Finches (family Fringillidae)
    *Chaffinch   *Fringilla coelebs*
    *Greenfinch   *Carduelis chloris*
    *Goldfinch   *Carduelis carduelis*
    *Redpoll   *Carduelis flammea*
Weavers (family Ploceidae)
    *House sparrow   *Passer domesticus*
Starlings (family Sturnidae)
    *Starling   *Sturnus vulgaris*
    *Indian myna   *Acridotheres tristis*

New Zealand wattlebirds (family Callaeatidae)
North Island saddleback   *Philesturnus carunculatus*
                            rufusater
North Island kokako   *Callaeas cinerea wilsoni*
Bell magpies (family Cracticidae)
*Black-backed magpie   *Gymnorhina tibicen tibicen*
*White-backed magpie   *Gymnorhina tibicen*
                            hypoleuco
Crows (family Corvidae)
*Rook   *Corvus frugilegus*

Appendix 2

Entry to public reserves

Reserves are popular places for birdwatching because they usually contain an undisturbed habitat with good numbers of birds. Different conditions for entry apply to each of the many classes of public reserve. The following notes are given as a guide to access conditions; details are set out in the various acts, regulations and by-laws. In case of doubt, or if you are planning a long-term study, it is wise to talk to the officers of the controlling authority.

Scenic Reserves. Free access; camping permitted

Historic Reserves. Free access; no camping permitted

Nature Reserves. Entry by permit only, issued by the regional office of the Department of Conservation; no camping

Scientific Reserves. Free access unless a gazetted notice states that a permit is required

National Parks. Free access; camping limited to designated areas; permit required for entry to any special "protected area" such as Takahe Valley in Fiordland National Park

Local Purpose Reserves. Conditions are set by the local body concerned

Government Purpose Reserves. Includes land which contains lighthouses, airports etc. Conditions are set by the department concerned

Esplanade Reserves give free access along a strip 20 metres wide (sometimes less) above high-water mark along all of the coastline, *if* the land has been subdivided since the passing of the regulations. Much of the coastline has been in the hands of one owner for a long time, and he or she owns right to the high-water mark with no public reserve. Where a map is marked "Sec. 58 strip", this refers to an equivalent reserve under the Lands Act (1948). At low tide there is always free public access along the beach below high-water mark.

Wildlife Refuges and Wildlife Management Reserves. Free access except where signs indicate a restriction, which is usually temporary

State Forests. A permit is not required for entry on foot to a State Forest, and there is limited access for vehicles on forest roads. Apply to the headquarters of the forest for information and permits to take vehicles on other roads. Naturally there are strict controls during periods of extreme fire risk.

Forest Parks. Free access; camping permitted in designated areas

Farm Parks. Free access; camping in specified sites (if any)

Appendix 3

Legal protection of birds in New Zealand

The Wildlife Act gives absolute protection to all birds with the following exceptions:
• Game birds
• Those listed as unprotected or partially protected
• Those listed as subject to the Minister's notification
• Domestic birds.

This means that the law takes the positive approach of granting legal protection not only to native birds but also to any bird that arrives here. If a migrant or cage escapee proves to be undesirable, separate regulations would be necessary to remove protection.

Game birds are currently black swan, Canada goose, mallard, grey duck, shoveler, paradise duck, pukeko, pheasant, chukor, grey partridge, California quail, brown quail and Virginian quail. An open season may be declared for any of these species to be hunted or killed (subject to conditions). At other times they are protected.

Unprotected species are all introduced birds except for the little owl, mute swan and the game birds, black shag, harrier and black-backed gull.

Partially protected birds may be killed when damaging land or property (normally crops). They are white-eye and southern skua.

The Minister's notification list covers those species which may be killed according to regulations which will normally specify places and conditions. It currently lists sooty shearwaters and grey-faced petrels (the two "muttonbirds") pied shag and little shag, Stewart Island weka on islands in Foveaux Strait, and other species on the Chatham Islands.

It is an offence to possess the skins, feathers or eggs of any protected species. Collection of the corpses of beach-wrecked sea birds is permitted under permit from the director of a New Zealand museum, who may then hold any specimens which are of value to the museum.

Appendix 4

Organisations

Ornithological Society of New Zealand (Inc.)
This is the only society solely devoted to the study of birds in New Zealand. Membership is open to anyone with a serious interest in birds, and there are currently about 1200 members including both professional scientists and amateurs at all levels of knowledge. As well as ordinary membership there is provision for family members and junior members.

The journal *Notornis* is published quarterly by the society. It contains articles on the birds of New Zealand and the South Pacific and short notes which deal with observations, rare bird sightings, etc. Once a year a large portion of one issue is devoted to "Classified Summarised Notes". This is a collection of all the bird sightings recorded by members over a twelve-month period, sorted under each species and acknowledging the observer in each case. *OSNZ News* is distributed quarterly with the journal. This is an eight-page newsletter covering events and society news and also contains short articles and observations. Activities organised nationally by the society include:

• A recording scheme for nest records of all species of birds
• Beach Patrols. This is the name given to organised and regular searching of beaches for dead seabirds. Regular patrolling of a beach and identification of all the bird remains found give an indication of what species are present off the coast in each season. Beach Patrol records have been kept for about 40 years and much valuable data has been accumulated.
• Moult Cards. Cards are available to record the state of moult on any bird which is handled. This relatively new scheme aims to collect data on the moulting patterns of all New Zealand species.

• Regular locality censuses are made of some key areas, and also annual counts of some species of special interest, such as the cattle egret. These become group activities for each region.
• A summer study camp is held each January in some part of the country.
• Labour Weekend camps are held each year to make co-ordinated surveys of birds and to measure the fluctuation in numbers of chosen species in particular areas.
• The annual conference in May moves around the main centres.

Regional representatives organise the activities of the society in 20 different regions of the country. These activities depend on the local group, but usually include a monthly meeting with an invited speaker, group outings for special counts, beach patrols, etc. Most regions have local newsletters.

All enquiries should first be directed to R.R. Slack, Hon. Secretary, Ornithological Society of N.Z., c/- Post Office, Pauatahanui, Wellington.

Royal Forest and Bird Protection Society of New Zealand (Inc.)
The main aim and activity of this society is conservation of the natural environment, and it is undoubtedly the premier conservation body in the country, with over 48,000 members. However, native birds have always been given special consideration and many New Zealand birdwatchers have got started on outings with Forest and Bird. There are 43 branches throughout the country which organise regular field trips, evening meetings and practical conservation projects. Programmes for these are usually available from the branch secretary well in advance. The society maintains bush reserves and lodges in many parts of the country and summer camps are organised.

The fully illustrated quarterly magazine *Forest and Bird* frequently includes articles which deal with endangered bird species.

Enquire from the National Secretary, Royal Forest and Bird Protection Society of N.Z. (Inc), P.O. Box 631, Wellington.

Miranda Naturalists' Trust
This trust was established to study and preserve the fauna
and flora of the Kaiaua-Miranda coast of the Firth of
Thames, especially the migratory waders which have given
the area an international reputation. A newsletter is
produced three or four times a year and an annual open
day at Miranda in February has talks, displays and
demonstrations of the features of the area. The Trust
leases land on the coast to give birdwatchers free access at
all times, and there is a shelter and a viewing hide. A
cottage in Kaiaua is available as accommodation for
members who want to stay in the area for weekends or
continuing studies. Enquiries to the Hon. Secretary,
Miranda Naturalists' Trust, P.O. Box 39-180, Auckland
West.

Junior Naturalists' Club exist in many centres. Contact
with these and any other local groups may be made
through the local museum or the branch secretary of the
Royal Forest and Bird Protection Society.

Appendix 5

Annotated bibliography

There are many books which make a contribution to field
identification by presenting photographs of a selection of
New Zealand birds in various habitats and situations.
Others will appear in the bookshops in time. All of them
add to the serious student's knowledge of the bird, even if
they have been designed for the coffee table. Borrow them
from the library for browsing over on winter evenings.
None takes the place of a good field guide, of course, and
photographs always have to give way to paintings when it
is necessary to show all the important features of a bird's
appearance.

The New Guide to the Birds of New Zealand, by R. A.
Falla, R. B. Sibson and E. G. Turbott, illustrated by
Elaine Power. Third Edition, for the Ornithological
Society of New Zealand. Published by Collins.
This is the only comprehensive field guide to New Zealand
birds. It covers every bird recorded even once in the New
Zealand region up to the time of publication; this may
create difficulties for the users unless they determine
whether the bird being considered is widely distributed or
just a straggler last seen 50 years ago. 315 species and
subspecies are illustrated in accurate colour paintings. The
text gives a full description of each, noting key
identification features and also voice, habitat and range,
and some notes on breeding. This field guide is accurate
and reliable, and no birdwatcher should be without it.

Collins Handguide to the Birds of New Zealand, written
and illustrated by Chlöe Talbot Kelly. Published by Collins.
230 species and subspecies from New Zealand and outlying
islands are dealt with, including some rare vagrants and a
few which must be considered extinct. Text is limited to

about 75 words on each bird, with no plumage Identification is aided by an accurate colour painting of each bird in its habitat. Special treatment is given to waders, seabirds and albatrosses, and some other difficult groups. This is a useful pocket guide at about half the price of the *New Guide*.

Reader's Digest Complete Book of New Zealand Birds, published by Reader's Digest/Reed Methuen.

This is a handsome big book, lavishly illustrated. Text on every species and subspecies recorded here was contributed by a large number of invited ornithologists. There is a colour photograph of each bird described.

The Atlas of Bird Distribution in New Zealand, by P.C. Bull, P.D. Gaze, C.J.R. Robertson. Published jointly by the Ecology Division of D.S.I.R., New Zealand Wildlife Service and the Ornithological Society of New Zealand.

Here you have in looseleaf form in a ringbinder cover distribution maps for all N.Z. birds except the rarities, compiled from the 10,000 yard grid squares which were counted during the years 1969-76. In addition a table gives the monthly distribution of observations of each species, and another lists both the number of squares in which each species was recorded and the number of cards for each species. Also included with the book are microfiches of the field cards to allow researchers to see the original data. Available from some booksellers, the Ornithological Society, or head office of Forest and Bird.

Southern Albatrosses and Petrels: An Identification Guide, by Peter C. Harper and F.C. Kinsky. Published by Price Milburn for Victoria University Press.

This is a specialist field guide to the birds of the Southern oceans, with valuable information on identification at sea. There are accurate drawings of wing patterns of the birds in flight and a key to diagnostic features.

New Zealand's Birds, photographs by Geoff Moon, text by Ronald Lockley. Published by Heinemann.

Excellent photographs in this book illustrate every species and subspecies, with a supporting text which deals with behaviour, choice of habitat, etc.

Index

Index

Habitats, pages 76-148; Districts, pages 150-224